TO THE ENDS OF THE EARTH

MARY GAUNT
PIONEER TRAVELLER

HER BIOGRAPHY

SUSANNA DE VRIES

© Susanna de Vries, 2009,2020

This book is copyright. Apart from any fair dealing for the purposes of study, research, criticism, review, or as otherwise permitted under the Copyright Act, no part may be reproduced by any process without written permission. Inquiries should be made to the publisher.

First published in 2010.
Print-on-demand edition published in 2020.
Published by Pirgos Press
Brisbane - Australia

National Library of Australia
Cataloguing in Publication entry: De Vries, Susanna.
MARY GAUNT — A TRAILBLAZING AUSTRALIAN

Collector's edition.

ISBN 9780980621686 (p/b)
ISBN 9781742984070 (ebook)

1.

Every effort has been made to trace owners of the negatives of historical photographs illustrated in this book, although taken before 1939 these are now out of copyright. Additional text has been specially written for this publication plus extra pictorial material. See
www.susannadevries.com

Cover and book design by Jake de Vries.

Contents

    Introduction and photographs
    Prelude — Outwitting Mussolini
1. 'Gaunts *never* give up'
2. Encountering prejudice at university
3. Finding Doctor Right
4. Mary postpones a visit to China
5. Africa — the 'Dark Continent'
6. Heading a band of naked warriors
7. 'Madame, you have the heart of a lion'
8. 'Murder Hill' and German Togoland
9. Black magic among the Ashanti
10. The male dinosaurs of London's RGS
11. Through Tsarist Russia to Peking
12. Inside the walls of the Forbidden City
13. A political assassination
14. The Great Wall of China
15. 'Behind every small foot is a jar of tears'
16. Chengde and the hunting palace of the Manchu
17. The temple of the Three Mountains
18. 'Please keep your last bullet for yourself'
19. Last days in China
20. Exploring the Amur River and Saghalien
21. On a troop train through Siberia
22. St Petersburg and after
23. Captured by Germans
24. The Gaunts in wartime
25. The final years of a cosmopolitan author
    Endnotes

INTRODUCTION
Mary Eliza Bakewell Gaunt
[1861-1942]

One hundred and thirty years ago Mary Gaunt became one of the first woman permitted to sign the matriculation roll of Melbourne University. Advised that women lacked the brains to study law or medicine, she enrolled in the Faculty of Arts to study literature. Mary and the twelve women who enrolled with her soon became aware their written work was marked down by biased male academics, desperate to prove women were not clever enough to be awarded degrees and should never have been admitted.

In 1882 at the end of her first year at university Mary Gaunt realising that the dice were loaded against women and neither she or the other female students would receive degrees, no matter how hard they worked, protested by leaving the university. History would prove her right: Melbourne University did not grant a degree to any of that first intake of young women, all of them hard working and intelligent due to their gender.

Mary Gaunt, always reassured by her teachers at school she had literary talent decided to become a professional writer. In the 1880s all: publishers, editors and literary critics were male and most regarded 'women's writing' as sloppy and sentimental. To protect themselves from wounding criticism, women writers like 'George' Elliot, Charlotte Bronte, 'Henry' Handel Richardson and 'Miles' Franklin used male pen names. Mary Gaunt and Edith Wharton were some of the few women who brave male critics and wrote fiction and articles under their own names rather than assuming a male identity. Mary's short stories for the Melbourne *Age* proved popular and could afford to visit London where she received a commission to write a novel set on the goldfields.

Back in Australia Mary continued writing and married when she turned twenty-nine. She was widowed young and under tragic circumstances. In 1901 short of money she returned to London, hub of the publishing industry, to earn her living as a writer of high quality fiction. She led her own expedition to West Africa in search of background material for African adventure novels, visited remote villages where human sacrifice took place. In 1909 her travel book *Alone in West Africa* made the name 'Mary Gaunt' famous in Britain and America.

In 1913, Mary had made a hazardous journey through China and Siberia to write *A Woman in China* and *Broken Journey*. They record everyday life in China when the fledgling People's Republic had replaced the Manchu emperors and China slid into civil war.

Between 1905-1919, Mary Gaunt became one of Britain's top selling quality female novelists, with a large educated readership and three travel books in print.

During World War One Mary had been a generous benefactor to wounded Anzacs in Britain at No 3 Australian Military Hospital at Dartford. She donated virtually all her savings to provide assistance to Belgian war victims who had fled to England. At the end of the war, short of money and suffering from asthma, Mary sold her Kentish home *Mary Haven*, invested the money and lived cheaply on the Italian Riviera where she spent the next two decades.

Mary's younger brother, Admiral Sir Guy Gaunt, a former head of British Naval Intelligence ,stayed with his sister in her villa at Bordighera. Mussolini's secret police became convinced Mary was a British spy placed there by her brother and she narrowly avoid being arrested and interned after Mussolini declared war on Britain. In 1940 she fled to southern France where she lived in the isolated village of Vence, her rented home was used as a safe house by the rescue network run by Varian Fry, the American 'Oscar Schindler' who was responsible for saving the lives of Jewish artists and British pilots shot down over France.

Mary Gaunt died in France, ignored in her home country but her literary merit and her courage as an explorer praised in a glowing obituary in *The Times*. Her death was virtually unnoticed in wartime Australia where she had spent the first 40 years of her life and written three exciting adventure novels set in lawless days on the goldfields of Victoria which are still in print .[1]

Top: The Ballarat lakeside house rented by William Gaunt for his family. This historic image shows the small tower in the centre where Mary and her brothers played as children on rainy days. *Strathalbyn House* was demolished and a smaller residence built on its site for the Bishop of Ballarat.

Left: A signed photograph of Mary Gaunt used as a frontispiece in one of her Australian novels. It is the only available portrait of Mary Gaunt. The photograph may have been taken shortly before her African expedition when she was in her 40s.
Courtesy the State Library of Victoria, who owns copies of many of Mary's first editions.

In the jungles of West Africa Mary was often carried by porters in a hammock.

The town of Elmina, with its former slave fort seen against the skyline.

Peking in the early 20th century, at the time of Mary Gaunt's arrival.

Mary Gaunt overseeing the loading of a flimsy 'Peking cart', which would take her to Jehol (Chengde). Peking carts were drawn by mules.

Mary Gaunt returned from Jehol in a 'wupan' on the River Lanho.

Top left: As there were no proper roads, Mary was carried in a mule litter on parts of her journey.

Bottom left: When visiting the remote Ming Tombs, Mary was carried by porters in a chair mounted on bamboo poles.

Mary and two friends take tea outside her home at the *Temple of the Three Mountains*.

Left: Chinese women with bound feet. The picture below shows the terrible effect of foot binding.

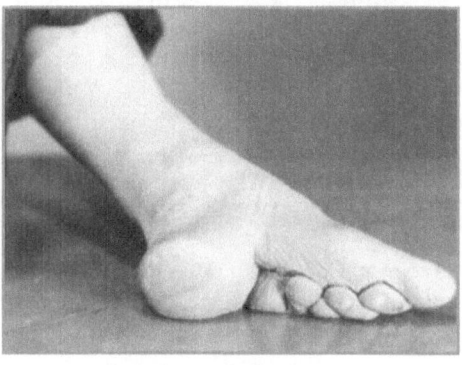

The ancient hilltop village of St Paul de Vence behind the French Riviera. Mary Gaunt rented a stone house in the neighbouring village of Vence rather than face chilly English winters. Photograph Jake de Vries.

The cemetery of St Paul de Vence where Mary's ashes were scattered. It is also the burial place of Chagall and D.H. Lawrence. Photograph Jake de Vries

PRELUDE
Outwitting Mussolini

Bordeghera, Riviera di Fiori, near Genoa, 1940.

At midnight Anselma, Mary Gaunt's elderly housekeeper, was woken by persistent hammering on the front door of the *Villa Camilla*. She hurried downstairs wondering who could be calling that late, fearing it might be the OVRA, Mussolini's secret police.

Anselma unbolted the door as she recognised the voices of the two Russian artists who lived in the adjacent villa. The couple had been good neighbours to Mary Gaunt for over a decade.

Opening the door Mary's housekeeper was aghast to see that the faces of the men were bruised and their hands bandaged. Stammering with fear and urgency the Russians insisted insisted they *must* speak to Signora Gaunt immediately. Anselma hurried them inside, asking them to wait in the salon while she went upstairs to wake her elderly employer, helped the eighty year old writer into her dressing gown and assisted her down the stairs.

As Ivan, the elder of the two, was in great pain, so his younger companion, Igor, related how they had been beaten up by a gang of Blackshirts while walking their dog after dinner. Fascist thugs had stamped on Ivan's fingers and killed their beloved poodle. Barely conscious, the two Russians had overheard the gang leader when he told his fellow Blackshirts that the OVRA would carry out house-to-house raids and arrest all foreign residents. Their leader had gloated that this was their last chance to beat-up foreign scum like these Jewish *omosessuali*.

Mary was shocked by Igor's story. She was aware of the danger of being arrested — three months ago Il Duce had declared war on Britain and France and her brother Guy had warned her to leave or she could be accused of spying for Britain. Some members of Bordighera's English-speaking community fearing arrest had already returned home.

Igor continued his story and related how after the Blackshirts had departed, he and Ivan had struggled back to their villa, cleaned and bandaged their wounds and buried their beloved little dog. In a great hurry they had piled their suitcases, paint boxes and unsold paintings into their car and on the roof rack. They intended to drive an artists' retreat in the hills behind Nice. At St Paul de Vence they had a Russian- Jewish friend from childhood days with a gallery that sold Ivan's paintings. He would certainly help them.

Aware that their neighbour of many years, the widowed Signora Gaunt, was bound to be arrested at dawn, Ivan and Igor realised they still had room in their little car for one person. They were offering Signora Gaunt a chance to escape on condition she was ready very soon and would only bring a small suitcase with her as their car was already bulging. .

Bordighera had been an English enclave since the days of Queen Victoria. Mary who hated the chilly damp of Britain had been loathe to leave Italy and her beloved villa.. But realising she could spend the rest of the war in an Italian jail, she saw the wisdom of leaving immediately while escape was still possible.[1]

As always, when faced with danger Mary remained calm. She thanked her neighbours for thinking of her, assuring them she would be ready to leave in half an hour.

Accordingly the Russians returned to their villa while Mary went upstairs to get dressed. The devoted Anselma packed a suitcase with Mary's medications, clothes and toiletries, her portable typewriter and a few pieces of valuable jewellery. She had just enough time to telephone several English friends and warn them of the house arrests that would be made at dawn.

As the Russians loaded car crunched over the gravel drive of the *Villa Camilla*, the two elderly women embraced. Anselma helped Mary down the steps and into the back-seat of the car. Devoted to her employer, Anselma placed her small suitcase and a canvas bag containing bread, slices of Parma ham, Mary's favourite *amaretti* biscuits and a thermos flask of coffee beside the artists' materials on the back seat beside the famous author.

The sky was still dark as Anselma wished them good luck and waved goodbye. The little Fiat sped through the streets of the seaside town where the windows of villas and shops were still shuttered, climbed the steep narrow streets, past the baroque church and the mediaeval towers on the skyline and out of the old town on the hill and through groves of the palm trees for which Bordighera was famous.

The bitumen ended at the Alta Via dei Monte Liguri, a pot holed track used by grape and olive pickers. The advantage of following this unsealed mountain road was the absence of border guards who inspected the passports of everyone crossing into Vichy France by the coastal road. The French government in Paris had surrendered to the Nazis and was under the thumb of the Gestapo, but Vichy France remained independent, so they were convinced they would be safe once they reached it. Mary, who had spent a great deal of time in Provence before coming to Bordighera spoke French fluently as did the Russians who had spent years working in Montparnasse. .

Dawn came up as they drove through terraces planted with vines and olive trees. On the seaward side, the land dropped away hundreds of feet below with no safety barriers and soon the gnarled silvery olive trees were replaced by the green-leaves of large chestnut trees.

As they neared the French border the landscape changed into *maquis* or scrub where barefoot boys herding goats waved at the car. Far below them was the Mediterranean, blue as lapis lazuli, and in the distance they could see a faint outline which must be the frontier port of Ventamiglia and its border guards.

Once Mary and her companions were several kilometres into neutral Vichy France they relaxed.

They stopped the car in the shade of a large pine tree and Mary poured coffee for the three of them. Ivan was still in pain from his swollen fingers and feared some had been broken. Igor had to hold the cup to his partner's swollen lips. They shared the bread and salami provided by Anselma and dunked the almond flavoured *amaretti* biscuits in their coffee. Through the open window came the smell of wild thyme and the drone of the cicadas. It was hard to imagine that across the border foreign residents were being arrested by Mussolini's secret police.

The sun, now high overhead, glinted on the dome of Monte Carlo's casino far below them on the coast. Turning off the dirt track they drove along the sealed *moyen corniche*, passing the small fishing port of Beaulieu, and the peninsula of St Jean Cap Ferrat, filled with luxury villas and then passed the largfer naval harbour of Villefrance. After a sharp bend they saw the magnificent sweep of the Bay of Angels. Ignoring signposts to the city of Nice the little car headed for the village of St Jeannet.

From the crest of a hill the mediaeval walls of St Paul de Vence rose before them, with tiers of red roofed houses topped by the square church tower. The smaller hilltop village of Vence was hidden behind another peak.

Their heavily laden car struggled up the hill to St Paul de Vence, passed through the arch in the ancient stone walls into a sunlit square where elderly men were playing *pêtanque*. In the deserted main street the Russians were shocked to see the art gallery belonging to their Jewish friend bore a sign saying *A Louer* (To Let) nailed across the barred and shuttered windows.

Back in the square Igor asked one of the *pêtanque* players for the address of Monsieur Paul Roux, the art loving restaurant owner whose collection adorned the walls of the restaurant. Directed to *Le Colombe d'Or* they drove down a winding side road where village women in long white aprons with coloured kerchiefs round their heads washing clothes in a stone trough.

They parked the car opposite an arched gateway set into in a high stone wall from which protruded the sign of a golden dove source of the inn's name — *Le Colombe d'Or*.[2]

The two Russians put on their black fedoras and helped Mary cramped by the journey, climb out of the car. . The younger of the two took one of his framed paintings to show Monsieur Roux, in the hope he might buy it, as due to their hurried flight they had not been able to withdraw any money from their almost depleted bank account. The artists escorted the small frail figure of Mary

Gaunt through the rustic door and inside *Le Colombe d' Or*.[3] Appetising smells were coming from the kitchen and the dining room. They sat at a table surrounded by framed works by some of the greatest twentieth century painters — Picasso, Matisse, Leger and Chagall.

Only when they were seated in a secluded corner did the artists remove their hats, revealing bruised cheeks and black eyes. While they were making their selection from an interesting menu of local dishes typical of the magnificent *cuisine* of Provence. Mary rose from the table and using her stick limped to the reception desk to change *lira* into French *francs*. She asked the receptionist to put through a call to Bordighera's International Library. From a friendly librarian she learned several of her elderly friends from England had been arrested at dawn and were being interned and held in a derelict prison on a windswept and rocky island off the Ligurian coast.[4]

***

Mary Gaunt, having escaped arrest was very grateful to her Russian friends and aware they had no money was determined to rent a house where all three of them could stay. Her phone call to her bank in Bordighera confirmed that on the orders of Mussolini bank accounts of all foreign residents were frozen. The manager regretted he had no choice but to comply with Il Duce's orders.

Mary realised she must contact her London bank, ask them to send the money from accrued royalties to France. As the southern half of France was still neutral there would be no problems with exchange control. Clearly the Russians could not sell their paintings in wartime and lacked other means of support. If necessary she would sell her few bits of good jewellery until the money arrived from England.

She returned to the table and broke the news that all bank accounts of foreigners had been frozen by order of Mussolini. Aware their funds were limited they selected from among the cheaper dishes, filled their glasses from a *pichot* of local wine raised their glasses and drank to the success of their flight from Mussolini's brutal secret police.

The three of them enjoyed examining the owner's magnificent excellent art collection on the walls of the restaurant, saw works by Chagall and Picasso and asked the waiter if they could talk to *le patron*.[5]

Paul Roux, restauranteur and amateur artist, arrived just as they were finishing their meal. The Russians explained they had trained at the Ecole Julien in Paris and known their fellow Russian, Marc Chagall who they believed was living in the hills near St Paul de Vence and congratulated Monsieur Roux on his excellent collection.

Monsieur Roux modestly replied that he was only a Sunday painter and most people considered him a far better *restauranteur* than artist! He enjoyed talking to artists and ordered the waiter to bring them coffee and cognac 'on the house'.

Above their table hung an impressive work by Fernand Lėger. Monsieur Roux explained that Leger's masterwork was displayed inside in winter and in summer occupied a special alcove in the restaurant's courtyard. Leger had been pilloried in an exhibition of 'degenerate artists' in Nazi Germany and been horrified when Petain's Vichy government announced they intended to strip French citizenship from any 'degenerate' artists. Terrified he would be sent to a concentration camp Lėger had fled to America.[6] The Surrealist Max Ernst had been interned in a camp but guards had been bribed to ensure his escape which had been funded by the American collector Peggy Guggenheim who was enchanted by Max's good looks and he had managed to reach New York.

Learning that the Russian Jews had known Moise Shagall before he took French citizenship and became known as Marc Chagall, Monsieur Roux revealed the famous artist was living quietly in the adjacent hilltop village of Gourdes, hoping his newly acquired French citizenship would protect him. Chagall's t his name was on Monsieur Fry's list so all expenses for his escape by sea would be paid by MOMA, New York's Museum of Modern Art.

'List! What list?' *Qui est ce Monsieur Fry?*' asked the Russians.

They were told Varian Fry was an American journalist who had arrived in Marseilles with a list of 200 celebrated Jewish artists drawn up by Alfred Barr, Head of MOMA, New York's Museum of Modern Art along with funds to organise their escape. [7] Fry's list included Jewish intellectuals, Jewish musicians and famous painters. MOMA were particularly keen to have Chagall in America before he too was arrested. But Chagall was working an a vast mural and with the dedication of a true artist did not want to leave his masterpiece unfinished. [8]

Since no more exit visas were being granted to Jews, Varian Fry was paying an art forger to create forged visas and passports. Word had Fry's escape network had reached the Jewish community so Varian Fry's office was deluged with requests for assistance from Jews desperate to flee to America. Fry and his volunteer helpers were doing their best to find 'safe houses' for as many Jews as possible while forged papers were prepared for them.

Monsieur Roux fished in his wallet and produced a business card engraved with the words VARIAN FRY, CENTRE AMERICAIN DE SECOURS, 60 Rue de Grignan Marseilles followed by a phone number and warned that should the French police learn the true purpose of the Help Centre, Monsieur Fry would be deported.

Madame Gaunt, an Australian travelling on a British passport was unlikely to encounter problems with the police if she explained why she had to flee from Italy. But Ivan and Igor should try to escape very soon or they could be interned. The French secret police were hand in glove with the Gestapo in Paris and making routine house searches.

They should phone Varian Fry's office for an appointment and say very little as his phone might be bugged. If the Russians could find the money he was sure Monsieur Fry could arrange visas and forged passports. Their gallery owner friend paid for forged papers and left on a boat bound for one of France's Pacific colonies and from there would take a boat to New York.

Mary and the Russians drained their cognacs in a sombre mood. Paul Roux regretted he did not buy paintings, only exchanged them for meals in his restaurant. Leger, Matisse and Picasso had eaten at *the Colombe d'Or*, given him paintings in return for meals and become his friends. He was happy to accept painting from the Russians for free meals but in wartime *no one* was buying paintings. The Gestapo were confiscating art from Jewish collectors and sending valuable modern artworks and Old Masters to be sold in Switzerland for sale and using the money to fund the Nazi war effort. It was scandalous but what could anyone do in time of war?

In answer to Mary's questions about renting a house, Monsieur Roux advised they would find the smaller village of Vence cheaper than St Paul. Besides Vence had the advantage it had no resident *gendarme*.

They drove to the hilltop village of Vence where Mary paid a deposit on the rental of a tall stone house in a narrow winding street with the services of a maid for six months and said her friends would soon be leaving for America where they had relatives but she disliked the British climate and would be staying in Provence, war or no war.

A few days later the Russians drove to Marseilles to see Varian Fry and ask for his help. As their names were not on the list of artists drawn up by the Museum of Modern Art, Varian Fry regretted he could not provide funds but promised to provide forged documents and a sea passage to America if they could find the money.

All the money they two artists possessed was tied up in their paintings and their car. As Monsieur Roux had explained no one was buying art in wartime. Mary sold her jewellery to support the three of them for several months while she waited for money to arrive from London and helped to fund the Russians to reach New York via one of the French colonies. . .

In April 1941, with forged passports and exit visas provided by Varian Fry's escape organisation , Chagall and his wife Bella made the same sea passage as the Russians and eventually reached New York. Out of gratitude to Varian Fry Chagall allowed his house in the isolated village of Gourdes to become a 'safe house' for Jews awaiting forged papers and for a few British bomber pilots shot down over France.[9]

Receiving no reply to letters addressed to the *Villa Camilla*, Mary wrote to her brother, telling Guy she needed her personal papers, diaries and notebooks left behind in the villa so she could finish her memoirs. [10]

Guy Gaunt's memoirs *The Yield of the Years*, relating his adventures on guns boats in far flung corners of the British empire to rescue British subjects had just been published. Guy was sympathetic to his sister's wish to finish her own memoirs.[11] From his home near Woking, Guy wrote to Mary telling her of a plan he had dreamed up to retrieve her papers. He would board a British naval vessel to the French naval port of Toulon, rent a car, drive to Nice, hire a motor cruiser and make the three hour journey by sea to retrieve the necessary papers and diaries from the *Villa Camilla*.

Mary was thrilled by his plan but insisted on accompany her brother — like many elderly people, the older she became the less scared she was of dying. Knowing her strength of character Guy knew better than to argue with his elder sister.

He boarded a naval vessel at Portsmouth for Toulon, hired a car, paid the outrageous black market price for petrol and drove up to Vence to collect his sister. A naval friend had chartered a fast cruiser belonging to Bolivian tin billionaire plus a couple of French deckhands. As the cruiser was registered in Panama and flew the Panamanian flag passengers could claim to be on Panamanian territory which might save them from arrest.

During his naval career Guy Gaunt had organised rescues of British nationals and as Head of British Naval intelligence in Washington, infiltrated a German spy network. Now retired but still active he welcomed the chance of another adventure. .

※

Mary kept no diary of their voyage. [12] With Guy at the wheel, they must have slipped out of the busy yacht harbour of Nice on the last night of October, 1940 and arrived at Bordighera soon after dawn on 1 November 1940, the religious festival of *Ognissanti, the Giorno dei Morti* or Day of the Dead. This was a public holiday so everyone in Bordighera went to mass and laid flowers on the graves of dead relatives including the police.

As they entered the harbour, Guy Gaunt, lean and distinguished in his dark blue yachting clothes and white cap, manoeuvred the motor cruiser alongside the dock before cutting the diesel engines. A *matelots,* rope in hand, jumped ashore to moor the cruiser.

It was almost seven o'clock and by now the sun had risen. Bordighera harbour was deserted, apart from several old men fishing from the sea wall. The fisherman went out each night with lights on their prows, returning at daybreak to unload their catch and spread their nets out to dry. Fishermen led a perilous life so most of them were religious. The *Ognissanti* mass lasted over an hour with another half hour for the tidying up and laying of flowers on gravestones of relatives and friends.

At Bordighera the French deckhands wheeled Mary in her chair down the gangplank and they ascended the steep road leading to the *Villa Camilla* Reaching the villa they found the shutters were bolted and barred against intruders. A typed requisition had been pinned on the top panel, announcing that the Italian Army had requisitioned the villa and the following week would arrive. They were just in time to save Mary's papers and a few treasured possessions.

There was no answer to Guy's knock. He unlocked it with Mary's keys, walked though the hall and opened the study door. No sign of Anselma. The bookshelves were almost empty, Mary's writing desk and chair covered by dust sheets. The leather-bound first editions of her books had gone. Mary's personal papers, diaries and the typescript of her memoirs, were also missing. Had

Anselma removed Mary's treasured possessions to a safe place, aware that young soldiers would be billeted at the villa?

Guy strode into the dining room where the table and chairs were shrouded in dust sheets. Table silver, bearing the Gaunt family crest, had vanished from the sideboard. In the drawing room, tucked into a corner of a mirror, Guy found a note from Anselma, announcing she was leaving Bordighera but no more.[13] Clearly Mary's housekeeper had not trusted young Italian soldiers to look after valuables and had hidden them away in storage. But where were they now?

To protect herself Anselma had not provided a forwarding address. As a childless widow, Mary knew Anselma spent her holidays with distant relatives in Rome or in the town of Reggio Emilia, near Bologna.[14] But finding Anselma amid the chaos of wartime Italy resembled searching for a needle in a haystack.

Guy propelled Mary's wheelchair across the marble floor of the hall,, opened the front door and peered out. No police were visible so they descended the deserted street to the harbour. The two elderly fishermen were still there, their floats bobbing in the calm water.

One of the deckhands pushed Mary's wheelchair up the gangplank, the other untied the mooring ropes nd jumped back on deck. Guy started the powerful diesel engines putting them in reverse. The twin propellers churned the sea into foam as uniformed figures sprinted towards the Panamian yacht, arms waving. Guy ignored them, pushed the gearstick forward and the cruiser surged forward across the harbour, out to sea and back to Nice. It was Mary Gaunt's final adventure.

CHAPTER 1

'Gaunts *never* give up'

The motto of Prince John of Gaunt, a warrior prince of England's Plantagenet dynasty and one of Mary's ancestors.

Mary Gaunt was descended from the royal dynasty known as the Plantaganets, famous for their courage.

Her father, William Henry Gaunt hailed from the town of Leek in Shropshire. Just before his twenty-first birthday, clever adventurous young William bored by work as an articled clerk in a law firm the provincial town of Leek, decided to sail to Melbourne. The year was 1851, the start of a gold rush in the new colony of Victoria. The lure of gold and making quick money saw many young men abandon everything in the rush to be rich.

William Gaunt took a passage on a wool clipper bound for Melbourne, capital of the brand new colony of Victoria. He claimed to his children that he chose to leave for Australia because adventure ran deep in the blood of the Gaunts.[1]

Mary's father explained to her that Prince John of Gaunt (1340 – 1399), Duke of Lancaster and Acquitaine and the third son of King Edward III [2] was a clever and ambitious man who married three times. His second wife was a Spanish princess from Castille so he had spent years in Spain and journeyed to the Holy Land at a time when travel in this area was extremely dangerous. [3]

Arriving in Melbourne, young William Gaunt found a town of unpaved roads and wooden dwellings. After obtaining a miners' licence he headed for the goldfields, staked a claim and started digging. Unfortunately Lady Luck proved fickle. Many former convicts, who could scarcely write their names, became wealthy while Mary's father acquired only badly blistered hands.

Since the Gaunt motto was 'Never give up' William continued to dig for gold for almost a year without much success before returning to Melbourne and using his legal experience to gain a salaried post with the Victorian Government's Goldfields Department. Acquitting himself well he was appointed Goldfields Commissioner in charge of the large mining camp at Indigo, near the lakeside town of Chilton. The post of Gold Commissioner was a prestigious and responsible one for a young would-be lawyer still in his mid twenties. He was given command of a band of mounted police who were a rough tough bunch who needed a firm hand to control them. William's job was to keep order over a large area where murder, theft and rape were prevalent and protect the Chinese gold miners whose lives were often threatened by Australian miners. As Gold Commissioner Mary's father was given a uniform that resembled that of a cavalry officer — a black jacket ornamented by gold braid, white breeches and black leather boots, polished every day by his batman.

William Gaunt also served as a magistrate and Justice of the Peace, sitting in judgement on the petty criminals his troopers had captured and brought to the tent which served as his office. A second tent served as the Gold Commissioner's sleeping quarters and dining room.

In 1857 as 'Protector of Chinese on the Goldfields' William Gaunt risked his life in the Buckland River Riots to save Chinese goldminers when a gang of ex-convicts threatened to kill the pigtailed Chinese miners by drowning them in the river and attempted to burn down their homes.

As children Mary and her brothers were fascinated by tales their father related of those lawless days on the goldfields and when she grew up Mary would use incidents from her father's time as Gold Commissioner in her short stories and novels about the exciting days of the Victorian gold rush. In Mary's stories,

William Gaunt was fictionalised as Commissioner Jocelyn Ruthven, a courageous well educated Englishman with a passion for administering justice, even under the harsh and difficult conditions prevailing on the gold fields.

Mary Gaunt, like her father, was a good story teller and she captured the essence of life in a mining camp during the gold rush, where men risked their lives or would kill lucky miners to gain possession of gold. The small leather bags of gold dust brought to the Gold Commissioner for safety were stored in strong boxes in a tent beside that of William Gaunt, guarded day and night by troopers from the mounted police until the gold went under an escort of armed troopers to Melbourne.

⁂

Mary Gaunt was born in the mining town of Chilton near the Indigo goldfields in the reign of Queen Victoria. She spent her early years in a house named *Woodlands*. In a strange co-incidence the talented novelist Ethel Richardson (better known as 'Henry Handel' Richardson) spent part of her childhood at Chilton in a house called *Lake View*.

In 1860, a year before Mary's birth, William Gaunt married Elizabeth Palmer of Yackendendah Station, a large property to the south-east of Chiltern. Mary's maternal grandfather was an enterprising Englishman, born in more humble circumstances than William Gaunt. He ran away to sea as a cabin boy and through hard work and intelligence rose to become the captain of a large merchant vessel owned by the East India Company. In mid-life Captain Palmer married a Welsh girl and purchased a property at isolated Yackendah in the high mountain country to the south-east of Chilton and raised his family there.

William Gaunt met Miss Elizabeth Palmer when sitting in judgement on a case in the area which featured a member of the Palmer family. After their marriage they set up house in Chilton to be near the Indigo goldfields. The new Mrs Elizabeth Gaunt, no doubt proud of her husband's ancient lineage and royal blood lines, talked grandiosely of the Gaunts' ancestral home, *Melton Hall*.

William's privileged childhood at *Melton Hall* was a fantasy created by Mary's mother to impress friends and neighbours. However William did have affluent relatives in the north of England who Mary would meet later. He also had an uncle serving as a High Court judge in Bombay, and it may well have been that William intended, if he did not strike gold to join his uncle in India.

John Gaunt, William's father, was a banker who seems to have suffered financial reverses and had a large family to raise and educate. This may have been why William Gaunt arrived in Australia with very little money. However his legal training stood him in good stead and he would eventually obtain a law degree from the new University of Melbourne. In March 1867, William Gaunt (by then Police Magistrate for Beechworth), inherited money from a relative and gave Joseph Challenor who lived in Leek power of attorney to act for him over his small inheritance. [4]

Contrary to Mrs Gaunt's fanciful tales of the ancestral home of the Gaunts the land records for the county of Staffordshire reveal William's aunt and uncle only bought *Melton Hall* in the village of Melton from total strangers a *year* before young William sailed away to Melbourne. He could at best only have spent a few months there. [5]

Blonde chubby Mary Eliza Gaunt was born on 20 February 1861. Her birth was a disappointment to her parents who had hoped for a son. The following year Mrs Gaunt gave birth to a second girl christened Lucy Georgiana in the days when sons were valued but daughters were seen as a financial liability and married off young.

Not until 1863 did Mrs Gaunt finally produce the longed heir, Cecil Robert Gaunt, who would always remain her favourite child. She lavished all her love on Cecil and paid scant attention to her Mary and Lucy, who she never kissed or cuddled.

William Gaunt and his young family were transferred from Chilton to the larger town of Beechworth where Ernest was born. He would become as close to Mary as a twin brother.

In 1865 William Gaunt and his growing family were posted from Chilton to the town of Sale as Magistrate and Justice of the Peace and would later be posed to the gold rush town of Ballarat where Mrs Gaunt gave birth to a third son, named Guy. Both boys had cheerful natures, good looks and a love of adventure. The trio were always very close and banded together against the spoiled Cecil, the eldest son and his mother's favourite.

Mary with her ash blonde curls and big blue-grey eyes was a typical mid Victorian child, wearing long black stockings, button boots and a white pinafore to keep her dress clean. This was an era when children were meant to be seen and not heard. The family were Anglican and attended church on Sunday as a matter of course rather than from any deep and abiding faith.

While Cecil Gaunt, the eldest but not the most intelligent son of a clever hard-working father, played with his collection of lead soldiers and dreamed of cavalry charges and medals, his younger brothers played with ships and dreamed of going to sea. Mary, something of a tomboy, did the same as her two favourite brothers. While little Lucy played with her dolls Mary climbed trees together with Ernest and Guy and read tales of adventure and foreign travel.

In 1869 Mary's father was appointed Magistrate for the entire Ballarat region. This post entailed a great deal of travel on horseback to meet out justice in isolated areas. In the same year, possibly while her father was away on one of his trips, a fire badly damaged the family's weatherboard home. In a short story Mary would use this experience to write about a little girl roused from sleep who fled from her blazing home in her nightgown as her father carried out the younger children while her mother wept.[6]

Repairs to the Ballarat house cost her father a great deal of money as he had not been insured for the full value. Eight year old Mary, as the eldest child, bore the brunt of her mother's attacks of nervous depression over their reversal of fortune. William was doing further study to gain registration as a lawyer so his children saw little of him.

Aged ten, Mary and Ernest developed a passion for China, where their maternal grandfather, Captain Palmer, had spent so many years of his sea faring career. Granny Palmer showed her grandchildren treasures which her dead husband had brought home from his trips to China. They included intricately carved ivory balls, one inside the other, enamelled boxes and a blue and white porcelain bowl, made in the imperial porcelain factory for the Emperor Yongle. Granny Palmer explained that the bowl had been plundered by a British soldier from Peking's Summer Palace during the Opium Wars. Their grandfather had bought the bowl from a British soldier when visiting Peking and it had been part of a large set ordered for the household staff of the great Emperor Yongle.

Mary admired the blue and white Ming bowl so much that Granny Palmer gave it to her, no doubt pleased that her granddaughter appreciated beautiful objects.[7] Mary and Ernest read a great deal about China, thrilled by the idea of eventually visiting Imperial Peking and the Forbidden City built by Emperor Yongle. The three of them formed a 'Travellers Club', pledging themselves they would one day go 'to the ends of the earth, see the Great Wall, hire camels and follow the Silk Road which stretched from Xi'an in central China through the Gobi desert, a bleak but beautiful area surrounded by snow covered mountains. They talked of meeting nomadic Kazak people with their flocks of sheep and goats, visiting the bazaars and oases of Central Asia, taking the train to Europe, travel to England and see Melton Hall and the town of Leek for themselves. They would also visit the British Museum which held so many treasures they had read about.

For Ernest and Guy the way to fulfil their dreams of travel and adventure was to avoid working in an office, like their father, but to go to sea. Mary wished she had also been born a boy — she believed that, being a girl, she would miss the opportunity to travel abroad and have an adventures life.

In the absence of reliable birth control, Elizabeth Gaunt continued to bear children year after year. In 1872 Elizabeth Gaunt bore a fifth son named Clive who, like Mary suffered from asthma. Mrs Gaunt had the misfortune to have a baby boy and a baby girl — Vere and Alice Maud — who died in infancy.[8] Her misery made her neurotic and hard to live with. Mary who, as the eldest girl, bore the brunt of her mother's depression. It is clear that continuous pregnancies and deaths of infants must have overwhelmed Mary's mother.

With a family of six to feed and educate William Gaunt did not buy a larger house but chose to rent a lakeside mansion at Ballarat, named *Strathalbyn House*, which had been on the market for some time as a Ballarat bank had been unable to sell it, due to a downturn in property prices.

Elizabeth Gaunt became so tense and depressed that on occasions Ernest, Guy and Mary were sent to stay with Elizabeth's mother, Granny Palmer. The children loved their Welsh grandmother who had a Gaelic flair for vivid story that telling, which Mary inherited from her.

Strathalbyn House, where the Gaunt family moved just as Mary was about to turn fourteen, delighted the children. The handsome twenty five room mansion was set in extensive grounds sloping down to Ballarat's Lake Wendouree. Residents of Ballarat thought the Gaunts must be very rich to live in such an imposing mansion. But the truth was that William Gaunt paid a very moderate rent for a six year lease. The property had been repossessed by a local bank after its owner-builder had gone bankrupt and they had problems finding a buyer. William Gaunt, a prominent barrister, was regarded as a trustworthy tenant and the lease made him responsible for all upkeep. However, repairs turned out to be far more expensive than he had imagined, because the mansion and grounds required a large staff to keep it going.

The house, described by the agents as 'a gentleman's residence' was approached by a long gravelled drive, bordered by cypress trees. *Strathalbyn House* had wide verandas which faced a fountain imported from Italy by the original owner. William Gaunt's combined study and library had a large bay window which overlooked the fountain.

To the left of the main house lay the shrubbery which masked a large vegetable garden and an orchard. William Gaunt paid two full-time gardeners and a gardener's boy to maintain the extensive grounds. A groom and a coachman looked after his horses. All the children learned to ride — should they fall off they were ordered to mount the horse again and ride on. Fear was not an emotion permitted to Gaunt children. However, Mary found that horses gave her asthma and she much preferred boating on the lake with Ernest and Guy.[9]

Strathalbyn House had a drawing room so large that when needed it could double as a ballroom. Each of the seven surviving Gaunt children had their own study-bedroom, with additional bedrooms for guests and a larger bedroom for Mary's parents. As was usual in the Victorian era there were only two bathrooms for the whole household. Jugs of hot water were carried from the kitchen to the bedrooms by housemaids along with the portable hip bath the children used.

Behind the green baize door that divided the main house from the servants' quarters was a large kitchen with an iron range. Off this was a larder complete with wire meat safes and hooks to hang game, a wine cellar, a laundry and an ironing room with overhead drying racks, as well as a fireplace where flat irons were heated as at that period there was as yet no electricity. Beside the ironing room was the sewing room with a large linen cupboard.

A kitchen maid did the dishes, the boot boy cleaned boots and shoes and helped the grooms with the horses. Mrs Gaunt, although worn out by childbearing, fell pregnant again. She was often confined to bed or resting on the *chaise longe* in the drawing room. With its high ceilings the drawing room remained cool during the summer but it was hard to heat it in winter.

Mrs gaunt had a difficult time with the birth of Lancelot (Lance), her fifth surviving boy. Lance was fourteen years younger than Mary and would be Mrs Gaunt's last child surviving child, because her next baby, William, would die in infancy.

William Gaunt, now working long hours as a lawyer specialising in mining cases, often complained of the high cost of staffing *Strathalbyn House*. As Mrs Gaunt suffered from attacks of 'nerves' her husband had to pay for a resident cook, a kitchen maid, several housemaids, a nursemaid for Clive and Lance. Mary and Lucy had a governess until they went to Grenville College. William Gaunt employed a groom and a coachman to drive him to his office. Other expenses were the fees at Melbourne Grammar for his three eldest sons. By the time they went away to the army and the navy, there were still the two younger sons to educate at Melbourne Grammar and university.

In the Victorian era Mary and Lucy were made to do the ladylike thing and ride side saddle.[10] Mary described her teenage years as

> ... bounded by our father's lawns and the young men who came to see us and made up our picnic parties to the bush around Ballarat... I acknowledge the delight to be found in sitting on the box-seat of a four-in-hand carriage on a glorious moonlight night, with four horses going at full speed... luncheon in the shade by the waterhole, with romantic stories for entertainment and a young man with admiration in his eyes to listen. Life was not bad. But it was not nearly as good a life as the boys in our family were having.[11]

Mary's interest in equatorial Africa began many years earlier when she was staying at her uncle's home *Mannerim Station*, near Geelong. She was reading a book from her uncle's extensive library, translated from Spanish, which related the story of a cabin boy named Carlos who worked on a Spanish galleon wrecked off Africa's Slave Coast. Carlos and several Spanish sailors had been rescued from Arab slave traders by members of the Ashanti tribe who took Carlos and his shipmates to Kumasi, the jungle capital of the Ashanti kingdom. The king's sorcerer ordered that the captives must be sacrificed in order to ensure the gods would provide a good harvest. The Spanish captives were tied to Kumasi's 'fetish tree,' a huge banyan whose branches were hung with human skulls and bones.

In the book, which made such a deep impression on young Mary, little Carlos was saved as King Prempeh of the Ashanti tribe wanted to learn Spanish and decided that Carlos would live in the palace and teach him the language.

Mary, always a keen reader was intrigued that the Ashanti king owned a large library with rare and valuable books. Mary had to stop reading as a crisis occurred — *Mannerim* homestead was threatened by a bush fire. Mary's aunt instructed her to take cooling drinks from the kitchen to the exhausted fire fighters. As the fire crept closer, the homestead became a refuge for friends and strangers whose homes had been burned out.

Once the danger had passed, Mary returned to her uncle's library but due to the chaos with so many strangers in the homestead the book about little Carlos had disappeared and was never found again. Mary never forgot the story of the shipwrecked Spanish galleon, the Ashanti king and the 'fetish tree' adorned by skulls. She wondered if little Carlos had spent the rest of his life at Kumasi or managed to return home to Spain?

Back at *Strathalbyn House,* Mary looked up the Ashanti tribe in her father's *Encyclopaedia Britannica* which confirmed facts in the story she had been reading at *Mannerim Station*. King Prempeh did have a library of books in his jungle palace at Kumasi. The Ashanti *were* Africa's wealthiest tribe as their tribal lands had rich seams of gold and they even had gold at the bottom of their rivers.

Searching for more information on little Carlos and the mysterious Ashanti tribe, Mary read Henry Morton Stanley's *Through the Dark Continent*. Stanley was a journalist-explorer who became famous after discovering the 'lost' Dr Livingstone alive and well in the centre of Africa. *Through the Dark Continent* was Stanley's account of several journeys in Africa and experiences with British troops fighting the Ashanti when Britain's General, Sir Garnet Woolsey, attacked Kumasi, the capital of Ashantiland.[12]

Mary read everything she could find about Ashantiland. She learned that in 1823 General Sir Charles McCarthy led a British attack on Kumasi but he was captured and killed by Ashanti warriors. To celebrate their victory over the British the Ashanti held a cannibal feast and honouring the general as a man of valour, Ashanti warriors ate his heart in the belief that the valour would pass to them. To placate savage gods and secure a good harvest for the coming season they hung the skull and thigh bones of the dead general from the branches of a huge 'fetish tree' in the centre of Kumasi.[13]

Mary, keen to discover what had happened to little Carlos, told her brother Ernest that, when she was grown up, she would go to Kumasi and meet the Ashanti. Her mother was horrified by Mary's passion for travel to heathen places like Africa and China. Mrs Gaunt was determined her daughters would grow up to be accomplished young ladies, attend a coming out ball at Government House in Melbourne and find wealthy husbands.

In the pre-television era the ability for upper class girls to play the piano was deemed important to entertain dinner guests and playing the piano and singing after dinner by candlelight thought to be one way a girl might attract an eligible husband. Mrs Gaunt made her daughters practice the piano for three hours each day, something Mary detested. Realising she had very little talent for the piano she developed a stratagem to read and play scales at the same time. While Mrs Gaunt sat in an adjoining room believing her elder daughter was practicing the piano Mary was thumping at the notes and reading a book propped on the music stand.

> I placed a travel book on Africa on the music stand and endeavoured to absorb it while playing my scales.... [My] desire for independence and foreign travel was considered by my mother to be most 'unladylike' and likely to spoil my chances of marrying.[14]

Until they turned fourteen Mary and Lucy were taught in the school room at *Strathalbyn House* by various governesses. Mary was then sent to Ballarat's Greville College for Young Ladies at the age of fourteen to seventeen. She, gained top marks in subjects that interested her, like history and English and French literature. She hoped to work as a teacher or once women were allowed to study at the all male Melbourne University to study law. Lucy who enjoyed science and biology, dreamed of a career in science but for the moment tertiary education was still denied to them as they were female.[15]

At Greville College both the Gaunt sisters were awarded prizes — Mary for literature while Lucy won the Science Prize. Mary believed that since she received good exam results this demonstrated she was as intelligent as her brothers.

Mary was annoyed at having to mind young Clive and Lance when their nursemaid had her day off. She believed girls were as intelligent as boys and should be treated equally. In 1874, when Mary left Greville College, girls were still not allowed to study at the all male bastion of Melbourne University.

Under Queen Victoria young women were supposed to be frail and feminine 'angels of the house' and to regard the male sex as inherently cleverer. It was dinned into girls that the role of women was marriage and motherhood, something Mary refused to accept as gospel and years later would proclaim this in her books.[16]

Cecil Gaunt was not as clever as his father or most of his siblings. But as the favourite son no expense was spared, so Cecil was sent to a prestigious fee paying school in England to prepare him for the entrance exam for Sandhurst Military College. Mrs Gaunt hoped that Cecil would become an officer in a fashionable cavalry regiment where his skill in horse riding counted more than intelligence.

After attending Melbourne Grammar for a year Ernest, unlike the spoiled Cecil, was left to fend for himself. He was sent away to Britain as a cadet in the merchant marine service in the hope he would follow his maternal grandfather's carreer. Cadets in the merchant marine were more like cabin boys.

William Gaunt hoped that Guy, who was witty, clever and good looking would follow him at the bar. But Guy had a wild streak — life at sea attracted him more than the bar, so he too joined the merchant marine. Ernest and Guy hoped to be able to transfer into the more prestigious Royal Navy. They studied and worked hard to achieve their aim. Guy Gaunt transferred to the Royal Navy in 1885, a year after Ernest. They would have stellar careers in the Royal Navy and ended up as admirals but Cecil never became a general and ended his career as a colonel.

After Ernest and Guy had gone away to sea Mary missed them badly and felt forlorn at *Strathalbyn House*. Clive and Lance were too young to be playmates, but her mother continued to use Mary as an unpaid baby sitter for them.

At this juncture the bank sold *Strathalbyn House* to the Anglican Church as a residence for the Bishop of Ballarat. The Gaunts moved to a smaller house in the same town. A few years, when William Gaunt was made a judge, later the family moved to Melbourne.[17]

Ernest served in Australian waters before being posted to a ship in the China Seas and Guy served on in English waters on a training ship, the ss *Worcester*. Both boys did so well they were allowed to transfer from the merchant navy to the Royal Navy. Young Clive was also doing well at Melbourne Grammar and it was hoped he would study law.

Mary hoped to follow her father's example and study law once the senate of Melbourne University made up its mind to admit female students. She was tired of being the daughter stuck at home helping her mother with household duties. She wanted financial independence and a career, an unusual aim for a young woman in the reign of Queen Victoria. Convention demanded that middle class girls were not allowed to work for money and were pushed into early marriages, a principle Mary detested.[18]

Mary's difficult relationship with her mother caused her angst and embarrassment. She resented her mother's clumsy attempts to marry her off and being regarded as a pedigree heifer, only suitable for breeding purposes. She disliked the kind of callow young men provided as dance partners at debutante balls.

Mrs Gaunt warned her two eldest daughters that, should their father die before they had found husbands, they would have to become poorly paid resident governesses or maiden aunts dependent on their brothers for a home and income. But Mary hated the idea that marriage at an early age would be her destination and miss out on the opportunity to travel.

Mary's mother claimed that men of any standing did not marry clever women and that marriage should be the aim of every young lady. She warned her daughters that if they appeared 'bookish' they could ruin their chances of a good marriage. They should flatter young men at dinner parties, ask them what they did, profess an interest in sport, flirt a little and they would receive proposals of marriage.

Mary was embarrassed that her snobbish mother boasted about the fact that her husband was descended from the Royal House of Plantagenet. She escaped from her mother whenever possible to shut herself away in her father's library where she read his books. William Gaunt, like Mr Bennett in *Pride and Prejudice*, also sought refuge from a fussy neurotic wife in the peace and quiet of his library, with the result that he drew closer to Mary.

Meanwhile Ernest and Guy were at sea. Although working hard, they enjoyed travel and adventure. Both young men wrote long letters to their sisters, relating stories of their adventures.

Ernest was visiting the ends of the earth, sailing with the British fleet which patrolled the China Seas as far north as Vladivostock. Guy had been given a place on a wool clipper that rounded Cape Horn and sent Mary exciting accounts of his stormy voyage and the amazing icebergs that dropped off into the turquoise sea around Cape Horn. Like Mary, Guy was a natural storyteller whose amusing letters opened up new worlds to Mary. Ernest showed a talent for navigation and foreign languages and was learning Chinese and Russian.

Mary missed her favourite brothers and read and re-read their letters from foreign ports with exotic names. She vowed she would travel overseas once she had enough money to do so. Meanwhile she did her best to improve her French, read as much French literature as she could find, including the exciting short stories of Pieree Loti and Guy de Maupassant. She tried writing a few short stories which she sent to Guy for his opinion.

Cecil Gaunt, had a commission purchased for him in a crack cavalry regiment and was off to India where he planned to play a great deal of polo.

By the 1870s the Gaunt family were living in the e Melbourne suburb of Malvern and William Gaunt was working as a County Court judge, Clive was attending Melbourne Grammar School, hoping to study law at Melbourne University and it was planned Lance would follow him there. Mary still wished to study law but the senate of Melbourne University still refused to accept enrolments from female students. The Vice Chancellor and members of the all male senate believed the quaint notion that as women's skulls were smaller than those of men, women did not have sufficient brain power to study law or medicine.[19]

Mary and Lucy Gaunt, clever and ambitious, were angry their mother insisted they stay at home and fill the traditional role of 'angels of hearth and home' and insisted that once Mary was 'out in society' she would chaperone her to dances and dinner parties to meet what her mother called 'the right people' and find a suitable husband. While their brothers travelled the world unfettered by convention the Gaunt girls must live No 15 Moorhouse Street, Malvern until they met Mr Right and had homes of their own.

Mary detested housework and sewing and the idea of a debutante season to meet suitable husbands as though she was a prize heifer suitable for breeding purposes was insulting. Lucy was now ready to leave school and as keen as Mary to attend Melbourne University and while Mary hoped to become a lawyer Lucy wanted to study science.

Mary found herself trapped in a very different world busy with dressmaker's fittings for ball gowns was launched into Victorian society at a debutante ball. Photographs show Mary and other debutantes tightly laced into wasp waisted off-the-shoulder gowns with full skirts of taffeta or satin.

On the plump side, though with a very pretty face, Mary was corseted into a wasp waisted white ball gown and elbow length gloves to attend her coming out at a debutante ball at Government House, given by Lady Bowen. It was a tight social world riven by rivalries between Melbourne 'new' wealth and old money. Mrs Gaunt's social pretensions always embarrassed Mary and she watched her eldest daughter like a hawk at debutante balls but saw no signs of any budding romance. Mary felt ill at ease in her wasp waisted gown and looked better in more sportive attire. She admitted she was bad at small talk and her teenage shyness could be taken for pride. Callow young men bored her stiff. In discussions with men who shared Mary's literary interests she could be interesting and entertaining but feared she would not find them debutante circles where the talk was all about the price of wool or property and social events.

Mary knew that in her mother's eyes, she had failed to gain a proposal from a wealthy young grazier and was a disappointment, the daughter who had money spent on her ball gowns to no effect and was no doubt heading for spinsterhood.

But there were greater worries. Judge Gaunt became embroiled in a financial crisis which would financially cripple him and caught up in the tense political situation caused by the stupidity of Premier Graham Berry over the question of whether politicians should be paid had slyly inserted a clause to this effect in his Allocations Bill asking the Legislative Assembly for funds. On 8 January 1878 when Mary was still in her teens fearing that giving politicians a salary would result in idlers standing for election as paid MPs made Victoria's Upper House reject Premier Berry's Allocations Bill for funds to run the colony of Victoria. Berry retaliated with a devious plan designed to bring the upper house into disfavour.

On Wednesday, 9 January 1878, ('Black Wednesday'), Judge William Gaunt and 300 other public servants were dismissed as Premier Berry, feared that with supply blocked his government's money supply would run out. *The Argus* and *The Age* complained bitterly of Berry's high handed action claiming it would have evil consequences for the sacked public servants. They wondered if and when the unfortunate public servants would be paid.

Dismissal meant belt tightening and domestic economies for Judge Gaunt, now approaching fifty, now going bald but with a luxuriant beard. He still had his two youngest sons to educate and a wife and two grown up daughters to support.[20] Judge Gaunt and other public servants received no salary for *six* months and at a time when no unemployment benefit was available.

The high-handed action of Premier Graham Berry of the Colony of Victoria in sacking so many public servants caused anti-government protests in the streets of Melbourne. The Victorian Premier refused to provide compensation for the public servants. Mrs Gaunt tried to live as cheaply as possible. Mary's father organised a petition to be sent to Buckingham Palace , asking Queen Victoria to act in support of dismissed public servants. For months the matter dragged without any payment to the unemployed public servants, many of whom were now borrowing form the bank to feed their families or selling their houses.

The experience made Mrs Gaunt vent her distress and anxiety on her eldest daughter. She told Mary unmarried daughters were a drain on the family coffers and at a time of financial crisis she must accept the first suitor who offered marriage. This s led to bitter arguments between the mother and her strong-minded teenage daughter. Mary would use this unhappy experience years later in her novel *The Uncounted Cost* in which the eldest daughter is told it is her duty to marry well since her parents who have educated her expensively have lost their money and the education of her brothers' took priority and she must marry a wealthy suitor who can help the family financially.[21]

After eight months without being paid a penny, Judge Gaunt realised his petition to Queen Victoria had failed and he most to cut his losses. The Gaunts sold their Malvern home, and moved back to Ballarat where William Gaunt set up in private practice as a barrister,once again specialising in mining laws. To do this

William Gaunt had to borrow more money from the bank. He knew that establishing himself at the bar would take time. William Gaunt felt he must warn his children that due to the house fire and his six months without a salary he had used up his savings and they must make their own way in the world — if he died young, any money in the bank and the family home, would pass to their mother who had no way of earning an income. Mary and Lucy must find husbands who would support them and his sons make a success of their careers as Ernest and Guy were doing.

In the Victorian era most upper class girls were married by the time they turned twenty-one and Mary and Lucy Gaunt, wanting to go to university were regarded as very unusual by their mother and her friends. Mrs Gaunt worried about Cecil, a junior officer in an exclusive cavalry regiment where the pay was relatively small and the officers expected to use family money to pay for the purchase and stabling of their polo ponies and large mess bills which often amounted to more than their monthly pay. She wished she had money to send Cecil and was constantly urging Mary to find a husband. Mary was made to accompany her mother e on a round of social calls, sipping tea, eating cucumber sandwiches and making politer small talk with the wives of Ballarat's leading dignitaries. Mary suspected these visits were arranged to enable her mother's friends to assess her as a suitable wife for their sons.

As the eldest daughter Mary had to bear the brunt of her mother's nervous attacks and mood swings and was embarrassed by her mother's clumsy and inept attempts at matchmaking. Instead of meeting Mr Right at dinner parties Mary was invariably seated beside Mr Wrong, Mr Rude or Mr Stupid.

Herr mother's matchmaking and petty snobbery embarrassed Mary so much, she refused to attend any more dances or boring dinner parties. She said that as Lucy was now 'out in society' her mother could leave her alone and concern herself with Lucy's marriage prospects as she was the more attractive of the two. Mary would sty home and concentrate on reading the books in her father's library, where she sought solace from her mother's constant fussing and complaining. It seems at this juncture she read as much history and English literature and works by Russian authors that she could find.

Mary insisted she would find a husband in her own good time. She insisted she would only marry if and when she fell in love. If she did not meet a man she could love she was happy to remain love she loved, she was happy to remain single and wanted what Shakespeare referred as a ' marriage of true minds' and a husband who would treat his wife as an intellectual equal.

Mary's writing contemporary, who wrote under the name of Edith Wharton) also suffered from a snobbish mother who claimed writing was an unfeminine occupation. Edith (born Newbold Jones) suffered a broken engagement and feeling depressed gave in to her mother's wishes and married a friend of her elder brother named Teddy Wharton who proved a most unsuitable and unfaithful husband. Teddy Wharton developed a passion for automobiles and the couple toured France and Italy by car. In the carefree days before World War One both Edith Wharton and Mary Gaunt wrote entertaining and informative travel books at a time when only the wealthy travelled abroad and there were few travel writers.

CHAPTER 2

Fighting prejudice at university

When Mary Gaunt turned twenty a reversal in policy of the senate of Melbourne University opened the university to selected young woman who had the qualifications to matriculate. Overjoyed Mary applied to study law thinking at last she would be able to fulfil her ambitions and become a lawyer and be able to travel overseas. It had not been her ambition to become a professional author, not only was it not ladylike as Edith Wharton's mother assured her but writing was a very hazardous occupation which was unlikely to furnish the money on which to travel, Mary's main aim.

Things became fraught at home when Mrs Gaunt, on the verge of menopause, bore another child named William Henry after his father but the little boy died in infancy, which caused Mrs Gaunt to go into a prolonged depression, and her anger over her eldest daughter's ambitions escalated.

By March 1881 Mary was delighted to escape to a new world at university where she hoped to be treated equally to male students. The senate of Melbourne University had agreed, albeit reluctantly, to admit female students and Mary had applied and the name of 'Mary Eliza Gaunt' was the second to be inscribed on the university matriculation register.[1] Hoping to study law and earn enough to travel overseas, Mary was excited to enter the hallowed halls of Melbourne University.[2]

She was therefore bitterly disappointed when told that female students could only study for degrees in arts or the humanities — law and medicine were deemed too hard for women's smaller brains to handle. Equally humiliating for the twelve women in the first intake, was the fact that the male students patronised them and bigoted male lecturers ignored their questions at the end of lectures and marked down their written assignments. The only staff member who took Mary seriously was Edward Morris, Professor of English Literature who told clever Miss Gaunt she showed great promise as a writer and should think about becoming a professional author.

Mary's decision to abandon her arts studies was not made lightly and she realised that the writing was on the wall. , not one of that trailblazing university intake of young women would be awarded degrees as was the case.[3] Most st of the lecturers (all male) had secretly vowed to downgrade the exam results of female students to prove that women should never have been admitted to university in the first place.[4]

Convinced she was doing the right thing Mary left Melbourne University at the end of first year, claiming she had had enough of prejudice against women and would pour her energies into writing. She was supported by Professor Morris who told Mary she was a natural writer and had the potential to become an excellent novelist if she worked hard.

Mary's sister, Lucy experienced similar discrimination against women when two years later she enrolled at Melbourne University. Lucy Gaunt and her fellow student, Bella Guerin who became a talented journalist received poor marks initially and were failed in examinations so that it took these two clever young women *four* years to gain a degree which should only have taken three had they been treated fairly.[5]

Professor Morris felt strongly that discrimination against women was scandalous. By now he was teaching at the same school that Mary's younger brothers attended and on a visit to Ballarat the professor saw Mary at home and gave her a complementary copy of a book whose publisher hoped to have it reviewed. By now Mary's self-confidence was at a low ebb: Professor Morris told her to write her review and send it to *The Age* who would pay her a fee if they published the review and this was a good way of getting her name known in the fledgling Australian literary world.

Mary was thrilled when Melbourne's leading newspaper, *The Age*, printed her book review under her own name — a rare honour for a woman in a male dominated era.[6]

Mary's lucky break came in 1887 when the London publisher Cassells appointed Professor Morris as commissioning editor for *Picturesque Australasia*, a four volume series designed to celebrate Australia's first hundred years of settlement. He decided that Mary Gaunt was the best choice to write seven chapters on different aspects of the colony of Victoria including one chapter about Ballarat, another on the Eureka Rebellion and several on Victorian explorers.[7]

Picturesque Australasia was published in 1888 and Mary was thrilled when Cassells paid her a handsome fee for her work. Her chapter titled *Gold* received praise for its vivid writing about the gold rush and the work of Gold Commissioners in keeping law on order among often desperate men in search of wealth.

Mary Gaunt earned more money by writing short stories for *The Age* and *The Argus* under a male pen name, based on the seafaring adventures of her brothers Guy and Ernest.[8] Her short story about her father's experiences in the Buckland River riots, when he confronted Australian miners carrying banners bearing the message 'Kill the Chinese bastards', was serialised by *The Australasian*. Serials in newspapers had been how Dickens and Thackeray originally published their novels.

Queen Victoria died in 1901 to be replaced by her wayward eldest son, Edward VII. Although the new king was a serial adulterer who deceived his wife with numerous mistresses very little changed in the double standards over female and male sexuality. Virginity continued to be greatly prized in brides while young men from wealthy families were able to use their money and power to 'sew wild oats' and take mistresses, a situation Mary would address in her novel, *The Uncounted Cost*.

Aged twenty-eight Mary Gaunt was regarded as 'an old maid' and had almost given up hope of falling in love as had Lucy.

Mary continued to earn money from her pen by writing short stories for the *Melbourne Age* and the *Argus* and plotting a novel set in Ballarat. Her mother never stopped complaining that her eldest daughter was wasting her time trying to be a writer and would end her days in poverty. But strong minded Mary Gaunt resisted her mother's pressure to make a marriage of convenience and Lucy took Mary's side in the arguments and recriminations that ensued.

Mrs Gaunt was amazed when after a whirlwind courtship, kept secret from her mother, , Lucy became engaged to a young mining engineer named Oatley Archer. The couple had met by chance when he was on holiday from Malaya. In 1890, they wed and sailed for Malaya where Lucy's husband worked for a tin mining company leaving Mary to face her nagging mother alone.

Fortunately for Mary her father had read her short stories, felt she had talent and encouraged her to continue with her writing. But in Australia with its small population and no major publishing houses a viable literary career for a woman seemed impossible. Serious books were published in London with a small 'colonial' edition shipped to Australia and Mary concentrated her efforts on short stories which were so good they found a ready market in Melbourne newspapers and magazines.

Lucy's letters home described how she enjoyed a very different kind of life in a company bungalow with Malay house boys waiting on her. The bungalow was on the edge of dense jungle where tigers roamed and she was happy and in love with her husband. After a year Lucy announced she was pregnant and Mary was thrilled when asked to act as the baby's godmother.

Ernest's letters described how he was learning Mandarin, now entrusted with compiling reports for British Naval Intelligence on the political situation in China. Aware Mary was fascinated by China he warned it was not an easy country in which to travel as there was such distrust and dislike of foreigners. The Chinese government isolated foreign residents in five treaty ports and several Legation Quarters, the largest of which was in the centre of Peking.[9] Ernest joked that he had finally achieved his goal and visited 'the ends of the earth' as the China fleet sailed north to Russian ports like Kamchatka, Vladivostock and Novobirsk.[10]

Yearning to travel to exotic places like her siblings Mary described how

> ...wander fever was in my blood and that of my ancestors and in the blood of my sister and my brothers. Brought up in inland Victoria, as children of a sub-tropical clime we dislike the cold but enjoy wandering in many countries. Anybody can travel on the beaten track and this only requires money to do so. The *real* challenge is to do something no one else has done, accomplished with difficulty![11]

※

By 1890 Mary had earned enough from short stories and magazine articles to buy herself a second class passage on a P&O liner bound for London. She hoped to see the sights of London and sell the manuscript of a novel set in Ballarat titled *The other man*. With limited funds she hoped to use the money from an advance by a London publisher to buy a train ticket to China via Moscow, join Ernest in Peking, and from there explore Inner and Outer Mongolia and visit the Ming tombs.

Ernest was due for shore leave and they planned to hire camels and follow the old Silk Route to Kashgar, Azerbijan and into Asiatic Russia — the adventure of a lifetime. Mary was convinced this would make a fascinating travel narrative if she could only find a publisher.

En route to London, Mary's liner called at Bombay (now Mumbai) where she visited Great Uncle Judge Arthur Gaunt and his children.[12]

Arriving in London during the last decade of the reign of Queen Victoria Mary stayed with relatives as it was deemed unsuitable for young women to live alone with no one to chaperone them.

※

Gaunt relatives and friends of her father invited Mary to stay in their homes and took her sightseeing to Westminster Abbey, the Houses of Parliament, St Paul's Cathedral, London's Savoy Hotel built on the site of Prince John of Gaunt's former palace and visited his tomb. Mary may have made an excursion by rail to Eltham to see the remains of the great palace of Eltham he had once owned and where decades later she would buy a plot of land and build a house and she went to visit Gaunt relatives in Shropshire and Sheffield.

Although the diary of her London visit is missing in what became Mary's best selling novel *The Mummy Moves* published decades later she named the British Museum as one of her favourite places in London. [13]

The London literary world proved hard to enter for an Australian. However the fact she was able to sell lively well written short stories to magazine editors in London and in Melbourne gave Mary Gaunt some additional money on this, her first visit to London. A magazine editor by the name of Kinloch Cook bought *a story of life at sea* from her, believing she was a naval officer. He recommended M. Gaunt to his friend, a leading literary agent, Mr Watt of Paternoster Row.

Mary followed up the recommendation and sent Mr Watt some of her writing signed as 'Mary Gaunt', but heard no more. It would take several years before Mr Watt agreed to take on a female client. However once she had an experienced agent advising her, he would play an important role in her literary career and helped her to become a financial as well as a critical success. Mary started writing books in the 1880s and was a very popular author up until the early 1920s, a long career for a novelist at a time when very few women were taken seriously in the publishing industry.

However success did not come easily and Mary's very first full length novel set in Ballarat did not interest London publishers. Failing to sell *The Other Man*, Mary lacked sufficient money to make that longed for trip to China so was delighted when Ernest arrived in London on extended shore leave, looking much older having grown a beard as a befitted a naval officer.

Together brother and sister paid a brief visit to relatives in Sheffield and in the village of Horton, near Leek. *Horton Hall,* where their father had lived for a year before departing for Victoria, was a manor house of time-tinged stone with peaked gables, diamond-paned windows and a walled garden.[14] *Horton Hall* had stone flagged floors with a few pieces of rush matting. But the house was damp, which gave Mary an acute attack of bronchitis. After being confined to bed and cared for by worried relatives she was glad to go back to London.

Mary was sad to say goodbye to Ernest on his way to County Clare to court Miss Geraldine Martyn whose family owned Geoghans Castle, near Cork. His Irish visit took place at time when young ladies had to be chaperoned in the presence of young admirers until an engagement was announced. As a naval lieutenant Ermest Gaunt did not earn much and had no family money or private income like many young officers. However he was hard working, clever and an excellent linguist and as a naval officer had the requisite social prestige.

The Martyns, lived in a castle surrounded by agricultural land which was rented out were far from rich. It was however understood by the end of the visit that there was a romantic 'understanding' between Geraldine and Ernest and that once he had been promoted and could support a wife, he and Geraldine would marry.

In London Mary made further attempts to sell *The other man* to London publishers but they claimed with its Ballarat setting it was too parochial to interest British readers Encouraged by advice from the Secretary of the British Society of Authors of which she was a supportive n member Mary submitted short stories to as many English and Australian magazines and newspapers as possible and a London-based magazine published her true story about a sea voyage to Nova Scotia. Mary's vivid descriptions of her brother Guy's adventures at sea made Mr Kinloch-Cook, editor of the prestigious *English Illustrated Magazine* excited by 'the superb and vivid quality of the writing'. Aware 'women's writing' was scorned Mary felt it wiser to submit her story under the pen name *'An Officer on Board'* and so Kinloch-Cook sent a cheque made out to 'Lieutenant G. Gaunt' to Mary's London address asking for more stories from Lieutenant Gaunt. He was stunned to learn that the brilliant story with its detailed descriptions of sailing tall ships was written by Lieutenant Gaunt's *sister*. Thise editor recognised Mary's talent for vivid writing and commissioned more short stories from Miss Gaunt.[15]

Hating the idea of failure and determined to sell *The Other Man* Mary contacted many other London book publishers but all their editors wanted were sentimental romances set on sheep stations where a pretty governess fell in love with son of the wealthy grazier. This was not a genre Mary wanted to excel in.[16] She wanted to write novels with female protagonists who lived adventurous lives and gained financial independence through hard work.

By now Mary's funds were running low. She swallowed her pride and wrote to her parents asking them to advance funds until she could sell *The Other Man* or the idea for *Black Dave's Girl* to a publishers but they refused. Her mother claimed all their spare money was needed for school and university fees for Clive and Lance and her behaviour was unfeminine. She should return home. In 1891 Mary approached London banks for a loan but in the male dominated era they refused to advance money to a woman.

Lack of money forced Mary to return to Australia. She left copies of the manuscript of *The Other Man* with two London publishers and the synopsis of her second novel *Black Dave's Girl* which was nothing like the usual female romance which ended in a happy marriage. Mary's realistic novel depicted the harsh life of a working class girl on the Victorian goldfields and was influenced by readings the realist novels of the French author Emil Zola.

By now Mary was thirty and had still to have a major success. *The Other Man* but it was eventually published in serial form in the Melbourne newspaper, the *Argus*.[17]

Acting on the advice of London publishers that there was great interest in the gold rush, Mary set her next novel on an imaginary goldfield called Deadman's Gully using incidents from her father's days in the rough tough days when he kept law and order as Gold Commissioner. While her father was encouraging, Mrs Gaunt told Mary she was wasting her time trying to be a novelist and that having her living at home was draining the family finances. Mary must think of her family and accept the first men who proposed marriage or they would end up as old maids, living in a shack with a cat and a canary. Mary retorted she would rather remain single until she met a man who could be a loving husband and her best friend, but sometime wondered whether such a man existed.

Towards the end of 1893 the Gaunts received the good news that Lucy had given birth to a girl named Mary Ellinor. Lucy hoped her elder sister would act as godmother by proxy to her little namesake as Mary could not afford the sea voyage to Malaya.[18] Nevertheless, Mary was delighted at the thought of being godmother and all her life took a keen interest in Mary Ellinor.

※

Mary Gaunt was still selling short stories and articles to Australian magazines, including *The Australasian* whose proprietor, William Hurst liked contributions from women which attracted women readers. Hurst paid e Mary Gaunt and Daisy Bates good money for articles and short stories. But it was painfully obvious that to support oneself as an adult novelist in Australia, which still had no major book publishers, was virtually impossible.

The idea that women were only capable of writing sloppy romances persisted and this led to many women writers publishing under male pen names. Even the strong minded expatriate Australian Ethel Richardson, nine years younger than Mary Gaunt did not dare to use to publish under her own name but used the pen name *Henry* Handel Richardson.

Mary started her literary career in the 1880s with successful novels set on the goldfields several decades before Ethel Richardson's controversial novel, *Maurice Guest* appeared in print in 1908 but with its theme of homosexuality in the music world. Ethel Richardson, nine years younger than Mary, spent years trying to be a concert pianist and was relatively unknown when Mary Gaunt was celebrated in London literary circles.

Mary's talent as a writer and story teller was applauded in the landmark publication, *The Development of Australian Literature* (1898) whose authors claimed that Mary Gaunt 'must be added to the list of Australian writers of note for her vivid descriptive powers' and her books continued to sell to educated readers for many years on both sides of the Atlantic and in Australia

. Not until 1929 when Mary's sales were declining did the publication of *Ultima Thule* turn Henry Handel Richardson into a well known author. *Ultima Thule,* , the third novel in Richardson's trilogy about a fictitious Irish doctor named Dr Richard Mahony was based on the life of Ethel's father, Dr Walter Richardson.

Even in the Jazz Age in 1929 Ethel Richardson's novel *Ultimate Thule* was seen as deeply shocking as in it Richardson described her father's harrowing mental and physical decline and this novel became a *success de scandale* comparable to Mary Gaunt's 'shocking' advanced novel , *The Uncounted Cost* was banned from circulating libraries in Britain which dared to question the sexual double standards expected of young men who could 'sew their wild oats,' with prostitutes or maidservants but to marry a virgin bride. During the reign of Queen Victoria on the throne some London critics were shocked by the crude and 'unfeminine' novels of Mary Gaunt including *The Uncounted Cost*, while others saw her a novelist who dared to question women's roles in society and stand up for women's rights.

Mary's novels with their feisty heroines had their critics among older members of the establishment. No doubt family members and her literary agent would have warned her that she must continue to keep the cause of her husband's terrible death a secret and it was widely believed Dr Lindsay Miller had died of cancer.

The novel 'Black Dave's Girl' (an international success under the title *Dave's Sweetheart* was Mary's first novel to be published in book form but like so many novels at that time initially it was serialised in the *Sydney Mail*. Like her serialised novella recounting events that occurred during the anti-Chinese Buckland Riots the novel included vivid details if life in a mining camp in the early days of the goldfields, details related to Mary by her father who had worked in this rough and ready environment.

Jenny Carter, Mary's female protagonist was an intelligent strong minded sensitive girl, the daughter of a shanty keeper selling 'sly grog' to gold miners. Stark poverty had denied Jennie a good education which could have seen her escape from the harsh life of the goldfields.[19] She married a police sergeant who despised Jenny's father and takes out his frustrations on Jenny. She escaped from an abusive marriage with a handsome gold miner. But Black Dave is no romantic hero of the Mills and Boone variety. Unknown to Jenny, Dave has an alcohol problem, in this starkly realistic novels Dave uses violence against Jenny and this novel ends just as bleakly as the novels of , Emile Zola, a writer Mary Gaunt read and admired. Jenny, like Tolstoy's Anna Karenina who runs away from her husband has dares to break the sanctity of the Victorian marriage bond for love but both women find no happiness in their love affair.

London publisher. Edward Arnold, who had excellent literary taste and would make a name for himself by publishing E.M. Forster's *Howard's End* and *A Passage to India* was the first to spot Mary's talent for story telling in a vivid and interesting way. had talent.

Edward Arnold wrote to Mary telling her he was proud to have the chance to publish such a remarkable book as hers. British critics , praised her good ear for realistic dialogue and her vivid descriptions of life on the goldfields. Edward Arnold changed Mary's original title from *Black Dave's Girl* to 'Dave's Sweetheart and told her it was 'a powerful and impressive novel which would do very well in Britain' butt it must have the title changed to gain a wider market and give it a title more appealing to women readers. They hoped to sell the American rights which would mean greatly increased royalties. Edward Arnold wanted to take an option on Mary's next novel advising it should take place on the goldfields currently a subject of fascination in Britain and America.

CHAPTER 3

Finding Doctor Right

Late in 1893, to celebrate the receipt of money from Edward Arnold, Mary took an unchaperoned holiday to the Victorian town of Warrrnamboul, a coastal resort and centre of a potato growing area where she had a school friend from Grenville College. As an author with books about to be published in London and New York Mary was introduced to a distinguished physician, a former director of medical services for a Melbourne hospital. Dr Hubert Lindsay Miller knew Judge Gaunt by reputation.

Dr Miller had given up a prestigious position directing the medical services of the Melbourne Hospital when his wife fell ill. In the hope the sea breezes and mild climate of the seaside town of Warrnamboul, near Melbourne, might help his wife recover, Dr Miller gave up a prestigious medical appointment and set up his own general practice in a private house in Korroit Street, Warrnamboul.

SOMETHING MISSING HERE (DID HIS WIFE DIE?)

Dr Miller was the son of an Edinburgh doctor, who had gained his medical degree at Edinburgh University Medical School and carried out post-graduate studies in Brussels. He spoke French fluently and had travelled widely in Europe. He was seven years older than Mary, had been widowed for eighteen months and was emerging from a long period of mourning.

Mary found Dr Lindsay Miller very interesting and easy to talk to. What made him attractive to Mary was not just the fact he was 'tall, good looking' (her words) and intelligent but the fact he shared her passion for reading and foreign travel.

When Mary told Dr Lindsay Miller that, as children, she and her brothers Guy and Ernest had signed a pledge they would travel to the ends of the earth one day. As she added that her brothers had fulfilled that pledge Lindsay laughed and said he hoped to meet them one day.

On her return home Mary kept quiet about her developing relationship with the intriguing widowed physician, fearing her mother would meddle in her affairs and spoil her romance.

Mary and Lindsay corresponded in secret and their relationship deepened over several months. Eventually, when certain of their feelings, they declared their love for each other and it was agreed they would marry at a quiet wedding in Melbourne.

The year 1894 was one of great happiness for Mary, *Dave's Sweetheart* set on the Indigo goldfields (Deadman's Gully Goldfields was Mary for them). The novel sold very well in Britain and Australia and received excellent reviews. The literary critic of London's *Daily Telegraph* called it 'one of the most powerful and impressive novels published this year' while *The Spectator* magazine's literary pages called Mary Gaunt 'a writer of great dramatic power' and hoped 'we may have before long another novel from the same pen.' The literary critic of London's *Daily Telegraph* hailed Mary Gaunt as a 'brilliant new author' and, along with several other eminent critics in Australia, urged Gaunt to continue writing novels.[1] The novel went into a second edition in the year it was published. Arnold's, considering it a classic work would reissue Mary Gaunt's classic goldfields novel in 1915 before paper rationing was introduced, convinced it would be read by Australian soldiers stationed in England and once again this paper back edition sold out at a time when Mary Gaunt was a very well known author.

Bolstered by the success of her novel as well as her short stories set in Victoria's gold rush days, Mary finally told her parents she had met her very own sweetheart, a widowed doctor desolated by the death of his first wife. Dr Miller and Anne

Isabella Murphy, his first wife had celebrated their union with a large white wedding in Kew attended by the cream of Melbourne's medical elite, paid for by his wife's father, Sir Francis Murphy, another Melbourne physician. Now Dr Lindsay Miller wanted a quiet wedding with the minimum of fuss, as did Mary. All the happy couple wanted was to be together.

Mary reassured her mother that Dr Miller had his own practice in Warrnambool and a post graduate degree in obstetrics and gynaecology from Brussels. In 1883 he had served as Medical Superintendent of the Melbourne Hospital before taking his ailing wife to Warrnambool.[2] For the past eighteen months Dr Miller had been lonely but that had changed when he met Mary and was keen to start a new life with her. He was seven years older than Mary, good looking, intelligent and mature. Mary, who was happier than she thought possible, treasured the ruby and diamond ring Dr Lindsay Miller gave her to mark their engagement.

On 8 August 1894 at a quiet wedding at St George's Anglican Church in Malvern, Mary Gaunt, daughter of His Honour Judge William Gaunt became the second wife of Dr Hubert Lindsay Miller.

Mary had a problem in deciding what to wear at her wedding. She feared that aged thirty-three and on the plump side she would look ridiculous in the meringue-like crinolines worn by most young brides. Perhaps she did not wish to invite comparisons with her husband's first wife. Mary had always been sensitive to the fact that her younger sister was regarded as the family beauty while she was the clever and witty one.

Mary decided on a suitably slimming outfit for the wedding, which she designed herself. According to the Warrnambool paper, her Louis XV style gown had a bodice of silver lace over a softly flared skirt with an underskirt pale pink with a long bias cut skirt of French lace. Mary carried a bouquet of pink roses but did not wear a veil. Only close friends of the couple and immediate family were invited to the ceremony of two people deeply in love with each other. Bride and groom escaped as soon as possible from guests and well wishers to honeymoon at Melbourne's bay-side suburb of Brighton before returning to Dr Miller's home and surgery at Warrnambool.

Mary's husband was a tolerant mature man who found his clever and amusing wife as fascinating as she found him.[3]

Delighted to be free of her mother's nagging, Mary enjoyed what she would later claim was the happiest period of her entire life. She enjoyed learning about various diseases and their cures and helping her husband in his home-surgery on the corner of Koroit and Henna Streets. Mary found she did not get queasy at the sight of blood when her husband performed minor operations or delivered babies.

In those prudish days, should Dr Miller need to conduct a gynaecological examination, his female patients had to be fully clothed with a female witness in attendance to prevent any hint of impropriety. This meant Mary was often present in the surgery to help her husband when the receptionist had gone off duty.

Dr Miller encouraged his wife to continue writing and was proud of her literary talent. Having travelled a great deal, he was more liberal minded than most Australian men of his era.[4]

Edward Arnold wrote to Mary, confirming they had sold the American rights to *Deadman's*. Arnold's would bring it ou*t* in Britain with a colonial edition to be sold in Australia and New Zealand and wanted the buy the rights to her third novel. (SEE NEXT PAGE) Mary was thrilled and so was her husband. At long last those years of hard work were vindicated. Professor Morris had been right and her mother had been wrong — she *did* have talent.

In 1895 leading London publishers Methuen and Company published *The Moving Finger*, a collection of Mary Gaunt's Australian short stories, several of which had already been published in Australian magazines and Melbourne newspapers like *The Age* and *The Argus*.[5] Critics from the quality press praised the writer's gifts as a story teller, her excellent ear for dialogue and lively prose. They hailed her as an important new author and story teller whose heroines affirmed the intelligence and determination of women.

Unlike many husbands of the Victorian era Dr Miller had no objection to his wife using her own name on her books and did all he could to encourage her writing career. Copies of *The Moving Finger* were shipped to Australia by Edward Arnold's Colonial Library where the book proved very popular.

Mary sent off to London a manuscript titled *Deadman's Creek*. Arnold who regarded himself as an expert in marketing, said the book was well written and vivid in its prose but the title must be changed to *'Deadman's*. He was adamant that as the British rarely used the word 'creek' and referred to them as streams it must be changed. *Deadman's* had a note of menace and mystery and would intrigue readers. Delighted that her publisher loved her writing and would publish her second goldfields novel, Mary agreed happy that her literary career was taking off.

Two years later, in, 1896, the literary critic Desmond Byrne in his book *Australian Writers* praised Mary Gaunt's novels and claimed that this Australian born writer 'had lifted the short story to an artistic level' not even approached by any other Australian writer.'

Several of Mary's novels and short stories, including another novel set in Australia, titled *Kirkham's Find*, whose heroine achieves financial success through bee keeping had British and Australian editions published during those first happy years of marriage at a time Mary had no idea of the tragedy that lay ahead. Her dedication of *Kirkham's Find* to Dr Lindsay Miller says a great deal about Mary's happiness when she wrote,

> To my handsome husband and closest friend in loving acknowledgement of the tenderness and sympathy which makes our married life so happy'.

Mary's novel *Kirkham's Find* was set in Ballarat and Warrnambool and had exciting scenes based on the experiences of William Gaunt as Gold Commisisioner and 'Protector of Chinese miners' who had quelled anti-Chinese riots at Packhorse to the south-east of Chilton. Mary's hero, Commissioner Jocelyn Ruthven was based on her father and in the book Commissioner Ruthven risked his life to quell the riots and save Chinese lives. She describes him wearing a dashing uniform of a cavalry officer, a black jacket with gold lacings white breaches and long black leather boots, riding around with a band of troopers quelling riots. Commissioner Ruthven, like William Gaunt, sat in judgement on murderers and thieves, many of whom were former convicts.

In this novel Mary did not limit herself to Victoria and wrote about gold rush in the Northern Territory where prospectors encountered Aborigines in the wild and were impressed by their hunting and tracking skills but behaved very callously towards them.[6]

In 1898 Mary's third novel set on Deadman's Gully goldfield appeared under the title *Deadman's: An Australian Story* and enjoyed critical acclaim and large sales in England, Australia and America. (REPEATED)

Writing under her married name as 'Mrs Lindsay Miller', Mary did her best to raise money for underprivileged women and wrote a series of articles for a very small fee hoping to raise public awareness of the need for donations to help the poor and needy at a time when there was no such thing as a welfare state. She became involved with various charitable projects and pro suffrage meetings as well as keeping chickens. She wrote an article advising country women they could gain financial independence by raising hens, selling eggs and keeping the money for themselves. All her life Mary would insist that women must develop skills to earn money or their would be no equality in their marriage.

During the early years of her marriage Mary widened her interests as a result of helping her husband in his surgery and wrote articles about social services and the new all Women's Hospital in Melbourne. She took a keen interest in this subject, realising the struggles these women had been through to study medicine at Melbourne University, where they had encountered great trouble gaining degrees due to male prejudices against women in medicine. At least it was a change from the days when Mary attended Melbourne University and Professor Balls-Headley, Professor of Medicine, had *refused* to let women study medicine, claiming that their brains would overheat if they studied, causing them to become infertile. He recorded this theory also in a textbook on women's ailments.

Several of the Women's Hospital pioneer women doctors, like Dr Constance Stone and her sister, had faced the same prejudices against women at university as Mary had encountered. Dr Constance Stone had such prejudice against her she had to finish her studies in America in order to be allowed to qualify as a doctor in Victoria. Mary continued to visit the hospital and raise funds for it and make donations herself when she received money for her short stories.

Mary was keen to help raise funds for the fledgling Melbourne Women's Hospital, run entirely *by* women *for* women. As most of the patients were too poor to afford paying hospital fees, the Women's Hospital relied on donations to survive. Mary did her best to raise money for this hospital and other charities by writing articles about the valuable work women doctors were doing. Encouraged by her husband, she wrote articles for the Melbourne *Argus*, intended to raise funds for volunteer organisations caring for the sick, the disabled and the poor. These were published at regular intervals in the early 1890s.

As Mrs Miller, Mary led a busy life with a home to run, meals to cook and some duties at the surgery. Fortunately, she was aided by a part time assistant and a local cleaning lady.

In an interview with the local Warrnambool paper Mrs Miller disclosed she lacked a proper studio or writing room and wrote on the kitchen table and hoped eventually to have her own garden studio where she could write her books without being disturbed.[7]

Research for these articles about social justice and feminist ideals opened Mary's eyes to the hard life of working-class women, who worried about feeding large families. Lacking access to reliable contraceptive measures or proper information about birth control, many of these women had born more then a dozen children. At her husband's surgery Mary saw many women who had prematurely aged as a consequence of frequent pregnancies and the harsh lives they led. They often arrived at the surgery nursing babies with two or more toddlers clinging on to them and, without doubt, another four or five children at home or working in low paid employment. She realised how hard it was for working-class families to raise enough to pay the doctor when illness or accidents affected them. Frequently, Dr Miller treated members of such families for free. Mary realised that her mother had also suffered a great deal in bearing nine children (three of whom died in infancy), but at least Mrs Gaunt had suffered in comfort.

Growing up in a middle class family and educated privately, Mary had been cushioned from the horrors of nineteenth century poverty. Now, as a doctor's wife, she saw for the first time the sufferings of working class women, most of whom married at sixteen or seventeen and stoically faced pain in childbirth and bore a child each year. She saw women with their faces bruised and battered and limbs broken by drunken husbands who had beaten them. It was an experience she never forgot.[8] When assisting her husband in his surgery, Mary saw how some men and women confronted pain and death with courage.

Mary was invited to join artistic and literary friends in a fund raising venture to help the Melbourne Children's Hospital. A group of artists and writers aimed to donated stories and artwork for a book to be titled *Childhood in Bud and Blossom*, to be sold to fund the work of the hospital. Among the illustrators were leading Melbourne artists like Walter Withers, Emma Minnie Boyd and her husband Arthur Boyd.

Mary donated a short story to the charitable project , *The Light on Goat Island* which was illustrated by Arthur Boyd. All contributors were invited to an evening launch of the book .

In 1898 Mary embarked on a new novel, her fourth on an Australian topic. It was set in colonial Sydney in the days of Governor Hunter —a turbulent world of convicts and emancipists. She stopped work on this projected book as he husband's behaviour deteriorated and put it away. She would not take up her work on this novel for two more decades.

After four years of a very happy marriage, Dr Lindsay Miller began to exhibit erratic behaviour and disordered thought. Mary must have been very worried and consulted medical friends who may have feared Dr Miler was s suffering from premature senile dementia rather than seeing it as a sign of the mental disturbance caused by tertiary syphilis. What was then an incurable disease has many recorded cases of striking wealthy young men who frequented prostitutes carrying the disease and medical students far too poor to think of marriage who often frequented prostitutes. In Edinburgh where Dr Miller studied medicine decades earlier there was a culture of heavy drinking among students usually in the Grassmarket, which teemed with prostitutes offering sex for a few shillings.[9]

The connection between syphilis and grand paralysis of the insane, though suspected by doctors was by the late 1890s not *definitely* established. As yet there was no Wasserman test to prove the lethal syphilis spirochete had entered the blood and no cure until the discovery of penicillin in the second World War so lunatic asylums were filled with inmates suffering the horrors of tertiary syphilis with progressively paralysed limbs, diseased spines and brains. Some had rotting nose bones as this dreaded disease ate away at the skull as well as the heart and other internal organs.

Grand paresis or paralysis of the insane damaged the brain and spinal cord, and this was t the *the diagnosis on the death certificate of Dr Lindsay Miller. [10])

Mary's husband died at Kew Lunatic Asylum in October 1900. The only sign of the disease in its primary stage had been a small chancre that developed on the penis or inside the body for a few weeks which was often overlooked or ignored.

During the secondary period which could last for decades the spirochete lay dormant but could infect female sexual partners. In the final or tertiary stage it caused a gradual deterioration in mind and bodily functions ending in insanity, paralysis of limbs and trunks and loss of normal bodily functions.

Since Mary did not write about this terrible period in her life one can only imagine her distress as the symptoms grew worse and her husband's whole character and behaviour changed. Initially, like Henry Handel Richardson's father, his behaviour must have been erratic and irritable and as a result patients left his practice and went elsewhere. [11] Tertiary syphilis had a latency period which could be as long as three or four decades and many sufferers were ignorant of the fact they had been infected.

This fatal disease affected rich and poor, beggars and prominent men, one of the most famous being Lord Randolph Churchill, son of the Duke of Marlborough. Having been infected as a young man by a prostitute Lord Randolph eventually had to resign as Chancellor of the Exchequer after his behaviour became so disturbed his parliamentary colleagues were embarrassed by him. His wife, Jennie., appraised of the problem by Dr Buzzard took her ailing husband on a voyage round the world to hide him from the eyes of the press and avoid embarrassing his parents, the Duke and Duchess of Marlborough.

For decades this diagnosis was questioned until Jennie Churchill's biographer Anne Sebba unearthed long-hidden case notes made by Dr Buzzard, Lord Randolph's physician, buried away from journalists in the library of the Royal College of Physicians. Dr Buzzards' case notes described Lord Randolph 'as well into the 2nd stage of gpi' the standard abbreviation for the diagnosis of 'grand paralysis of the insane' a disease of the brain and spine. It was usual in cases of prominent men not to mention the word syphilis on the death certificate.

Anna Sebba's biography of Jennie Churchill gives a detailed description of the physical and mental decline of a syphilitic and the progressive numbness that afflicted Lord Randolph Churchill's hands and feet. It resembled what occurred with Ethel Richardson's father, Dr Walter Richardson. In this case both wives soaked the numb and paralysed limbs in hot water for hours at a time to give the sufferer some relief. To pay for private treatment by a physician and a private room in Kew Lunatic Asylum Mary sold their Warrnamboul home and rented a house at Kew to be close to the asylum. Probably like the other wives she soaked the numbed limbs in hot water for hours, one of the few things she could do for the man she had loved so much. [12]

In 1899 Dr Lindsay Miller occupied a private suite hidden away from other patients and having held the post of Medical Superintendent of Melbourne's leading hospital was well known in medical circles. Given the horror with which 'Cupid's disease' was regarded in 1900 Mary must have told as few people as possible of the real cause of her husband's decline into insanity. Like Lady Jennie Churchill, Mary was warned she may have caught the disease from her husband. This was the case was the case with Danish writer Karen Blixen who died of syphilis having been infected by her husband Baron Bror Blixen. Mary's fellow member of the British Society of Austhors, e novelist Violet Hunt was infected after an affair with her editor , Oswald Craufurd at Messrs Chapman and Hall. Mary must have been warned by her doctor of the doctor at the Kew Lunatic Asylum she could have been infected and have worried over the possibility but fortunately for her she escaped infection by lethal sexually transmitted disease, the AIDS of its era .[13] So great was the shame of syphilis that even mentioning the word was taboo for ladies. Penicillin which would eventually provide a cure for syphilis was not invented until 1942.

A harrowing portrait of her father Dr Walter Richardson, confined to a lunatic asylum with his limbs paralysed and reeking of gangrene appears in Henry Handel (Ethel) Richardson) in her novel based on fact titled *Ultima Thule* (though she does not mention the word syphilis and implies her father's death was due to dementia.) . The numbness that gradually spreads to her father's limbs is alleviated by soaking in hot water for hours and Ethel's mother went to the asylum to do this for her husband. Henry Handel Richardson was haunted by shame that her father had died of syphilis for the rest of her life.

In 1900 Mary Gaunt, with a dark secret she had to hide, had to sell their combined home and surgery in Warrnamboul to pay large hospital and medical bills at a time when there was no such thing as medical insurance and pretend that her husband was suffering from cancer. She rented a house in Princess Street, Kew to be near the Lunatic Asylum. In the same way as other wives of syphilitic men Mary alleviated her husband's s numbed limbs but soaking them for hours in hot water. [14]

Using money from the sale of their matrimonial home, her only asset, Mary paid for an expensive private room so her husband had a proper bed rather than a straw mattress and decent meals served on proper plates as public patients in Kew Lunatic Asylum were treated like animals.

Shortage of staff saw those who were violent chained up left to lie in their own filthy or in padded cells as they could no longer control th Some who became aggressive were strapped to a evice known as Dr Benjamin Rush's restraining chair or bled until they became weak, two methods of control in the era before calming psychiatric drugs were invented. [15]

In the case of Dr Lindsay Miller since no blood test existed in 1900 which could positively identify the syphilis spirochete, to spare relatives the word syphilis did not appear on the death certificate and his death certificate referred to 'a disease affecting the spine and brain.'

⁂

As Dr Miller's wife there would have been n fears Mary may have been infected with what was then known as 'Cupid's disease' spread by sexual intercourse. Some women were infected with syphilis by their husbands during the secondary stage, including the Danish author of *Out of Africa*, Karen Blixen infected by her husband, Baron Bror Blixen who like her husband died of tertiary syphilis.

Dr Miller died at Kew Lunatic Asylum on 30 January, 1900, the diagnosis on the death certificate 'disease of the brain and spine' a tactful way of describing syphilis.

The terrible sufferings of her husband took its toll on Mary. She returned to her parents' home in Ballarat y depressed and grief stricken. In *Alone in West Africa*, written a decade later, Mary describes herself as 'sick and miserable, and how much she missed her husband after his death though to all intents and purposes she 'lost' the read Dr Miller once he was committed to Kew Lunatic

Asylum and he was no longer the dignified confident physician she had married.

Rather than going overseas immediately Mary retreated to her parents home to sort out her financial position as being declared a lunatic and unable to manage his own affairs had died intestate. Mary found herself homeless, money and trained to do nothing but write short stories and books. After running her own home at Warnamboul she found it impossible to endure her mother's constant criticisms.

Mary remained tight lipped about her husband's death and far too proud to ask for money from her parents.[16] She determined to support herself in the hazardous world of writing, the only world she knew. She had problems sleeping, ate little and like most people who are depressed lost concentration. Mary r described herself as 'sick and miserable' knew she must rebuild her life and continue writing.

Aged forty, after working very hard as a writer and a doctor's wife and secretary-assistant , Mary was left with a meagre annual income of £30 a year and one hundred pounds in cash, enough to buy herself a passage on another P and O liner to London. This was still the centre of the publishing and literary world, , home of George Bernard Shaw's New Woman who was demanding the right to vote and a chance to gain higher education and careers. In 1900 out to change society were grouping together in female organisations and residential clubs like the Lyceum in Piccadilly which Mary would join.

After an uncomfortable voyage in an interior cabin as this was cheaper than one with a porthole Mary arrived at Tilbury Docks. She caught a train to St Pancras and searched for relatively inexpensive lodgings. While Australian authors like Katherine Susannah Prichard and Louise Mack were enchanted by the historical aspects of London Mary disliked its climate and unfriendly atmosphere. y. Perhaps this dislike was a result of her misery over the terrible end to her marriage but she described returning to ' cold unfriendly London' with its ' grey pavements' as a widow with little money, who had suffered deeply and had very few friends in England. She did have Gaunt relatives in Shropshire who she scarcely knew but with whom she sought to establish a rapport. She described how she tried to ' pick up the broken threads of my literary aspirations'.[17]

The idea of travel to Europe and China so kept her going. London was still the centre of publishing. She would find a publisher, make money and go by a train to Russia and China and carry out their childhood plans developed with Ernest to travel the Silk Route through the Gobi desert to Asiatic Russia.

Years later Mary Gaunt described in *Alone in Africa,* her state of mind as a widow. ' I was penniless, homeless and alone. Had I stayed in Australia quietly I had exactly thirty pounds a year to call my own but I wanted *to see the world.*[18]

And see the world she did! With little money but plenty of determination but far from athletic, in spite of being asthmatic and overweight, Mary Gaunt would become one of the most renowned travel writers of the early twentieth century.

The effect on Dr Miller's widow of the harrowing end to her love match was profound. Raised as a conventional Anglican but never devout after the sufferings of her husband she rejected the idea of God. Like Ivan in the *Brothers Karamazov,* (and Mary read widely in Russian and French literature both at university and in the library of the British Museum) Mary came to believe that the existence of suffering contradicted the idea of a benevolent deity who cared about mankind. Either there was a god who did not care so was inherently evil or God was a illusion created by man out of fear of the unknown. She became interested in the fear theory when studying the power of sorcerers and black magic in Africa.

Her cynicism about organised religion affected her feelings about missionaries in Africa who she felt would have done better to have stayed at home.

However when Mary was in Outer Mongolia and stayed for some time at a medical mission the sincerity and devotion to duty of medical missionaries nursing the sick and dying Chinese and risking their own lives in the process moved her deeply. Her novel

A Wind from the Wilderness relates the story of doctors in a medical mission there and it would be published in 1919.

Watching French nuns nursing Chinese women and children in a cholera epidemic affected the cynical Somerset Maugham and caused him to incorporate their dedication inspired by their faith his Chinese novel *The Painted Veil* which was published a year later than *A Wind from the Wilderness*, Mary's most appealing novel for the modern reader.

At the start of *Alone in Africa* Mary Gaunt revealed how much she missed her late husband. He had died in 1900 but the brilliant physician she had married 'died' a year earlier as this terrible disease overtook and changed him into a very different entity when she was forced to commit him to the Kew Lunatic Asylum.

Mary's harrowing visits to her husband in his private room at the barracks-like Kew Lunatic Asylum can only be imagined. In an era when syphilis was too shocking to mention Mary locked this harrowing experience away inside her and went to London to make a new life for herself. What little money remained after Dr Miller's death was invested in an annuity which provided the grieving widow with the princely sum of thirty pounds per annum. Like Somerset Maugham who refused to practice medicine even though he had studied it for five years and preferred to live from writing.

Writing came naturally to Mary Gaunt as Professor Morris had noted. Like Somerset Maugham she believed the subconscious mind enhanced the creative act and took over sometimes at night when the writer was sleeping and resolved problems from the previous day.

Both of these talented 'natural' writers sat down with a book of unlined paper and the words flowed from the ink in their fountain pens. Both had iron self control and a sense of discipline and set themselves the e task of writing at least 1,500 words per day.

On her previous visit to London Mary had discovered the delights of the British Museum library which was free of charge to readers applied for a ticket. The British Museum and d foreign travel would be her consolations for leaving Australia.

CHAPTER 4

Mary postponed her visit to China

'*A perceptive study of men and women which deserves to be successful*'.
The Times, London, 3 February 1910, reviewing *The Uncounted Cost*, the banned novel of colonial life by Mary Gaunt.

Mary found life in crowded noisy foggy London expensive and missed tranquil Warrnamboul with its sea views and golden wattles in blossom. All she could afford to rent on the meagre amount of her savings was a furnished bed-sitter in a Kensington basement, the cheapest accommodation in a respectable area which in the days before hotels and foreign students took over was beloved of maiden ladies and professional couples in the tall narrow houses, where coachmen and horses occupied the mews to the rear.

Mary chose to live in Kensington as she liked open spaces around her. Kensington Gardens and the Serpentine were attractive to her. Londoners in 1900 s warmed themselves with coal fires, London streets were lit by gas lamps, the wealthy drove around in landaus or the smaller broughams pulled by only a single horse like the Prince of Wales t on his secret visits to the homes of married mistresses. Those who could not afford to maintain their own transport like Mary Gaunt hired hansom cabs or walked.

With her passion for the British Museum it is surprising Mary did no chose to live in Bloomsbury like Sydney writer and former journalist Louise Mack who also sailed to London in 1901, determined to write a 'literary' novel which would garner good reviews and make her famous. Louise Mack starved in a Bloomsbury attic to write *An Australian Girl* in London, but it was poorly promoted and did not make her any money. Cold, hungry and with holes in her shoes Louise Mack abandoned 'literary' ambitions for a well paid job writing slushy romances for the women's section of the *Daily Mail,*

In Kensington Mary lived frugally in a chilly rented bed-sitting room Mary wrote the outline and sample chapters of another novel, renewed contact with London publishers who did not seem interested in her work. At this critical period managed to survive by writing short stories for Melbourne papers (where her name was well-known) and sending stories to British magazines about the adventures of her brother Guy Gaunt at sea.

Cold, lonely and suffering debilitating attacks of bronchitis and asthma in winter Mary Gaunt refused to earn good money by writing sentimental twaddle like Louise Mack who had sold out to Mammon and Lord Northcliffe. Fortunately for Mary she had kept up her ties with Australia and readers and editors of the Melbourne *Argus* and *Age* still wanted her short stories set on the Victorian goldfields.

In the pre-telephone era, letters keep Mary in touch with her siblings. She learned that Cecil Gaunt had made an very good marriage while serving as a cavalry officer in Bombay, His wife was the daughter of General Moorsom, and Helen's private income and his father-in-laws connections helped Cecil's army career and deemed an excellent choice of wife for her favourite son by Mrs Gaunt.

Guy Gaunt, who shared Mary's talent for story telling had little time to do so as a lieutenant in the Royal Navy. He had been singled out for commendation when serving in a cruiser off the Philippines and as Mary arrived in London became a hero for his courage and leadership skills when commanding the ss *Porpoise.* In those days British gunboats were sent to quell revolts in far flung places and Guy arriving at the Samoan capital of Apia went ashore with a band of armed men leading an expedition to defend the British Consulate against an attack by rebels. The British press described how 'Gaunt's Brigade' aided by Samoan loyalist troops kept the British Consulate and its staff safe from attack. The charismatic Lieutenant Guy Gaunt was mentioned in despatches for bravery under fire. In 1904 Guy married a wealthy widow named Margaret Worthington, daughter of Sir Thomas Wardle. While Mary's husband was in Kew Lunatic Asylum Ernest, married Geraldine Martyn... whose parents were Anglo Irish gentry the hereditary owners of Geoghan's Castle in County Clare and in 1900 became a hero of the Boxer Rebellion leading a band of marines into Peking to relieve the beseiged and starving British Legation staff and was also promoted to the rank of captain.

Mary was very proud that her favourite brothers were doing well in the navy . Living in London on very little money was chilly and uncomfortable for Mary but vital for her success in the literary world as all the main publishers were there. Mary was never very fond of London and called it 'cold, grey and unfriendly'. She, longed for the space and warmth of Australia and was homesick for friends in Ballarat and Warrnamboul.

She wrote her thousand words each day and edited the previous day's work and prepared short stories for The Age and The Argus who still wanted her work. She was trying to find a topic for an international novel that would have the same success as *Kirkham's Find*. When finally she achieved her aim and had become a very successful writer, Mary admitted how lonely she had been in those early years in Kensington.

> I had no one to speak to from morning to night so I wrote and wrote and wrote... I was sick, miserable and lonely. I longed for Warrnamboul where the sun shone and roses climbed over the wall and white pittosporum blossoms filled the air with their fragrance... I did not go back to my father because my pride would not allow me to call myself a failure and because all the traditions of my family were against giving in. But I was very near it, very near it indeed.[1]

In her chilly bed-sitter Mary lived frugally on the cheapest food available and cups of tea. The boom of the early 1880s haad ended in bank crashes in the 1890s, banks were reluctant to lend and British publishers reluctant to risk more novels set in Australia. They told Mary the market had changed since she wrote her two goldfields novels and the public wanted novels set in England butt Mary found this hard. The wide open spaces of Australia and goldfields or sea faring adventures were what inspired her.[2] Determined not to return to Australia as a failure she repeated her father's maxim, 'Gaunts never give up!'

She attempted a novel about her ancestor, Katharine de Roet Swynford, and her complex relationship to her lover, Prince John of Gaunt trapped in a marriage of convenience to his cousin, Duchess Blanche of Lancaster, who eventually died of the plague when Katherine was in her late twenties with two children by her late husband. But Prince John was not allowed to marry Katharine who lacked the necessary blood royal. He was ordered by Edward III to make another highly politicised marriage of convenience to the daughter of the wealthy King of Castille. Only after she died did Prince John of Gaunt return to England and marry Katharine Swynford, mother of his four adult bastards by which time Prince John and Katherine were middle aged. Prince John of Gaunt was able to have his illegitimate sons made dukes and died three years later.

Mary enjoyed researching the historical background and re-visiting the Savoy Hotel on the Thames Embankment, once the great Savoy Palace home of John of Gaunt and his duchess and the ruins of Eltham Palace, his hunting lodge in Kent. But the historical sources Mary consulted varied widely in how they regarded Katharine Swynford, the royal mistress who broke centuries of tradition to become a royal wife. Some praised her sweet nature and the fact she spoke English, French, Flemish and read Latin. Others reviled her as a scheming *femme fatale* who had wormed her way into Prince John's bed and gained ideas above her station in life.

Widowed again after his second wife died and having failed to gain the crown of Castille, Prince John returned to his long-suffering mistress and four adult children who scarcely knew him. He did finally marry Katherine when two of John of Gaunt's illegitimate sons by her were given dukedoms. One became Duke of Beaufort and built a stately home called Badmington. Katharine's third son was created a cardinal. but a decree forced these right royal bastards to style themselves 'Beaufort' rather than Gaunt to avoid jeopardising the succession of their father's legitimate heir, Henry Bolingbroke(, who would rule as Henry IV).

Mary Gaunt's ancestors claimed descent from an illegitimate grandson of Katherine and John of Gaunt who dared to use the name Gaunt in defiance of the parliamentary edict.[3]

Guy found Mary's research fascinating. He and joked that it gave them the right to claim the Duke of Beaufort as a distant relative so en masse they should all pay the duke a visit at his stately home? . Other English and Australian relatives were not amused. Illegitimacy was almost as shameful as syphilis (which until the invention of the Wasserman blood test in 1904 for syphilis Mary must have feared she could have caught from her late husband since the spirochete can be latent low for many years.

Gaunt relatives implored Mary not to turn their family history into a novel which could make them the butt of lewd jokes and with her own dark secret about the cause of her husband's death which she did not wish to be made public, either in deference to their feelings or as a result of a veiled threat Mary shelved the projected novel and never returned to it.

She still hoped to visit China to write a book about the country. However but letters from Ernest who had served in a ship of the British China Station d pointed out most of the Chinese distrusted foreigners. The Boxers, (Society of Righteous Fists) had sworn to kill any foreigners on Chinese soil for offending their gods. The situation was tense and wives and daughters of Legation officials were being sent home for that reason.

The Boxers believed that the long drought and subsequent famine, were caused by the anger of their gods over the presence of foreigners in China importing a 'new religion' called Christianity. They saw it as a religious duty to kill all foreigners in China and end the drought and attacked mission stations in remote parts of China and beheaded over 100 American and British missionaries and Catholic priests and killed female teachers on mission stations, missionaries' wives and the Chinese children who were their pupils. On the orders of a provincial governor who detested all foreigners more, missionaries, Catholic priests and their converts had been summoned to his Viceregal palace and beheaded.[4]

On 20 June 1900 Mary read a despatch by the Australian Dr George Morrison, Peking correspondent for *The Times* in which Morrison reported violence had exploded, triggered by the murder of Baron von Ketteler, German Minister to the court of Dowager Empress Cixi. Boxer troops had rampaged through Peking, burning down Protestant and Catholic churches where thousands of terrified Chinese converts had fled for safety.

By now the British navy in the China Seas (of which Ernest Gaunt was part) had become involved as Boxer troops marched on Peking's Legation Compound aiming to kill all the foreigner diplomats and clerical staff sheltering inside the walls. The Boxers managed to kill two members of the British Legation and wound a few dozen diplomatic staff before being driven off by an ancient cannon, the only weapon the British possessed.[5] Boxer troops supported by Imperial troops sent by Empress Cixi, besieged Peking's Legation Quarter, killed staff from the British Legation and burned Protestant chapels and Chinese shops selling foreign goods. They attacked the Catholic cathedral where almost 3,000 Chinese Christian converts sheltered during the fifty day siege with a dozen British soldiers to protect them.

Meanwhile Ernest Gaunt set off for Peking commanding a ship full of British marines and Indian troops bound for the port of Taiku, the nearest to land locked Peking to relieve the besieged staff inside the British Legation.

Meanwhile the Boxers had built a huge ramp in an attempt to scale the walls that surrounded the Legation Compound. The defence of the British Legation was organised by, Dr George Morrison and Mary was following his despatches avid for news about Ernest but his despatches from Peking ceased abruptly as Morrison was now inside the walled Legation Compound helping defend the half starved inmates against the Boxers and Imperial troops sent by Dowager Empress Cixi, ruler of China.[6]

Ernest and the men under his command n braved the stench of the sewers and entered the walled city of Peking via this underground route and led a daring attack on the Boxers. [7]

George Morrison's despatches could not get through to *The Times* but, on 16 July 1900 *The Times*, rashly printed an unverified report from Shanghai headed *Massacre in Peking*. It claimed the head of the British Legation, all legation staff, George Morrison had been murdered by the Boxers and the Legation Compound was in ruins and published Morrison's obituary. Terrified that Ernest could have been killed, Mary waited anxiously for news.

It would be weeks before Mary learned Ernest was alive and George Morrison not dead only badly wounded. They had met in the war-torn Legation Compound and both hailing from the colony of Victoria had become friends.

On 2 August 1900 Mary read George Morrison's despatch from Peking. *The Times* listed the huge damage done in the siege to the Legation Compound. Mentioned in despatches and promoted to British Naval Attache the gallant Captain Ernest Gaunt awarded the C.M.G (Companion of the Order of St Michael and St George) and would be given command of a battleship,

The Boxer Rebellion and the financial penalties on China would cause the downfall the Qing dynasty which led to China becoming a republic. Mary was still determined that once she had the necessary money she would visit China and take the Silk Road back to Europe.

⁂

Mary, was still searching for a topic for her next novel found it at a meeting of the British Society of Authors where she met a would-be author, a retired colonial official named John Ridgewell Essex who had had written scholarly articles on African tribal lore, customs and fetish magic. He hoped to use his knowledge to write novel set in West Africa but now he had the necessary time to do so had reached the conclusion lacked the literary skills to do so. Aware of his limitations, the elderly ethnologist said he would be delighted to share his knowledge with the widowed Mrs Miller if she would work with him on his projected novel about a young doctor in Africa. To prove how popular a topic Africa was with readers, Ridgeway Essex loaned Mary Gaunt copies of several popular books by Rider Haggard, *King Solomon's Mines* and the sequel, *Alan Quartermain.* Using his knowledge of Africa Henry Rider Haggard, once a poorly paid colonial official like Ridgewell Essex was now a wealthy author able to resign from the colonial service.

Mary decided to take a chance on Ridgewell Essex and his knowledge of Africa and using her skills as a storyteller turn his rather turgid plot into a saleable novel. By now she had enough of renting and was determined to buy land near London and build a house, unusual for a woman in the days when banks never lent money to women. It was vital t his novel was well promoted and made money if she was to own her own home.

Mary worked with Ridgewell Essex on *The Arm of the Leopard, a West African Story* He proved an excellent source of information on fetish magic, tribal customs and language but a boring writer as Mary had suspected and had to re-write the material he gave her. The protagonist was Dr James Craven, a coloured graduate of Oxford Medical School with high ideals a bout helping the Africans who confronted a group of scheming European crooks and adventures planning to cheat the Africans out of their gold and diamonds.

Events in Africa were arousing a great deal of interest in Britain. France, Germany and England were trying to grab mining concessions from the Africans: Africa was now full of rogues from all over the world, searching for or gold and diamonds and as Rider Haggard and Joseph Conrad were realising Africa, 'The

Dark Continent' was fertile ground for novels of adventure and romance.

An editor at William Heinemann, read a few chapters and a synopsis sent by literary agent Mr Watt liked it and bought the rights to a joint novel by Marty Gaunt and Ridgewell Essex,, titled *The Arm of the Leopard,* The book was published in 1904 as Mary discovered she had not been infected by syphilis and could live a normal life free of the cloud that had hung over her.

The British economy was booming, Mary was an excellent promoter of books and the gripping adventure novel with its air of authenticity sold very well. A colonial edition was printed in London and shipped to Australia where Mary already had many readers.

Working together harmoniously Mary Gaunt and Ridgewell Essex produced a second novel set in Africa during the Boer War, *Fools Rush In: An African Story* published by Werner Laurie in Britain and America with a colonial edition shipped to Australia. The book received excellent reviews and they decided to write a third novel once again featuring the exploits and adventures of Dr James Craven with local colour by Ridgewell Essex and accurate medical background and dialogue by Mary.

In 1905, Clive and Lance Gaunt arrived in London having left Melbourne University with first class honours in law to work in legal offices in London to gain experience. Ernest and George Morrison had maintained their friendship by letters. Through the intervention of Ernest, Lance Gaunt fell in love with George Morrison's younger sister, Violet and they planned to announce their engagement, both George Morrison's widowed mother and Judge and Mrs Gaunt regarding a marriage to the daughter of a former headmaster of Geelong Grammar as a most suitable match.[8]

Later that year, in October 1905, Judge Gaunt, suffered a mild stroke and collapsed in court. Instead of going hospital Mary's father insisted on being taken home where he died from a second and more massive stroke.

Judge Gaunt had been widely respected by members of the legal profession, and had a wide circle of friends. having been chairman of the Ballarat Club for many years.

On the day Judge Gaunt was buried at Ballarat Cemetery the Union Jack flew at half mast over the Ballarat law courts. His funeral was attended by the prominent citizens of Ballarat but the sad fact was that none of his children attended as they were all overseas.[9]

The shock of her father's death left Mary grief stricken and guilty she had not been able to return home before his untimely demise. Mrs Gaunt announced that with all her children overseas she was selling the Ballarat house and going to stay with relatives in Africa. Lance had deferred his marriage to Violet Morrison until early in 1906 and Clive went back to the Far EASt and although he announced his intentions of marring Hilda woujld not do so for many years.

An invitation to spend Christmas and New Year with Mrs Horsefall, a widowed friend of Guy Gaunt at her Liverpool home was something to look forward at this miserable time for Mary, still grieving for her father.[10]

The Horsefall family owned a large trading company on West Africa's Gold Coast (now part of modern Ghana). Mary was made welcome and shown Mrs Horsefall's views of the Gold, Mahogany and Ivory Coasts with their golden beaches, palm trees and rivers lined with jungle foliage. Their Liverpool home contained an interesting collection of West African artefacts including *biyeri*. These were carved masks and ebony fertility figures with massive heads and metal discs for from Ashantiland, magnificent carved heads from Benin and photographs of naked Africans at work and dignified Africans in long flowing patterned robes. Mary learned were these were kings or headmen of the wealthy Ashanti tribe who had profited from all the gold in the rivers of the British-Ashanti Protectorate lands.

Seeing these photos of Africa brought back her childhood dream to wanted to follow in the steps of Welsh explorer and journalists Henry Stanley. She wanted to see for herself the palace of the King of the Ashanti and the fetish tree in the Ashanti capital of Kumasi and see if it still had human bones hanging from the branches. She wanted to learn what had happened to little Carlos. Had he been murdered by the sorcerers or returned to Spain a wealthy man.?

Once the New Year celebrations were over, Mary returned to cold foggy London. As a second generation Australian , she hated the grey days of winter and felt she did not belong in England but was an outsider. Her longing for warmth and sunlight deepened as the chilly English spring of 1906 was followed by a miserable wet summer. Judge Gaunt's will revealed that Mary' moher, rs Gaunt in addition to the family home inherited all the money in her husband's bank account and his mining shares. Each son received a small legacy and Mary and Lucy received books from their father's library. Ironically enough by now the Gaunt boys had well paid careers Lucy was married. Mary the widow who had sold her home to pay her husband's medical fees was doing well with two African novels but she was painfully aware that a writer is deemed as good as their last book and it was possible her fame would not last. [11]

At this juncture she might y have returned to Victoria but there was no longer a family home left for her to return to and all her brothers were overseas. Mrs Gaunt had sold the Ballarat house kept the money and was planning to move to East Africa.

※

To Mary's relief her mother showed no wish to come to London to live with her. Mrs Gaunt, who had lauded the virtues of being the Angel of the House and homebody had amazed her children by selling up and sailing for Rhodesia to live with relatives planning to live on the interest from selling the family home and investing the money.[12]

The death of Judge Gaunt was followed by another shock. Lucy's husband, Oatley Archer, a young man with a good career ahead of him and regarded as very healthy died suddenly from a heart attack. '

Mary was very worried about Lucy and hoped she might come and join her in London but with two young children to raise and educate Lucy Archer, a young widow left Malaya and returned to Victoria. Having obtained her degree from Melbourne University at a time few women managed to do so, Lucy Archer was appointed resident Principal of Melbourne's Trinity College Hostel for Women, (later Janet Clarke Hall). This post meant Lucy had a home in the college and would be able to educate her son, Pat and Mary's young namesake, Mary Ellen in Melbourne.

Soon after Mary's arrival in London Guy came back for a short holiday and they visited the Egyptian galleries of the British Museum, both of them fascinated by the mummies. Urged on by Guy she had written a 50,000 word crime novel had it typed up and circulated to her siblings, to be read by family members and friends as a Christmas present.

Fortunately for Mary who was once more casting around for a plot for a novel was that Mr Watt, her literary agent read *The Mummy Moves*. He assured Mary that handled properly d *The Mummy Moves*, could make her a great deal of money as readers in Britain and America were fascinated the topic of the Pharoahs, the Pyramids and Egyptian mummies.

Mr Watt insisted Mary Gaunt extend her detective novel to 80,000 words. Mary did as he asked but heard nothing more. The British winter of 1906 was exceptionally cold and damp and Australia seemed a very inviting destination to visit and once again Mary thought about returning to Australia to see her sister now they were both widowed. Mary planned to take a boat to Adelaide and meet Lucy there during her sister's long summer vacation. The adventurous sisters could make an overland expedition through what was at that time n known as the Northern Territory of South Australia.

Having enjoyed success with her chapters in Cassell's *Picturesque Australia* Mary was convinced she could write a book about the north of Australia including the new overland telegraph stations connecting Australia with the world. She and Lucy would go by train as far north as possible and then buy horse and buggy across the desert to visit vast cattle properties in the Northern Territory, some of which were larger than Wales.

Mr Watt as Mary's agent put this idea for a travel book to Mr Laurie at Werner Laurie who was not keen on the idea of an Australian travel book. Nor for very different reasons were Messrs Methuen, the second publisher Mr Watt contacted on Mary's behalf. Early in 1905 Methuen had published an outback novel titled *We of the Never-Never* by Mrs Aeneas Gunn, set in the Northern Territory. The author, Jeannie Gunn, a widowed school teacher married to a station owner called Aeneas Gunn had written the book to incorporate her experiences as a station owners' wife on the remote Elsey cattle station.

. *We of the Never Never* sold well in London but Methuen were not happy with the idea of *two* books set in the Northern Territory on the market at the same time. They rejected Mary's projected book on the Territory so she abandoned the idea of coming 'home' to see Lucy and her young niece and nephew.

The vastness of Africa, like the vast open spaces of Australia appealed to Mary. Travel was booming among the wealthy and the newly affluent middle classes. Somerset Maugham, determined not to practice medicine but become a full time writer had written *Liza of Lambeth* set in the London tenements he had visited as a medical student which made very little money.

. Now he established a pattern of travel and writing using Seville as a base Maugham exploring Spain on very little money on horseback and by train and donkey cart and wrote *The Land of the Blessed Virgin* (a title which discouraged many buyers), although it was the best book on Spain by an English writer since Richard Ford's 1845 *Handbook for Travellers in Spain*

With no publisher wiling to pay her an advance to return to Australia and write a travel book and now associated by readers with Africa Mary decided to go to West Africa in search of material for e another novel set there and at the same time write a travel book set in several African colonies.

Mary was a good organiser and travel planner, aware she needed capital to organise an expedition to travel the vast distances and by now had found suitable land and hoped to build a house and stop paying out rent for the rest of her life. On a visit to Kent see the ruins of John of Gaunt's Eltham Palace,, Mary had saw seen signs indicating that the former hunting grounds with their magnificent oak trees were to be subdivided and sold off.

Mary wanted to buy land in this attractive wooded area which was close to London but needed capital to build a house. She hoped that a visit to Africa would inspire more novels and was encouraged in this aim by Constance Smedley and Christina Gowans White, leading lights of London Lyceum Club and of the British Writers and Authors Club who urged Mary to buy the land which would appreciate as it was near a railway station. The members of the London Lyceum wanted progress for women but did not believe in violent protests. They met in their elegant residential club, held meetings and discussions and enjoyed its attractive surroundings and Mary found encouragement and companionship there.

※※

In the booming Edwardian era, book publishing was no longer the preserve of gentlemen with large libraries of leather bound books. It had become big business thanks to an increase in spending money and literacy among the newly prosperous middle classes. ;Educational evening institutes designed for working people and cheap editions in hard and soft backs helped created a much larger market of new readers in circulating libraries.

As is often the case, Mary's best selling novel was not her best work. Mary wrote to Guy with the good news *The Mummy Moves*, the crime novel which her younger brother had encouraged her to write as a joke present for her siblings at Christmas would not win literary prizes but was selling like hot cakes in Britain and America and film rights had been sold. Film rights plus his plays were what made millions for Somerset Maugham. However the Hollywood film company who had optioned *The Mummy Moves* went broke during World War One and the film was never made. Nor was a film of A Wind in the Wilderness which were it to be filmed today like Maugham's The Painted Veil with its fascinating story and Chinese backgrounds would probably be a huge success and bring back the name of Mary Gaunt to prominence while *The Mummy Moves* would be seen as dated.

Mary's novel *The Uncounted Cost* was a success on all counts, praised as a a ;literary' novel by leading critics, (something to his chagrin Maugham never achieved probably due to envy by the literati of the huge sums Maugham earned from films of his books and plays and from *Of Human Bondage* and The *Razor's Edge*.] .

American rights Mary Gaunt's *The Mummy Moves* were sold to Edward Clode in New York for a vast sum for the times to be paid in three instalments over the next three years. So Mary was able to pay off her land and give the builder a generous deposit to start work.

Mary who suffered badly from asthma attacks during the English winter decided to use her windfall for a holiday in Nice where the winters were mild. This elegant town, once owned by the Principality of Savoy had an English language lending library, an opera house, superb shops and a second hand book market on Sunday mornings. In spring wattle known as 'mimosa' was sold in Nice's flower market in the Cours Saleya. The sea air of Nice and the mimosa reminded Mary of Warrnamboul where wattles flowered on the hills behind the seaside town.

She had enough of gas rings, bed sitters and prying landladies. With royalty payments for two African novels and foreign rights sold for *The Mummy Moves* she no longer had to live in a cramped bed-sitter in Kensington basement. While waiting for her Eltham house to be built she moved to far larger and more comfortable premises near the Brompton Road close to Harrods Emporium, which prided itself on selling 'everything that Londoners wanted. At long last she could afford elegant clothes and shoes and good luggage.

In January 1909 Werner Laurie bought out a third joint Gaunt-Ridgewell Essex novel, *The Silent Ones* which once more featured the adventures of Dr James Craven, a graduate of Cambridge and Heidelberg Medical Schools. Mary modelled Dr Craven's career on the experiences of her late husband. He had studied medicine and worked with coloured doctors in Edinburgh and been indignant over the racial prejudice they encountered. One reason for the success of *The Silent Ones* the fact that Ridgewell Essex's accounts of African customs and beliefs on sorcery and fetish magic were incorporated into the plots and which gave them the stamp of authenticity. But Ridgeway Essex's years in Africa and bouts of malaria had taken their toll and t was no longer a well man and felt he was not capable of another novel but did manage a few more short stories.

Reviewed by *The Times* literary critic *The Silent Ones* was described it as 'realistic and vivid novel, praised by *The Scotsman* and *Blackwoods Magazine* and awarded a literary prize in Edinburgh. The literary critic for *The Scotsman* noted that 'the antagonism of black and white is developed in a masterly fashion and the novel has distinct ethnological value.' London's *Review of Reviews*, claimed *The Silent Ones* was 'a gripping novel filled with vivid detail and it was impossible to give the book higher praise.'[13]

Mr Laurie, a canny Scots businessman, realised steam trains were opening up foreign travel in Europe to a wider market. He wanted to bring out more travel books, a genre supplied by male authors in an era when 'ladies' were not meant to travel unchaperoned could Mary Gaunt, his popular novelist not take a chaperone with her to Africa to keep up appearances. Mary Gaunt was enraged at yet another manifestation of the 'double standard' was determined to visit Africa alone and write a book highlighting this in the title.

Mary had written three popular novels *set in* Africa so Mr Laurie finally had to admit her idea for a travel book about West Africa was viable from the commercial point of view but warned her it could be dangerous and she might not return from 'the white man's grave' with its tropcial fevers.

From Mary's point of view a journey to West Africa meant escaping another chilly winter in London. However other 'colonial hands' to whom she confided her plan were horrified to think a white woman would travel around Africa unchaperoned accompanied by semi- naked African porters. She must have a male relative to protect her but Mary refused to listen.

With royalty cheques from three best selling novels coming and a reputation as one of Britain's most popular novelists Mary could now afford to take hansom cabs everywhere, buy new clothes, presents for Lucy's children, enjoy dinners with Ridegewell Essex and his friends, whose reminiscences furnished background material for African short stories. She wrote a few more with Ridgewell Essex but the days of joint novels were over.

With money in the bank Mary was able to pay an architect to draw up plans for a house on what had once been the hunting grounds of Eltham Palace and design a garden studio where she could write in peace.

Once the plans were approved, Mary engaged a builder and agreed to pay him in three instalments. Eltham had a station whose trains went to Charing Cross. She would not be isolated from friends at the Lyceum Club or the London and British Museum libraries where she carried out research. It would be easy to visit her agent and her publishers by train and at last she could have a garden of her own.[14]

Having paid off the land and given a progress payment to the builder to start work on her house Mary was short of cash to organise her African expedition. She hoped to visit six or seven British colonies, inspect disused slave forts and make a long expedition to the jungle area north of Kumasi, to visit the mud brick palace of the King of the Ashanti.

Every since her childhood when she read the story of little Carlos she had wanted to visit Ashantiland, (now under British rule and renamed the British Ashanti Protectorate). Mary returned to the West African galleries of the British Musem, to study the *biyeri* — small female figures made of ebony given to Ashanti girls to assure their fertility and used as fetish charms by the sorcerers who dominated many of these remote village and did her best to learn all she could about Ashanti customs and beliefs. She saw artefacts of solid gold captured by British troops at Kumasi during the Ashanti wars — boxes of solid gold ornamented with Ashanti designs in which , Africa's wealthiest tribe, carried the gold dust found in their rivers which they used as currency. She hoped to visit disused West African slave forts and learn about the slave trade and include a chapter on them in her travel book.

Reading accounts by previous explorers like Henry Moreton Stanley Mary realised they had relied on African porters to carry crates of tinned food and camping equipment so she must do the same. Stanley's African expedition had been funded by a newspaper but Mary knew no newspaper would fund a mere woman to explore the former kingdom of the Ashanti.

Tropical diseases against which Europeans had no immunity abounded and cures had still to be found. Roads were often non-existent.

These obstacles made West Africa an irresistible challenge to Mary who like her brothers thrived on danger and excitement.

She read an article in *The New York Times* titled 'A White Lady Visits the Masai' about an eccentric and very wealthy American named May French Sheldon who had toured the lands of the Masai and climbed Mount Kilimanjaro wearing long skirts and high buttoned boots. But Mrs Sheldon had been lucky to have her expedition funded by an obliging but absentee husband. She was born aloft through the tribal lands of the Masai in a wicker palanquin lined with swansdown cushions. The imperious American explorer employed 300 African porters to carry herself and her trunks filled with expensive clothes, a feather mattress, a porcelain dinner service, silver cutlery and 1,000 tins of assorted delicacies so she could dine in luxury in the jungle and was carried across crocodile infested rivers in a canvas sling born by four Africans.

Clearly Mary Gaunt was not able to emulate Mrs French Sheldon's luxurious expedition on her tight budget. She would have to rely on the hospitality of colonial officials since there were no hotels or government rest houses in many parts of East Africa. Travelling up the Volta River she hoped to be able to camp in disused copra or cocoa warehouse or sleep in a native hut and she was determined to visit the unexplored jungle that lay to the north of Kumasi.

Some ex-colonials from West Africa were shocked by Mary Gaunt's plans to go to Africa without a chaperone and hire Africans as her bearers. But once they realised nothing would dissuade Mary, they advised she should buy in England crates of tinned corned beef and tongue if she did not want to live on roasted monkey or the barbecued flesh of hippos. Naked African warriors would act as her porters, guides and hunters as they had done for Mrs French Sheldon. No doubt this ch would shock the inmates of various Government Houses but this the only way she could manage to journey through jungle, up the Volta River and in the remote lands of the Ashanti where tinned food was unobtainable and she could easily get sick on the local diet.

Mary was advised to buy pots of English jam and marmalade, tins of soup, bags of porridge oats and jars of a spicy anchovy paste known as 'Gentlemen's Relish' available at Fortnum and Masons. She should take with her boxes of Huntly and Palmers biscuits, bread being largely unavailable in the jungle. She would be expected to provide basic rations for the porters and, when necessary patch up their wounded feet. The British colony of Ghana where she would spend most time had only one hospital at Sekondi so her medical chest must be well stocked and she should take a medical encyclopaedia in case of emergencies.

Walking would be difficult in long skirts through waist-high grass or in deep mud and advised Mary that she must behave like royalty or the porters would refuse to obey her since women were generally despised. She should take a supply of small coins (threepenny pieces were best) as her African he porters would expect payment each evening or could turn mutinous and abandon her in the jungle.

Mr Laurie found Mary Gaunt's desire to visit West Africa — the 'white man's grave' very odd. He warned Mary that the English author, Mary Kingsley had toured Nigeria and Gabon and written two popular travel books before returning to Africa where in 1900 she had died from typhoid fever. He related what Mary

Gaunt regarded as a sick joke, claiming shipping companies only sold one way tickets to passengers to West Africa as the death toll was so high.

'Gaunts *never* give up. They *thrive* on danger' Mary insisted.

She planned to disembark at Dakkar in French speaking Africa and hire native bearers to explore the Gold, Ivory and Slave Coasts (modern Ghana) and visit several former slave forts. After that she would explore the remote Volta River by tramp steamer and dug out canoe, visit Sekondi on the Gold Coast and then to remote Kumasi, capital of the British Protectorate of the Ashanti and then return to the coast and catch an Elder Dempster boat back to Liverpool.

Mr Laurie said he was happy to commission a book of her travels illustrated by her photographs and another African novel, this time written only by Mary Gaunt.

What worried her publisher — Mr Laurie, a canny Scots businessman — was the fear Mary might die before completing both books. He did not like the idea that a middle aged overweight lady, prone to asthma and one of his most hardworking and versatile authors could easily die in Africa so saw it as a poor risk to pay Mary a large advance for going there in case he never received the promised manuscripts.

After tough negotiations with Mr Watt, Mr Laurie grudgingly increased his advance but only a little. Publishers of that era were very tough as Maugham and others would complain. Half jokingly Mr Laurie repeated the advice often given to African travellers to 'remain on good terms with missionaries as they were the ones who would have to bury her!'

Mary was shocked to learn a sea passage to Africa cost a great deal more than she had allowed for in her budget. Fortunately Sir Charles Lucas, an old friend of her late father came to the rescue. As head of the British Colonial Office, Sir Charles persuaded the chairman of Elder Dempster Shipping lines, to give Mary Gaunt free return passage to West Africa. Sir Charles described Mrs Lindsay Miller (the name on her British passport, as there were no Australian passports in 1909) as an excellent writer whose books would bring tourists to West Africa and benefit the Elder Dempster shipping line.

Sir Charles provided Mary with a letter of introduction to the African trading company, Messrs F and A. Swanzey, owners of warehouses and river steamers. Swanzey's managing director offered Mrs Miller, the name she used to give her more credibility, free transport on their steamers up the Volta River and on the Congo. Sir Charles wrote to several British governors he knew telling them of Mrs Lindsay Miller's arrival in their colonies.

CHAPTER 5

Africa — the Dark Continent

Wanderlust was in my blood and in the blood of my brothers and sisters. All of us loved adventure. Mary Gaunt, *Broken Journey*, 1917.

On a foggy morning in November 1907, Mary left Euston Station to catch the train to Liverpool, where she boarded d the Elder Dempster liner, ss *Gando*.[1] She took with her what she had been told were essentials for an African explorer — a set of maps in a long metal cylinder, a canvas folding bed and folding bath, a roll of mosquito netting, a heavy glass plate camera, a folding brass tripod, chemicals for developing photos, a compass to chart bearings and a well stocked medicine chest and encyclopaedia.

Having worked in her husband's surgery, Mary felt she would be capable of doctoring herself and any porters who needed her assistance in remote areas where there were no doctors

Photographs to illustrate her travel book were another problem. In the pre-digital era, photography involved a great deal more than pressing a button hence the need to bring with her jars of suitable materials to develop black and white films.

Privacy from male porters was another problem On Ridgewell Essex's advice Mary bought a large folding screen behind which she could obey the calls of nature in private. She decided that wearing ankle length skirts and matching high necked blouses of cream coloured 'holland linen' would make her look like a respectable 'lady explorer'. Mary knew she must maintain her ladylike status to be taken seriously and treated well by colonial officials who would provide government accommodation and other assistance. But she was aware it was important to wear modest clothing to prevent the wrong impression being formed by male colonial officials. She had no wish to be seen as a 'scarlet woman' but was determined to be taken seriously as an explorer.

For weeks she would be alone in jungles with naked African porters who wore nothing but penis sheaths, a shocking idea for most Edwardian ladies. But Mary as a doctor's widow who had worked in her late husband's surgery was not shocked by the idea.

Beige 'holland linen' had the advantage of being cheap as holland' was made to cover window blinds and cool to wear in tropical heat. However like all linen it crumpled badly and Mary had no way of ironing linen clothes in the jungle.[2]

In addition to her long linen skirts Mary wore high button boots as a defence against snakes, leeches, piercing thorns and malarial mosquitoes. At London's Army and Navy stores, she bought a white a pith helmet or 'solar bowler' covered with mosquito netting.

Since trousers were scandalous on women Mary wore a pair of Ernest's discarded trousers *under* her long skirt for protection against mosquitoes and leeches but did not mention the fact to colonial officials (or their wives) fearing they would regard her as a woman of ill repute and refuse to assist her.

Hoping to save money by staying at various Government Houses via the good offices and letters of introduction from Sir Clive Lucas, Mary's trunk included the fripperies of the *belle époque* — long formal evening gowns, satin slippers, rustling taffeta petticoats and rose trimmed hats.

Mary intended to stay in West Africa for eighteen months. Financially it was a great help she was able to travel free on coastal and river steamers, owned by Messrs F. and A. Swanzey. She planned to use dug out canoes paddled by African warriors on the Upper Volta River and when the going was rough emulate Mrs

French Sheldon and be carried in canvas sling across rivers by the African porters. She would take the newly constructed railway from Sekonidi on the coast to the gold mining area of Tarkwa and Kumasi in the Ashanti Protectorate.

On board the *ss. Gando* bound for West Africa, Mary Gaunt met an important figure in the colonial world,, Sir George Denton, Governor of the small colony of Gambia, returning from leave in Britain.

Seated at the captain's table in her evening finery and jewellery, Mary, who was an excellent raconteur and mimic, proved herself an entertaining dinner companion. She charmed the elderly Sir George into inviting her to stay as his guest at Gambia's Government House and called him 'the nicest governor a lucky colony ever had'.[3]

As a result of an invitation from Sir George, instead of disembarking at French speaking Dakar, Mary and her baggage and crates of supplies left the ship at Bathurst, capital of Gambia. She went ashore with Governor Sir George Denton and was greeted by a brass band and escorted to Gambia's Government House in style.

Mary enjoyed lavish hospitality at Bathurst's Government House. a comfortable residence, designed for the tropics with large airy rooms and wide verandas. Her bed was enclosed 'in a mosquito proof cage made of wire netting' as malaria and yellow fever, carried by mosquitoes, had killed many government employees in the past. She was fascinated by Bathurst's native local houses, made from closely woven bamboo in a process the natives of Gambian called *'crinting'*.

After spending a few weeks at Bathurst, Mary decided to explore the Gambia River. However the governor's yacht, the *Manskillah*, was on the slip having repairs carried out, so Mary had to use a grubby overcrowded commercial steamer, called the ss *Mungo Park*.

The tramp steamer was captained by an alcoholic Frenchman with a roving eye, so Mary was careful to lock her cabin door each night. The small river steamer, ideal in an area where there were no roads, carried a cargo of cotton cloth imported from Manchester and a cargo of sugar, salt and coffee, which its owners were trading in return for ivory, cocoa beans and palm oil.

There were only two cabins, the largest one reserved for the captain. Mary was given the only other cabin, a small cramped one under the wooden deck hot as an oven which smelt of stale beer and tobacco. The remaining ninety passengers were from various African tribes. They slept crowded tightly together on bed rolls on top deck, accompanied by their babies, chickens and goats.[4]

At Fort St James the Gambia River narrowed and as they passed the old slave fort the Africans started wailing and moaning, aware how many of their relatives had died in that grim place, now an ivory trading station.

After a four day journey up the winding mosquito infested river, Mary was glad to leave the steamer and its drunken lecherous captain.

She continued her journey upriver in a long canoe, made from a hollowed-out log, paddled by naked warriors who chanted and sang in unison as they paddled. Among the mud and mangroves that lined the river banks Mary saw basking crocodiles which slithered into the water as they passed. Venomous snakes hung in loops from branches overhanging the river.

In spite of Ernest's trousers worn under her skirt to protect her thighs and calves large grey mosquitoes feasted on Mary's ankles. She prayed they did not carry a deadly fever. In a clearing in the jungle, the appearance of a leopard created an uproar among the paddlers. Terrified cries, shrieks and incantations to the gods indicated the Africans were terrified the canoe might overturn and thrown them all in the river. Mary was the only one who ke[t calm: the canoe righted itself and they continued the journey upriver.

After her return to Bathurst's Government House, Mary boarded the coastal steamer *Zaria* which hugged the coast until they reached the British colony of Sierra Leone. Mary landed at

Freetown the capita and was impressed by the sheer h size of its harbour, which must be even larger than Sydney Harbour.

Armed with a letter of introduction from Sir George Denton, Mary was invited to stay at Freetown's Government House. Other dinner guests, included two Forestry Officers, a Medical Officer and a few British and French traders. The government employees, wore full evening dress (very hot under the circumstances) with medals for the men and jewels for the ladies, regardless of the tropical heat and humidity. The menu was stodgy — like a British or Australian dinner roast beef, roast potatoes and Yorkshire pudding. None of the colonial officoals had brought wives to Africa for fear of mosquito or water born diseases. One claimed he felt his wife was 'far too delicate' to cope with African conditions.

From her questions to the staff at Government House Mary learned that several of the married British officials lived with African women who were never acknowledged by the white community who regarded what they called 'miscegenation' as a crime, an attitude Mary found obnoxious.

Following a three year period of duty, these Englishmen would return to their wives in England and leave their mistresses and any children they had produced behind and forget them.

This adulterous and hypocritical lifestyle gave Mary an idea for an novel featuring a British colonial officer who takes an African mistress as a convenience but falls in love with her and plans to divorce the wife who had refused to follow him to Africa. He wants to make an honest woman of the African mistress but in trying to do the right thing becomes a social pariah and outcast from the white community.

Mary knew that such a story would create a furore in Britain and relished the fact various church groups would denounce it. As Oscar Wilde had noted, adultery among the upper classes was tolerated but never mentioned, , King Edward VII being one of the leading adulterers. But while adultery was tolerated among the upper crust, divorce was a scandal and divorcees outcasts from polite society. Mary felt this was wrong. She had no strong religious feelings to hold her back from writing what was happening in the African colonies and , felt she was being true to her calling as a writer by writing a novel that told the truth about a problem.

From Freetown Mary took a coastal steamer to the colony of Liberia on a ship owned and operated by Messrs F and A Swanzey, who were generous in offering her a free passage thanks to her letter of introduction from her father's old friend, Sir Charles Lucas.

Liberia had been founded by America's President Monroe as a place for or freed slaves to rebuild their lives. Due to the generosity of American philanthropists and church groups, back , in 1822 freed slaves had been shipped to Africa to lead a new life in Liberia and the capital city of , Monrovia named in honour of America's President Munro.

{MAP OF WEST AFRICA IN ALBUM COULD BE INSET HERE

Seated in the ship's tender looking across at the town of Monrovia, Mary described the scenery as 'very beautiful with blue sky, blue sea, snow white surf breaking on the sandbar and a hillside with small houses peeping out from among the verdure'.

On paper Liberia seemed a magnificent social experiment and Mary was hoping to find it a tropical paradise.[5] However she was disappointed — Monrovia was neglected and had streets choked by weeds, manure and garbage. Flea-bitten dogs scavenged for dead rats and refuse and reeking sewage ran down the gutters. She described Monrovia as

> ...an outrageously ill-kept town with no proper roads, only dirt tracks knee deep in weeds, the houses built of wood or corrugated iron with broken windows and crumbling wooden balconies... Never have I seen such a dreary neglected town which would be pitiful anywhere in the world. The inhabitants of Monrovia are eternally at war with the tribesmen in the land behind them' [who they had displaced by force and enslaved some]. I met half a dozen African prisoners dressed in rags, chained two and two with iron collars round their necks and their guard... as ragged a scarecrows. Lower Buchanan [the area below Monrovia] reeked of human occupancy as they do not trouble

overmuch about sanitation in Liberia. I saw three cows and half a dozen razor backed pigs on the dirt track described to me as the principal street'.[6]

Mary pitied the women of Monrovia who led miserable lives, in general treated like slaves by their husbands. She visited three different churches made from rusty sheets of corrugated iron and wondered which denominations had donated the money to build them. She also raised the question in the chapter she was writing on Monrovia why the original donors had not thought to provide enough money to maintain buildings they had funded.

As Mary attended a Sunday morning service in one of the tin churches, sickened by the stench of stale sweat and unwashed bodies.

> God forbid that I should scoff … but here, cleanliness is divorced from Godliness. I can honestly say that in my life I have never seen a dirtier rags than those worn by the congregation who sang hymns so beautifully as to bring tears to my eyes… These descendants of a once enslaved people now take slaves [for themselves] in their turn. Women are saleable commodities in Liberia. For a trifling consideration, a bottle of gin or a few sticks of tobacco, families hand over a female child who, taken into a household without pay, becomes to all intents and purposes a slave… I can only say that I have seen no evidence of plantations… You cannot buy fruit in Monrovia, no chickens, no eggs. Bananas and limes have to be imported, meat is to be only to be had at rare intervals and the living is dear… the Liberians after nearly ninety years of self-government, compare badly with the Mandingo or the Jolloff of Gambia and the Ashanti.[7]

Delighted to be leaving Liberia, Mary boarded the *ss Chama* for the long voyage to the former Portuguese settlement of Axim.

On board the steamer she made friends with a young British Forestry Officer who was also bound for Assini on the coast. They agreed to share expenses and contracted to hire porters from the headman of the Beyim tribe. Thirty strong men were needed, working in relays, to follow the potholed coastal track to Assini, on the borders of the Ivory and Gold Coasts (modern Ghana).

Each night Mary and the Forestry Officer would pay their half share of the porterage fees in the octagonal bronze coins the British called 'threepenny bits'. Mary carried her small coins in a velvet bag and when she was alone was careful to have her pistol tucked into her waistband or in her reticule .According to native custom the daily rate was agreed with the tribal chief and he took a percentage of the fees in return for arranging the contract.

The tropical humidity and heat were intense and at times Mary, although used to the heat of a Ballarat summer, felt ill with heat. African porters used to the steamy heat carried food supplies and alcohol and the survey and camping equipment of the Forestry Officer.

Mary's equipment including a tent and bedding roll, a crate of tinned food, another crate containing fresh eggs, oatmeal for porridge, boxes of biscuits, jars of marmalade and a crate of fresh fruit purchased in Axim market. She also took with her assorted pots and pans, her canvas bath, the canvas folding chair and table, her maps, camera and shipping trunk full of clothes. The Forestry Officer had brought heavy earthenware jars contained fresh water and bottles of whisky, gin and claret. He also travelled with a tin case contained his white tropical uniforms, personal belongings and a far smaller case containing boots and shoes.

The Forestry Officer's tent was so heavy it needed three porters to carry it. When they stopped for the night they discovered the Beyim men had left the wooden ridge poles behind, so the Forestry Officer's tent could not be erected. Propriety made it impossible for the young Forestry Officer to share Mary's tent. As there were no inns or government rest houses he had no alternative but to sleep in the open, covered by a mosquito net.[8]

Mary and the Forestry Officer breakfasted at dawn, while a light mist hovered over the sea on porridge, fried eggs, sweet biscuits and marmalade and bananas, pineapples and oranges.

Mary started out by walking, but thorny branches tore her long skirt and scratched her feet and ankles. It was not long before the heat and humidity brought on an attack of asthma (in the days before inhalers a severe asthma attack in the wilds ould have been fatal). After Mary had finished wheezing and regained her breath, she was carried in a hammock along a blisteringly hot sandy track. It was fringed by coconut palms and covered with tangled creepers that tripped up the unwary.

On the outskirts of small fishing villages they saw the graves of African villagers made in shallow sand. Wild dogs had dug up the bodies and Mary found it gruesome that bones and sculls were protruding from these graves. The tropical heat and humidity were exhausting but finally their small expedition staggered into Assini on the Tano River where yellow fever and malaria were a constant danger. Mary described how

> ...down this great river come great mahogany logs that rival in size and value the logs of Honduras and Belize. The Tano enters the sea via a lagoon behind Half Assini. The lagoon is surrounded by swamp in which crocodiles abound so fierce they have been known to take the paddler's arm off as he stoops to his stroke. Then men who paddled showed marked reluctance to jump out and push when we ran aground on a sandbank.[9]

There was no government rest house at Assini where accommodation in his government bungalow was provided by a young English official, so ill from yellow fever he was unable to crawl from his sickbed. The dinner table was enlarged by the arrival of a band of shady adventurers. Mary realised with distaste, were hoping to make their fortune from African gold and diamonds and exploit African natives in the process.

Leaving the Forestry Officer to conduct his business at Assini, Mary prepared to make the gruelling return journey without him along the pot-holed 'King's Highway' and set off with porters recruited from the Beyim tribe whose rates of pay had been negotiated in advance. In mid journey they sat down and refused

Africa — The Dark Continent

to continue unless Mary doubled their pay, breaking the contact negotiated by the Forestry Officer and the Beyim chieftain.

Mary had been warned by the Forestry Officer that this kind of blackmail was often practiced on employers regarded as weak. If Mary gave in to the demands of the Beyim they would raise their fees higher the next day. And then if she refused these former warriors could easily overpower her, steal her bag of coins and vanish into the night, leaving her alone with swamps full of crocodiles on one side and dense jungle on the other or murder her and take the rest of the money.

Mary knew she had to keep calm to deal with this dangerous situation. With one hand on the pistol tucked into her waistband and keeping her voice low and firm, Mary said she regretted she could not pay any more than the original contract negotiated with their chief.

When the Beyim warriors muttered angrily among themselves Mary replied calmly if they broke the contract, she would hold their chief responsible for the safety of luggage that had to be left behind. The chief would be billed for any loss or damage.

The mention of payment for damage settled the matter. The Beyim picked up their loads and set off again and the return journey accomplished without further incident.

From Axim Mary took a coastal steamer to Sekondi, a port founded by Dutch slavers in the sixteenth century when it was called Fort Orange. Over a century later the Dutch government sold the fort t to the British government. Mary noted with annoyance that the British had made no attempts to improve the squalid conditions for African workers at what had become a busy port and rail terminal and said as much in her manuscript.

The rail line to the gold mines of Kumasi had been completed back in 1897. Allgold mined in the interior of the British Protectorate of the Ashanti was exported through Sekondi which had a high death rate from tropical diseases, most married men had left their wives home so there was a large male population lacking women.

Sekondi had only one hotel which was the sole watering hole for all miners. Mary, short and plump in her ankle length cream linen skirt and a demure high necked blouse, received a ribald reception from drunken British and German miners who harassed her with lewd comments and gestures.

Mary feared a drunken goldminer might break into her room during the night as the door was so flimsy. She was grateful for the invitation from Nurse Oram, the matron of Sekondi Hospital to stay in the walled compound of the small hospital. Mary and Australian born Matron Oram talked for hours — discussing was the need for more hospitals and schools for Africans and how the British government might be shamed into providing them.

CHAPTER 6

Heading a band of naked warriors

After her stay at the hospital with Matron Oram, Mary wanted to visit the coastal settlement of Chama, nine miles to the east of Sekondi. Discovering that no coastal steamers were due there for many weeks she was forced to spend money hiring a fresh set of porters to accompany her on foot to Chama.

Most available Beyim men had been hired as bearers by British troops, who were on manoeuvres in the Ashanti Protectorate while the rest of them flatly refused to work for a woman.

Eventually Mary managed to hire seventeen surly naked Mendi warriors to carry her baggage for nine miles along a track on which the jungle had encroached so far that it was now almost indistinguishable.

The emblem of the Mendi tribe was a wild boar and the tall naked warriors who were acting as Mary Gaunt's porters wore necklaces of boar's teeth round their necks and nothing else. As they had a fearsome reputation Mary approached the local District Officer, asking him whether he could spare an African policeman from another tribe to accompany her.

The District Officer sent a native policeman from the Ga tribe, so small he resembled a pigmy. As another precaution Mary employed an African servant-cum-interpreter, named Grant, who had been educated by missionaries and came warmly recommended by them.

Mary knew that the Ga were enemies of the Mendi, who for centuries had massacred the inhabitants of Ga villages. She could not see the pygmy policeman as much help in an emergency. But the die was cast — she had to continue with the Mendi porters regardless of the danger.

At the appointed hour for departure, Mary was dismayed to find the Mendi cook had vanished. So had all the food. She decided that, at a pinch, she and the remaining porters and Grant could survive on her tins of food and, hopefully a few freshly caught fish. The topical heat was overwhelming and the air so humid it made Mary feel nauseated and faint. Fearing the onset of asthma again, she retreated to the hammock and was carried by four strong young Africans.

On reaching the next village the sound of chanting and beating of drums signalled a funeral in progress. The porters asked to stop beside the river for a drink of water. The Mendi warriors put down the crates, drank from the river before vanishing into the jungle in the direction of the drums.

Alone in the jungle Mary waited and waited. Her unease mounted as the hours went by. The sound of drunken revelry in the next village grew louder and louder. Eventually the four hammock boys staggered back with bloodshot eyes and waving hands, clearly intoxicated by palm wine.

Mary scolded them and clambered into her hammock. Laughing and giggling the porters staggered and stumbled over the potholed jungle track. As the gloom deepened the porters stumbled into a clearing on the edge of the jungle and were faced by a deserted government rest house, raised on stilts above a concrete platform. The light from a half moon revealed two forlorn figures sitting on the platform — two of the missing Mendi porters but the rest had vanished, along with all the food.

As it was far too hot and humid to sleep inside the rest house, Mary decided to spend the night on the veranda where it was cooler. She sat in her folding chair, listening to the soothing sound of the surf. In the background she still heard the sound of the drums, but it was no longer as menacing as before. She decided to write up her diary s by candlelight. As the missing porters had taken all the food, Mary had eaten nothing since that morning and was very hungry but had to make the best of it.

Later that night the porters staggered in with their loads, intoxicated from drinking too much palm wine. To Mary's horror the naked warriors with their boar's teeth necklaces crowded onto 'her' veranda, dumped their loads. Laughing and gesticulating in their drunken state, they prepared to spend the night beside her. Were she to fall asleep and be raped, Mary could imagine District Officers relating the story with lewd guffaws, claiming she had been asking for trouble travelling in the jungle without a male relative to protect her.

Whatever the outcome, sleeping on a veranda beside naked drunken Africans would make a saucy story and damage her reputation should it reach the ears of the District Commissioners at Sekondi or Kumasi. The gossips would claim widowed Mrs Miller had been looking for a virile African lover to replace her dead husband.

Mary always kept calm in emergencies. She walked to the second rest house, found the elfin Ga policeman, who was as drunk as the porters. She demanded he and her servant clear the veranda of drunken men and support her when she ordered the warriors to go away and spend the night at the nearest native village.

Confronting the tall muscular porters aided by the petite policeman and Grant, her manservant she kept her voice firm and made herself as tall as possible and assumed a very imperious manner. To her surprise and delight they obeyed her when she told them to walk to the adjacent village and sleep there.

After the porters had departed , Mary celebrated with a 'midnight feast' of coffee, tinned tongue and tinned apricots served by the faithful Grant with whom she shared her repast. The air was thick with mosquitoes, so she had to cover her camp bed with netting. Exhausted by the stresses of the day she fell asleep.

The next day brought more problems. Mary had planned to depart at daybreak when the temperature was cooler. She had ordered the Mendi porters to start at 5.30 am. At the appointed time there was no sign of any of the porters. The only men who presented themselves were Grant who had drunk no alcohol and the elf-like Ga policeman who was clearly suffering from a mammoth hang over.

Accompanied by the petite policeman, Mary walked through the deep sand to the neighbouring village. She was furious that that the porters, who were being well paid by African standards, had once again ignored her instructions.

It was now 7.00 in the morning, the sun was starting to get hot and instead of being ready as requested, Mary found the former warriors enjoying a leisurely breakfast of cooked fish and rice. They were laughing and singing and it was clear would not be ready to leave until the sun was high in the sky and the temperature blisteringly hot.

Mary realised that unless she asserted her authority her porters would have the upper hand, as being warriors they carried long curved knives and could easily have murdered her as she could not defend herself properly against a band of them with only one small pistol.

Mary was scared but knew she must not show any fear so she ordered the petite Ga policemen, 'Throw away their chop. Now!'

He hesitated, Mary stamped her foot to emphasise the point.

The hapless policeman had to choose between a band of tall naked warriors armed with knives and a petite but determined white woman. To her relief the Mendi porters did not retaliate when the policeman threw away what was left of their breakfast. They started to load the crates of food, Mary's camera, bath and tripod and the medicine chest. Meanwhile Mary kept hold of the bag containing the coins to pay them that evening and every evening for the next few days.

They were following 'The King's Highway', which in spite of the grandeur of its name, grew worse and worse. The porters with their heavy burdens struggled through soft deep sand. Some cut their feet on sharp rocks which lay hidden under the sand so Mary had to disinfect and bandage their wounds. The 'King's Highway' led through the hills with rocky outcrops so steep that Mary was in danger of being tipped out of her hammock.

Chama turned out to be a straggle of thatched huts, scrawny goats, chickens and smiling children, where Mary spent an uncomfortable night in a dirt-floored hut with a thatched roof. All night long she was bitten by fleas and driven mad by the whine of mosquitoes.

The next day Mary felt ill but continued her journey over hilly country, reaching Kommenda at two in the afternoon. The town had an old decaying stone fort, where they halted for lunch. Mary's table and chair was set up in the courtyard and feeling slightly better she ate some of her tinned food.

They were heading for the slave fort at the port of Elmina which Mary hoped they would reach by nightfall. But the porters insisted they wanted to spend the night at Kommenda, because they were 'no fit' to continue work while she could stay in a flimsy rest house beside the fort.

Having been told by the Forestry Officer that the Kommenda tribe were not to be trusted and had a reputation for robbery and rape Mary did not fancy spending the night in a flimsy hut. Once again she could not show any fear or that could prove fatal.

With her pistol tucked into her belt and holding the bag of threepenny pieces like the status symbol, she sent for the village headman. She asked if he could supply her with fresh porters whose fees she was prepared to pay in advance from the bag of coins in her hand and showed him one of them.

The headman readily agreed. Mary sent for the Mendi warriors' spokesman and told him that those men who were 'no fit' or unwilling to work would have to go back to Sekondi at their own expense, as she had hired porters from Kommenda to take her to Elmina.

Mary's strategy worked. She engaged two Kommenda men, but the Mendi warriors announced they had made a miraculous recovery and would now be fit enough to take her to Elmina.

Although the Mendi porters still severe hangovers from the previous day's drinking and were ill tempered and surly as a result they left Kommenda after lunch for a 19 kilometre trek to Elmina. Mary was determined to reach Elmina by nightfall aware it had a government rest house not wanting to risk another night in the jungle with the hung over Mendi porters.

At dusk, as they saw the lights of Elmina twinkling in the distance, Mary's hammock carriers stumbled and dropped the hammock so Mary tumbled out of it on her head and bruised her neck and shoulder. She picked herself up with as much dignity as possible and declared angrily she would walk the remaining distance to Elmina and would reduce the porters' wages.

As Mary walked away over the rough track, carrying her bag of coins in a canvas holdall, her anger gradually subsided. Hearing a rustling sound in the waist-high grass she realised it easily come from a venomous snake. To her relief she heard the voices of Grant and the hammock boys behind her and hey caught up with her. The stress made Mary start wheezing, the prelude to a full scale asthma attack .Grant insisted she climb back into the hammock so that the porters could carry her the rest of the way. Wheezing badly and worn out by the humidity and heat Mary was so grateful she promised to reward them with a bonus.

Reaching Elmina, originally settled by the Portuguese, then purchased by the Dutch who sold it to the English Mary was carried down the main street in style. It was bordered by large stone houses built in the time of the Porguese and above and to the left loomed a walled fortress called St George's Castle. They crossed a drawbridge and entered the central courtyard of the imposing former slave fort, the largest on what had once been known as 'the slave coast.'

Mary knew that a flimsy government 'rest house' was built into one of outer walls of what the British renamed St George's Castle overlooking the surf and decided to camp there. By now she was totally exhausted but had stopped wheezing but s aware she needed permission to sleep in the rest house asked to see the custodian of the now vacant fort, believing him to be an African.

CHAPTER 7

'Madame, you have the heart of a lion'

Mary was greeted by a surprised Scots academic and historian, working as custodian in order to finish his research paper on the slave trade. Dr Duff, was a red-haired, freckled Scot who told her he was amazed to find a lady so far off the beaten track. He was even more amazed to discover Mary Gaunt was doing research for a travel book on West Africa and hoping to do another on its slave forts. [1] Elderly Dr Duff was aware what harsh country Mary had traversed. He said admiringly, 'Madame, not one woman in ten thousand would have endured the journey you have just made. You have the heart of a lion and the brain of a man'.[2]

As a confirmed bachelor Dr Duff was wary of most women but admired Mary's courage, determination and resilience in making such a hazardsou and difficult journey. He suggested she stay in the empty rooms of the former governor in St George's Castle as she would be far safer there than in the government rest house, which lacked a fence or protection against the thieves who preyed on visitors. Mary accepted his kind offer with gratitude.

After she had bathed, rested and changed into clean clothes, she and Dr Duff enjoyed his simple evening meal together and talked till midnight. Like Mary's late husband, Dr Duff had been born in Edinburgh and had studied at Edinburgh University and knew by reputation her late husband's father, an academic in the medical world, which created a bond between them.

Dr Duff discussed his researches into the African slave trade on which he was preparing an academic treatise. He was a great help to Mary, providing details from antique books in Portuguese and Dutch.³

Dr Duff explained how the Portuguese settlement of San Jorge da Mina (later renamed Elmina) became the headquarters of Portuguese traders who used the fort as a base to export gold, ivory and slaves to Portugal and parts of South America.

The Dutch captured Elmina from the Portuguese in 1637. They used the fort as a trading centre in African wild animals as well as slaves. Like the Portuguese the Dutch kept the captive chained to rings in the walls of the cellars of the fortress. Dr Duff told Mary that from the 16th century onwards when the first African slaves were captured (often by rival tribes) until the slave trade died out in the 1850s he estimated some r 50,000,000 Africans had been captured and brought to various forts along the 'Slave Coast'/ Only one in three slaves survived imprisonment in the slave forts or the long gruelling sea voyage to America or the West Indies where so many died packed like sardines below decks. Mary was deeply shocked to hear such vast numbers of slaves had been involved.

Dr Duff added that in 1872, Elmina now the property of the British Government who renamed the fort St George's Castle had a British garrison who s dug a moat around the castle for protection, but failed to realise malarial mosquitoes would breed in the water and malaria and yellow fever decimated large numbers of British soldiers who garrisoned it. So many deaths meant an outcry in Parliament and the British Government finally abandoned the fort.

Dr Duff estimated over four centuries some 3,000,000 slaves were exported from Elmina, along with a large amount of gold dust. African slaves and the gold were traded for Caribbean rum, sugar and tobacco from the West Indies where the slaves were sold to the sons of leading British families who owned and ran sugar plantations.

In West Africa American and British traders did a substantial import trade in textiles and musket rifles from Britain and traded them with wealthy tribes like the Ashanti and Yoruba who had gold dust to purchase guns. Armed with the imported musket rifles they had purchased from the British the Ashanti and the Yoruba conducted raids and captured their weaker neighbours, like the Timini, the Mendi and the Ga and brought their captives to St George's Castle for sale. Aided by Arab traders, the Ashanti and the Yoruba continued the slave trade long after it had been abolished by British and European governments.[4]

Mary was fascinated by Dr Duff's knowledge. They talked until late at night while Mary made notes which she would use in several future books. She was shown by a servant to a suite of rooms furnished with heavy Dutch furniture but which lacked glass in the windows. [5]

The following morning Mary had breakfast with Dr Duff and gave him a jar of her precious Cooper's Scottish marmalade which he greatly appreciated.

After breakfast Dr Duff showed Mary around St George's Castle, reputed to be haunted by the ghosts of slaves who had died in the cellars. Dr Duff explained to Mary how on arrival the captive entered by 'The Door of No Return' which had a human skull embedded in the wall above the door as a warning not to try to escape. The captives were taken to a special cell and branded with an identification number on the arm. The Cell of the Condemned had another skull and crossbones inserted into the stone lintel. Any captives Africans who caused trouble were starved to death and their corpses thrown into the sea as a warning to the other inmates.

Dr Duff estimated only one African captive in three survived imprisonment in the fortress of Elmina. The more attractive female slaves were given a bath then taken to the apartment of the Portuguese Governor for his sexual gratification. If they fell pregnant they were given a house in the town of Elmina and entrusted to the Jesuits to teach them to speak Portuguese and became housemaids.

After the fort was sold to the British in 1872, British soldiers who garrisoned what was now named St George's Castle claimed that sighs, groans and shrieks could be heard at night from the dungeons. This was where several thousand slaves e had been chained up in the dark for months at a time. Those that managed to survive the waiting period once a slave ship arrived, were loaded into the crowded holds and shipped to the cotton plantations of America and the sugar plantations of the West Indies.

Dr Duff, a Scot who had little love for the English, traditional enemies of Scotland said it was scandalous that so many of the plantation owners came from titled English families, who were keen to hide the fact the source of their t wealth was due to their involvement with the slave trade.[6]

Unfortunately, Dr Duff knew nothing about little Carlos and the crew of the wrecked Spanish galleon. However he confirmed part of the story. Ashanti sorcerers had made human sacrifices under the 'fetish tree' at Kumasi and in other villages to ensure good harvests. The wealth of the Ashanti came from their river gold from which they had purchased so many Danish muskets and sold men from the Ga, the Fanti, the Timini and the Mendi, and sell them to Portuguese, Dutch and Arab slavers.

Armed with their long barrelled Danish muskets the Ashanti had fought the British in a series of wars, the last war being eight years ago when the Ashanti massacred many of the Ga and surrounded the British garrison att Kumasi and would have killed them. Fortunately, reinforcements had arrived from the coast in time. But now the ancient kingdom of the Ashanti was a British Protectorate and becoming prosperous gold mining town. It was believed the new king even had a picture of King Edward VII on the wall of his mud brick palace and claimed him as a friend.

Dr Duff told Mary that to the north of Kumasi lay Africa's 'heart of darkness' where no white woman had ever ventured and wily sorcerers still wielded enormous power over simple villagers. Human sacrifices were still made by the Ashanti in these remote areas and when a village headman or king died his wives and children were buried alive alongside him like the Pharoahs of old or the Ming emperors of China.

These gruesome details, intended to deter Mary from visiting the area, had just the opposite effect on a woman who loved danger and rarely suffered from fear. Mary Gaunt remained determined to go north from Kumasi and learn more about 'fetish' magic and local customs.

After expressing her gratitude to Dr Duff for his hospitality and sharing his knowledge, Mary and her bearers set off for Accra, coastal capital of the Cape Colony (now part of Ghana).

The track led through sand dunes covered in coarse grass and past scattered fishing villages where thatched mud huts nestled among groves of coconut palms.

Eventually Mary and her party arrived at the untidy straggle of woven huts and shanties known as the town of Cape Coast. Decades earlier, Governor General Sir Charles McCarthy had set out from Cape Coast on what would prove a fatal expedition against the Ashanti. He had been captured, beheaded and sacrificed under Kumasi's fetish tree.'

The governor of Cape Coast Colony was away but Mary received a warm welcome from the local Medical Officer. Contrary to the general custom, his wife, a trained nurse, had insisted on accompanying him to West Africa and they invited Mary to stay with them in their bungalow. The Sekondi porters were paid off and about to return home. Mary tried to negotiate a contract for a fresh gang of porters but , was confronted by surly Cape Coast men who refused to work for a mere woman regarding this as below their dignity.

In despair Mary tried to engage their strongly built wives to help her. Initially the women seemed keen to work for a 'white missus' but refused to sign a contract. At the appointed hour for departure the wives arrived, laughing and smiling and told Mary that they were sorry but were 'no fit' to work. Mary suspected that their husbands were responsible for their sudden change of heart but as she had no contract with them had to accept their decision.

After more protracted negotiations, two Kommenda porters and several of the former Sekondi porters agreed to work for Mary Gaunt in return for greatly increased fees. A new contract was signed, the loads were lightened by selling some of the tinned food, since Mary had discovered, contrary to advice provide by Ridgewell Essex and others, she could manage perfectly well without tinned meat and would be able to buy fresh fruit and vegetables and the odd chicken in the villages they passed through. She took with her sacks of rice and a small bag of salt, which was valuable to be carried by the porters.

Eventually Mary and her porters continued their journey along a rough track made centuries earlier by the Portuguese. The next disused slave fort on Mary's itinerary was Annambu. According to Dr Duff, this large and handsome fort made of mud bricks was the home of a cultured African, an erudite man who was the owner of a library of rare books about West Africa. Mary envisaged a man like King Prempeh, g in the story of little Carlos and was keen to meet this keen bibliophile. She went to see him but, was disappointed to be told by the king's servants he was away on his farm in the interior.

Mary, often critical of the British administrators, was full of praise for the Cape Coast Colony where British officials were consulting with the local chiefs to build and equip schools for African children and adults, who showed considerable enthusiasm and aptitude for learning to read and write.

Sometimes when her team of porters passed through African villages Mary had to intervene in quarrels between the porters and the local villagers over pilfered food. She found to her dismay that it was often her porters who were ly the culprits and she had to pay for the chickens or fruit they stole.

The 115 kilometre journey from Cape Coast to Accra took several days. Through an interpreter Mary learned that Accra was quarantined, due to an epidemic of yellow fever. Fortunately, by the time Mary and her entourage reached the coastal town the epidemic was almost over.

The Acting Governor of Accra regarded Mary's arrival with mixed feelings — he clearly believed an unchaperoned white woman travelling with semi-naked African porters was scandalous. However Sir Clive Lucas had advised him that Mrs Mary Miller was a judge's daughter, the widow of a doctor and a well known author so he could not write her off as a fallen women and ignore her. Mrs Miller would be collecting her mail at the Accra office of Elder Dempster lines. In the absence of the Governor the e Acting Governor and his wife discussed Mary who presented a tricky social problem.

Finally the Acting Governor decided that they would make an exception for widowed Mrs Miller and invite her to stay at Government House which Mary found amusing since they were prepared to invite to Government House white men living ' in sin' with African women they had no intention of marrying. women. Possibly the Governor changed his mind as he did not want to feature in Mary Gaunt's forthcoming book as having refused to let her stay with them and forced her to stay in an evil-smelling tavern in Accra.

In a crested envelope Mary found a letter awaiting her arrival at Elder Dempser's Accra office inviting to stay a Government House. It was situated about five kilometres outside Accra in what had once been a Danish trading fort called *Christiansborg*.

Mary arrived there and was shown to her room by a uniformed flunkey and asked what she planned to wear that evening so the maid could iron it for her and reminded that formal evening dress was *de rigeur*.

In the large dining room Mary found the men wore black tail coats with stiffly starched white shirts and medals pinned to their jackets. Mary and the Acting Governor's wife (the only women present) wore long flowing silk or chiffon evening gowns, jewellery and satin evening shoes with high heels.

The menu for their four course dinner was typical of the Edwardian era and most unsuitable for a hot climate. White gloved uniformed staff served cr thick brown Windsor soup for the first course followed by roast meat and several vegetables and a sherry trifle topped with custard. Mary having dined with her parents at Melbourne's Government House was unfazed by finger bowls and waiters in tail coast and white gloves. However in the tropical heat she would have preferred to have eaten salads and a platter of tropical fruit but nevertheless was grateful for their hospitality rather than staying in a mud hut filled with disease bearing insects .

> 'I really think it was noble of the Acting Governor to invite me, for he had no sympathy with my mission, and though far too polite to say so, regarded a woman travelling on her own a pernicious nuisance … Government House Accra known as Christiansborg, had been bought from the Danes sometime in the 1870s… There was a ghost at Christiansborg, built as Government House, and then, because some governor did not like it, became a lunatic asylum before n reverting to being a Government House . Christiansborg Castle is so close to the seashore that the surf tosses its spray against the windows … The heat was so oppressive that I could not sleep and moved to the veranda where the air was cool. But I could not sleep there as it was a public passageway… they kindly gave me for my abode a tumble-down bungalow just outside the castle walls. It was like a little fort, loopholed for defence and on top of the fort was a wooden bungalow rapidly falling into decay. I engaged a cook and ran my own establishment to my own satisfaction. The bungalow was close to the seashore. I opened the windows wide and let the cool healthy fresh air blow over me day and night and I felt wonderfully well. I believe that to ensure good health in West Africa you must have plenty of fresh air. Accra, the principal town of the Ga people must have been a town of great importance for three nations built their forts here. The English had James Fort, now the prison, the Dutch fort was now a police barracks, while the Danes had Christiansborg Castle, three miles from Accra …which lies within a few degrees of the equator and has few shade trees. The sun blazes down on hot red streets lined with bare white houses and the glare makes one pant.

Mary was exhausted from so much travel in n blistering heat and humidity. She spent a month resting and recovering at Christiansborg preparing for another arduous journey on her way to the upper reaches of the Volta River.

Obtaining porters once again was a problem as then local men flatly refused to work for a woman. In desperation Mary had to make a large hole in her funds to hire one of the few lorries available in West Africa. She watched her baggage and equipment loaded onto the truck. She sat beside the driver, as the truck lurched and bumped over the rough track to Dodowah. where Mary was to meet African porters previously engaged by the Acting Governor negotiating with the chief of the Kroo tribe for the next leg of her journey.

A tiring journey over a potholed stony track had left Mary badly bruised as she bumped around. At Dowdah she was confronted by sixteen tall Kroo warriors who had been awaiting her arrival for four days. By now they had run up a large account she was expected to pay, eating and drinking at her expense. The Kroo warriors were naked other than for small penis sheaths. They had been contracted by their chief to accompany the white lady on a forty-four kilometres trip to Akuse — their contact would expire once Mary Gaunt's expedition reached the capital of German owned Togoland.

CHAPTER 8

'Murder Hill' and Togoland

'Mary Gaunt is rich in intuition, vivacity and narrative skills, recording her vivid personal impressions in this remarkable book.' Literary critic of *The Daily Telegraph*, October, 1912 in a review of *Alone in West Africa*.

Although night had fallen and Mary was exhausted from her bruising journey over rough ground in the truck in the high humidity, she decided to leave for Akuse immediately. She made this decision so that the Kroo warriors who carried the expedition's baggage and food supplies could travel by moonlight which would be much cooler than by day.

They set off for Krobo Hill in the tribal lands of the Krobo who for centuries had been enemies of the Kroo tribe. Mary did not know that Krobo Hill had a sinister history of murder and human sacrifice but soon realised the porters were nervous of crossing the hill.

Eventually Mary learned the secret of 'Murder Hill.' Every Krobo youth underwent a rite of passage to manhood, which required him to kill a man on Krobo Hill and donate the corpse given to Krobo sorcerers for use in 'fetish magic'. ceremony . Her porters told her through their interpreter that Krobo Hill was haunted by the ghosts of the dead seeking revenge on their murderers. These ritual murders usually n took place just before the burial of a chief as Krobo tradition e required a large number of bodies to be buried with the dead king to serve him in the after life.

> ...on Krobo Hill the fetish priests [sorcerers] held great orgies, and for their ghastly ceremonies and initiations caught any stranger reckless enough to pass the hill... at the end of the last century the British Government intervened. Their soldiers took Krobo Hill and scattered the fetish priests and their abominations... [but] only three years ago a negro clerk on his bicycle was traced to that hill and no further trace of him found. His hat was in the road, and the Krobos declared that the great white baboons that infest the hill had taken him. This was hardly reasonable... the clerk was strong and young, a fitting offering to accompany to his last resting place a dead chief whose obsequies the Krobos were celebrating at the time.[1]

The Kroo porters were scared of the murderous Krobo who greatly outnumbered them and wanted to wait for daylight before entering the haunted area of 'Murder Hill' where so many of the Kroo had vanished. Mary was told that Krobo sorcerers not only wanted the bodies of 'servants' rpses to buy with dead chiefs but regarded human sacrifices and the sprinkling of human blood on the ground as a means of ensuring plentiful harvests and the fertility of Krobo women.

Mary kept her hand on her pistol all the time they were crossing Murder Hill but in spite of dire predictions of an attack they crossed the hill without incident and reached Akuse before nightfall.

From Akuse Mary and the Kroo porters continued along the banks of the beautiful Volta River traversing palm plantations from where the palm oil was exported to Britain and France and exotic tropical fruits flourished like weeds.

> The Gambia River is interesting, the Congo is grand but the Volta River is entrancingly lovely. Its quiet reaches are like deep lakes in whose clear surface is mirrored the calm blue sky, the fleecy clouds and hills clothed in the densest green. Beneath the vivid

blue sky are tangled, luxuriant feathery palms, tall cotton trees bound together with twining creepers and trailing vines. Here are broad leafed banana trees, handsome mangoes, fragrant orange trees, patches of lighter coloured cocoa and cassava. Men fish from canoes, boats return with cotton cloth for the factories run by negro agents of the great trading houses.[2]

Mary's team of warriors trekked across wild and sparsely inhabited country with Mary born aloft in a kind of palanquin before they came to rubber plantations. Mary was shown how the trunks of the rubber trees were scored with knives, so the milky latex could be tapped and drained off in small cups attached to the tree trunks.

Along the upper reaches of the remote Volta River Mary stopped to visit a hospital and research station run by the Basel Mission. Here dedicated Swiss medical missionaries were trying to discover how to prevent the spread of sleeping sickness which had killed so many Europeans and Africans convinced this fatal disease was caused by the bites of the tsetse fly.

The first symptoms of sleeping sickness were blinding headaches, which n led to a swelling of the brain and high fever which sent the victims to sleep, hence the name sleeping sickness. The progress of the disease was slow as it could take as long as six months for victims of sleeping sickness to die.

Mary was told by mission doctors, who were working on a cure that his dangerous disease was caused by the flukes of the 'guinea worm' an organism prevalent in most African rivers. The doctors warned Mary about the importance of boiling all drinking water — the flukes were invisible to the naked eye they were believed to be the cause of fatal liver damage. Many African natives, whose canoes had overturned in rivers or lakes, along with their European passengers had died in agony as a result of imbibing water containing these flukes.

Mary was impressed by the research carried out by the dedicated Swiss medical missionaries. Although her money was running low she made a donation to their work from the bag of coins she carried with her to pay the porters, as she believed what they were doing to be important research for the future of Africa.

Further up the Volta River (which now has a damn across it and has become a large lake on the map that accompanies Mary's African travels) one of the branch managers of Messrs F and A. Swanzey, the trading company who owned mines and river steamers, who, contacted by Sir Clive Lucas kindly provided a free passage for Mary and her porters. She was grateful for the help of various managers of Messrs Swanzey which represented a considerable saving for her. By now her bag of small coins was almost exhausted and needed to go to a town where she could cash a bank draft and obtain more coins to pay her bearers.

After leaving the river steamer owned by the ubiquitous Mesrrs. Swanzey, Mary spent an uncomfortable night in a disused cocoa store, also owned by Swanzeys.

The interior of the cocoa store smelt of the cocoa beans. Mary heard the scuttlings of rats and spotted rat dropping , Grant, her efficient African servant boiled up pans of water on his charcoal stove so she could take a bath in the portable canvas bath which was turning out to be most useful.

Mary was disconcerted to find eyes peering at her through chinks in the wooden walls. As she emerged from the bath, wrapped in a towel, she was amused to hear spectators discussing in pigeon English what they had seen of her at her toilette.

Some Edwardian ladies would have been shocked but Mary was made of sterner stuff and described with the incident amusement

> I did not know if they found it satisfactory but at least the show was free. That is unless Messrs Swanzey's agent had charged them for it in advance![3]

The following day Mary's porters hacked their way through unmapped jungle. The road climbed steeply to the peaks of the Ranges they had to cross to reach the border of German owned Togoland. Mary took her bearings and drew a rough map of the area. She was surprised to find nothing marking the boundary between British territory and the German colony of Togoland.

> I had been warned I should have to walk across the Eveto Ranges as no hammock-boys could possibly carry me. I decided the walking had better be done very early in the morning and arranged to start at half past five as soon as it was light. I cannot think the Eveto Range is perpendicular but it seemed to be so... The track twisted and turned among holes and roots and rocks. After ten minutes it was brought home to me I was a fool to have even *attempted* to travel in Africa.[4]

It seems extraordinary that a middle aged woman who suffered from asthma would even consider the strenuous ascent of one of the steepest mountain ranges in West Africa,. a long way away from any medical help.

Whenever Mary Gaunt started wheezing and felt an asthma attack coming up she would lie flat on her back. As Dr Duff had noted, Mary had the heart of a lion, but overweight and asthmatic she lacked the physique of an explorer. Most asthmatics of her age would have given in, but Mary was determined to explore the German colony of Togoland, an area unknown to most British readers before making the long trip to visit Kumasi, the place she had longed to see since she was a girl.

After crossing into German territory Mary noticed a great difference between the German run colony and colonies run by the British. In Togoland there was as in most colonies only one road but was well-tended and straight and wide enough for two carts to pass abreast. On either side, with typical German neatness and precision, the grass verges had been neatly trimmed.

Unlike most of the African villages on the British side the first village on the German side of the border was neat and well maintained. The streets were bordered by flame trees with beautiful orange flowers. Underneath the flame trees were rustic seats made from split logs ideal for travellers. Even the goats and sheep looked neater and cleaner in Togoland than in Britain's African colonies Mary thought.[5]

***

A chance meeting with the German Commissioner led to an invitation to stay with him and his wife in their neat clean bungalow. The Commissioner's attractive young wife provided fresh coffee and delicious home made German cakes and pastries. Mary, looking at her rosy cheeks and bright eyes, asked how long she had been there.

'Not long,' was the reply, 'Only a year and two months. But it's so nice here we are asking the Government to let us stay for the full two years. We love it here. There is so much to do!'

Mary found the German Commissioner's wife's reply a contrast to the moans about heat and lack of amenities from the few English wives she had met. Most of the British wives were counting the months and days until their husband's next leave 'home'.

By now Mary realised that she was vulnerable alone in the wilds where she could easily be blackmailed for higher wages by her porters as had happened to other explorers. This time the German Commissioner was kind enough to supervise contract negotiations with the chief for a fresh crop of porters. After Mary had reached an agreement with her new porters she thanked the kind young German couple and said goodbye to them.

Her next destination was Kpalime, a neat little town where she dismissed her porters and took the newly built railway to Lomé, the capital of Togo situated on the Bight of Benin. She had been told by John Ridgewell Essex, that Togo was in a very pretty part of Africa. With his interest in fetish magic and mind control practiced by African sorcerers he told Mary that Lomé had a fascinating sorcerers' market, selling potions made from monkey flesh and jungle plants. The sorcerers claimed s they had potions to bewitch and seduce women and charged accordingly and even offered for sale stronger mixtures could secure the deaths of enemies.

Mary searched for the sorcerers' market, hoping it would provide local colour for her next novel set in t Africa. To her disappointment she found the Germans authorities had forbidden the sorcerers to set up their stalls. Lome market only contained women in colourful dresses with red bandanas on their heads selling fruit and vegetables.

The centre of Lome had been built on a swamp, drained under the supervision of German engineers. It had attractive gardens and modern bungalows for its small colony of resident German officials and the neat streets were maintained by African prisoners from the local gaol. Mary was full of admiration for the cleanliness and orderliness that prevailed and how well the Germans had conserved the magnificent trees and preserved the natural beauty of the countryside. She wrote,

> A beauty spot to the Germans is a beauty spot, whether it be in the Fatherland or in remote West Africa, while in contrast the English in Africa seem indifferent to aesthetics or beauty.[6]

Mary's glowing descriptions of German Togoland in comparison with Britsh colonies meant *A Woman in Africa* was translarted into German and sold well there. as the Germans were proud of their 'model' colony and keen to read a description of it.

What Mary could not foresee was that when Germany invaded France in 1914, French troops stationed in French African colonies would invade Togoland, and d rename it Togo. Under the French administration all the Germanic neatness and cleanliness disappeared and the colony became unkempt and dirty.

※

After leaving German Togoland, Mary headed for the Ashanti Protectorate. The local office of the ubiquitous Messrs F and A Swanzy kindly provided Mary with another free passage on a steamer that took her from Lomé along the coast and back to Sekondi.

'MURDER HILL' AND TOGOLAND

Kumasi, capital of the ancient Ashanti Kingdom, lay some 200 kilometres north of Sekondi. Mary took the new railway to Kumasi, made a stop at Tarkwa, a gold mining area run by the British.

Tarkwa was a desolate town without a single tree and very little grass. Having grown up in gold mining regions of Victoria and heard her father recount his experiences on the goldfields, Mary knew a great deal about goldfields life and its problems of alcoholism, constant fights, shortage of women, prostitution and venereal diseases.

She found that many gold miners at Tarkwa suffered from dengue fever, transmitted by mosquitoes. They also suffered from filariasis a water born disease that caused a painful and incurable swelling of the limbs, known as elephantiasis in which the limbs swelled up to huge proportions.

Mary followed the advice of the Swiss medical missionaries on the Volta River and boiled all her drinking water and made her porters do the same. dysentery and typhoid were prevalent in the mining town now part of Ghana. The flukes and eggs of the 'guinea worm', undetectable in water had killed many gold miners who drank or swam in it.[7] Gold miners and colonial officials at Tarkwa risked their lives working in what they called 'a tropical hell-hole'. By now Mary must have realised what risks she was facing remembering the family motto, 'Gaunts never give up' refused to turn back. She was about to achieve her childhood dream, reach Kumasi and visit the mud brick palace of the king of the Ashanti and the 'fetish tree' under which so many men had been sacrificed to pagan gods.

CHAPTER

Black magic among the Ashanti

Kumasi was even more humid than Takwa since it lay closer to the equator. The British had imported machinery to extract gold from deeper levels than the Ashanti could penetrate. With the royalties from the gold the new Ashanti Protectorate had paved the streets and built brick shops and offices. It was a very different place to the primitive jungle settlement in Ashantiland described in the book Mary had read as a child at her uncle's Geelong sheep station.

She was met by servants of the Chief Commissioner and escorted past armed guards to the Commissioner's Residennce in the former British fort of Kumasi. Here she was welcomed by Chief Commissioner Fuller and his young wife, one of only two white women in Kumasi, the other being the wife of an English missionary. The Kumasi fort had been enlarged since the last Ashanti attack which had taken place eight years previously.

As they went to the newly built annexe on the upper level of the fort where Mary was allocated a bedroom by Mrs Fuller who showed Mary the original gun emplacements from the former Danish fort of Christiansborg whose guns had defended the British garrison from the ferocious Ashanti.

At dinner time, Mary heard how one Ashanti rebellion had begun in wild country to the north of Kumasi with an Ashanti massacre of their enemies, the Ga. British traders, Swiss and German missionaries and hundreds of Ga survivors — men, women and children — sought refuge in the British fort which was soon overcrowded to the point of suffocation.

Outside the walls of the fort hundreds camped hundreds more Africans with their wives and children, terrified survivors of armed attacks by the Ashanti, hoping the guns of the British garrison would save them.[1]

Food supplies at the fort and in the refugee camps ran low. The officer in command of Kumasi garrison, Major Armytage, sent a native runner to the coast to tell Major Beddoes the Ashanti were on the warpath. But nothing more was heard so Major Armytage r had to decide whether to abandon the fort and face an eight day walk through the jungle where the Ashanti, who specialisedd in jungle warfare, could kill them with ease.

The alternative was to remain inside the fort and hope British troops would arrive before the garrison and those sheltering around the fort starved to death.

Several of the younger officers, aware how little food remained, decided walk to the coast, reckoning it would take them eight days to get there. Aware that, if they were captured, the Ashanti would torture and murder them, they took with them capsules of potassium cyanide preferring to commit suicide rather than fall into Ashanti hands and have their genitals cut off before tjeu were beheaded.

Meanwhile inside the British fort, brave Major Armytage and his garrison had almost given up in despair until they heard the sound of bugles and realised that Major Beddoes and relief forces were arriving to save them.

Mary was fascinated by a story and made notes to include in *Alone in Africa,* and felt that a visit to the unexplored area to the north was absolutely vital and was sure it would also provide material for a novel.

Over the next few days Mary explored Kumasi to see how much had changed since the Ashanti had revolted against British rule. She found the export of gold had brought even more wealth to the Ashanti and wrote that Ashanti warriors and their wives had 'taken very kindly to trade'.

She visited small shops full of cotton goods from Manchester, kerosene lamps, brooms, brushes and sewing machines, staffed by men who had once been warriors. Some of the Ashanti could afford to employ men from the Hausa and Krepi tribes, to act as salesman or porters. Mary described an Ashanti warrior turned businessman

> ...stalking about Kumasi in his brightly coloured toga, sure that he is a man of great importance among the tribes; Ashanti chiefs parade through the streets sitting in chairs carried on their men's heads, with tom-toms beating, immense gaily coloured umbrellas twirling, their silken clothing a brilliant spot in the brilliant sunshine, their rich gold ornaments marking them off from the common herd.[2]

Mary was told that the palace with rows of books belonging to the King Prempeh, the savour of little Carlos, had been burned down by the British and replaced by a smaller palace, built by a subsequent king.

Mary did her best but could find no record of little Carlos or the Spanish sailors sacrificed under the 'fetish' tree. This giant banyan had been chopped down by the British as soon as they arrived at Kumasi. Sir Garnet Wolsey's troops were amazed by the size of the Ashanti king's mud brick palace and the vast library of books in several languages owned by the king.

Mary now realised with a shock the hypocrisy of at the underlying motive for the British attacking the kingdom of the Ashanti for a second time was not to avenge the murdered Ga and assure their safety but to ensure the British Army held the area and kept the Germans and French out so that British mining companies gained access to Ashanti gold. The current Ashanti king had sworn an oath of loyalty to Queen Victoria and built himself a new palace to replace the one the British had burned down. British interests took over gold mining in the area and using British capital and expertise were able to mine underground for gold, something the Ashanti had not been able to do. They paid the Ashanti a small royalty on the gold that was exported (but the royalty would decline over the years as the gold mining companies became greedier and greedier for more profits and had to mine deeper).

Mary was fascinated by the tall graceful Ashanti women in their long silk robes and matching turbans as well as their heavy gold bracelets and exquisite gold rings. The Ashanti women gathered around Mary, the first white woman they had ever seen. Politely they asked if they could touch her linen skirt. Accustomed to wearing the finest silk and patterned cotton they had never seen linen before.

Through an interpreter the Ashanti women asked the whereabouts of Mary's husband and how many children she had, fertility being greatly valued in their culture. They shyly offered condolences when Mary said her husband was dead and had no children.

Mary greatly admired the spirit of these African women who unlike those from other tribes had won the right to considerable independence, conducted business on their own account and kept the profits, which they spent as they saw fit.

Mary described Ashanti women as 'rich and self-supporting, happy, contented and sure of themselves'. The women were proud of the fact they were overweight as this showed the world they could afford to eat well unlike tribes were the women were half starved. They spent lage sums on clothes and jewels, loved and cared for their children and seemed content with their lives, in contrast to downtrodden wives from other tribes Mary had seen in other parts of West Africa.[3]

Under British rule Kumasi had become a thriving trade centre for rubber and gold.[4] The building of the railway from Sekondi had had a health benefit. The wholesale felling of trees around the town, leaving a wide corridor bare of trees in a deliberate effort to eradicate the tsetse flies that killed so many Africans and their cattle. By now a journey that once took the Ashanti eight days on foot through dense forest only took a single day by train.

Mary noted that British officials had done their best to break the power of sorcerers. The ground beneath the branches of the fetish tree,, once soaked in blood and covered in bones of human beings sacrificed to savage gods was now paved over and the banyan chopped down.

Around what had once been the area where the men and women to be sacrificed had been tied to other trees were small shops staffed by members of other tribes paid by the Ashanti to work for them.

British officials lived in pleasant bungalows surrounded by trees and shrubs and streets corners bore signs with names like 'Kingsway' and Stewart Street.' Mary saw British run schools in the centre of Kumasi and an ancient Arab town known as the *zonga*, built by Arab slave traders.

※

Mary had now been travelling for eight months under difficult conditions and was very tired but her zest for travel undiminished and determined to see the wild and primitive jungle villages to the north of Kumasi.

'Go to Odumanse' advised Chief Commissioner Fuller 'You'll be the first white woman to visit the area — it's so interesting. I'm sure you won't regret going there.'[5]

With a retinue of naked warriors from the Krepi tribe carrying her supplies and photographic equipment Mary went up country with a porter who spoke broken English designated to act as her interpreter.

Mary hoped to talk to local chiefs and their sorcerers or shamans who wielded enormous power in this remote forested area, known as 'the Northern Territories of the Ashanti.' Here the spirits of the dead were venerated and sorcerers still had the power of life and death as did their chiefs.

Dr Duff had warned Mary that, even in 1910, human sacrifices still took place in this remote area, the real 'heart of Africa' and she would be the first white woman to venture into these villages.

In the dense rain forest Mary was overawed by the majesty of the immense tree trunks that surrounding the track that her porters hacked through the dense jungle hung with looping vines.

These mighty trees that dwarf all other trees in the world have taken hundreds of years to their growth. When George I came to England from Hanover the trees were young and slim and now that George V is on the throne they stretch up their tall crowns to the brilliant sunlight... That road is like nothing else in the world. My hammock and its porters were dwarfed by the great roots and trunks of the trees and became as tiny as ants. Overhead was a narrow strip of blue sky but only at noon did the sunlight reach the roadway below. We travelled in shadow which was pleasant in the ferocious heat. Looking down the road I could see the trees straight as a die, tall pillars ahead of me. Close at hand the mighty buttresses that supported them rose up to the height of ten men and between them were matted together thick creepers and vines. There must have been orchids for sometimes I smelt their rich sensuous smell while at other times I smelt mice and knew there must be colonies of fruit bats overhead.[6]

At Ofinsu Mary stayed the night in a native hut. She crossed the Ofin River in a canoe, aware if it turned over she risked dying from infection by guinea worm. On the far side of the river the forest was even denser than she had seen before. The trees were so awe-inspiring she felt as though in a cathedral dwarfed by these mighty trees.

In the remote village of Potsikrom, goats, pigs and scrawny chickens wandered down the only street. Mary spent the night in a native hut and slept badly, her fair skin covered in bites from insects. She feared she might have been bitten by a tsetse fly and die of sleeping sickness. But it was too late. There was no cure or antidote. All she could do was hope the nasty red swelling on her arm was not caused by a bite from a tsetse fly.

Mary found a large gathering of Ashanti celebrating the crowing of a new chief who was carried in procession to his 'crowning' under a large red umbrella. Mary learned that the British had been unable to stamp out the tradition whereby the dead chief had been buried with his wives, who were still alive.

The natives of the village were excited to see a white woman for the first time. To honour the white lady's arrival, the first most of them had seen, Ashanti warriors fired their long barrelled Danish-made muskets into the air which was soon blue with smoke.

The new chief presented Mary with a sheep, an elderly chicken and some ripe bananas. Custom decreed that she had to respond with an equal gift, which in her case was money and tins of tongue and Fortnum and Mason's chicken soup, seen as delicacies by the delighted chief. After Mary had given presents to the chief, there was more banging of tom-toms and dancing, and everyone seemed to be smiling and nodding at her. Mary was the centre of attention and observed wryly she had never received so much admiration — not even on her wedding day!

She gave the live sheep to her native porters who killed and roasted it for their dinner. Mary ate the scrawny chicken for dinner, after Grant, her faithful servant from Accra, had boiled it up for her. Coronation celebrations continued all night with more Danish made muskets discharged and tom-toms beaten *ad nauseam*, so Mary had little sleep in the village 'rest-house'.

The next morning a long line of native women waited outside the rest house to catch another glimpse of the first white woman they had ever seen. While Mary ate her breakfast they peering at her through a palm-frond partition. These women aroused Mary's sympathy as they lacked the privileges of their wealthier sisters at Kumasi. She observed how badly they were treated by their menfolk and used as slaves by husbands and fathers.[7]

On their departure, Mary and her Krepi porters were escorted by the chief and his warriors. Tom-toms were beaten, red and green umbrellas twirled, and once again those Danish-made long barrelled musket rifles were fired into the air in salutation.

As they departed a procession of villagers followed Mary, waving goodbye until finally the forest enveloped them. She crossed the Tano River by canoe to reach Sunyani and stayed in the thatched bungalow of the Provincial Commissioner. He explained over the dinner table how life was changing, even among the remote jungle Ashanti. A Medical Officer now came out from Sekondi Hospital twice a year to tour their villages and teach the mother's better health practices, warning the women they *must* boil all drinking water and telling the men it was vital to drain the swamps where mosquitoes bred.

The last stop on Mary's journey was Odumanse. Once more a welcoming procession of warriors came out to greet her, yelling and firing off their Danish musket rifles until the air was filled with acrid blue smoke.

Odamanse was merely a straggle of thatched round mud huts with holes for windows and doors. The women, tall and statuesque wore nothing but strings of beads cut from bamboo and incised with designs darkened by fire. A group of men surrounding the chief, seeing Mary's camera, asked her to take their photographs.

Mary obliged.[8] She observed that the head servant of the chief wore a gold chain bearing a heavy breastplate of solid gold. She learned that this was a badge of honour for being close to the chief, but such honour came at a price — on the day of the chief's death the young man would be beheaded. The head servant was regarded as the 'soul' of the chief and along with the chief's wives who were by custom beheaded or buried alive him , the head servant would be killed so he could accompany his master to serve him in the after life.

The visiting Medical Officer was about to leave the area before the rainy season began. He volunteered to accompany Mary back to Kumasi, an offer she accepted with pleasure. The young doctor had cut his hand and the wound was festering so it was vital he was back in Kumasi before the infection worsened. In the era before antibiotics were discovered there were numerous deaths from blood poisoning when even small wounds became infected.

The Medical Officer and Mary retraced their steps as rapidly as possible, due to the urgency of the situation. On the third day, while crossing a river, they were caught in a heavy rainstorm and their dug out canoe almost capsized. This was very dangerous in view of so many crocodiles on the bank or in the water crocodiles. They could also have been infected with liver disease from snail flukes. Although Mary was not a strong swimmer she remained calm and did not move until the swaying canoe righted itself.

The following day they reached Kumasi, where the Medical Officer left Mary in order to attend to his wounded hand which had become badly infected. She never knew what happened to this pleasant young man. Had he died or was he still alive and helping save more lives? Years later she learned he had died of blood poisoning.

Mary caught the train back to Sekondi and, having no wish to encounter more drunken miners in the only hotel in the town, stayed in the hospital compound for the second time as the guest of Matron Oram. [9] (Years later she learned that Matron Oram had distinguished herself serving in France in World War One and the young Medical Officer had died from blood poisoning.).

After a brief stay at Sekondi, Mary said goodbye to her loyal servant Grant as she prepared to board the luxurious Elder Dempster liner *Dakar* for her return voyage to England.

As the ship lay at anchor off shore, Mary and what remained of her luggage had to be paddled in a dug out canoe through the heavy surf — it was the final exhilarating experience of her African expedition.

CHAPTER 10

The male dinosaurs of London's Royal Geographical Society

The voyage to fog-ridden Liverpool gave her ample time to read her notes and diaries to decide which of her many and varied experiences would appear in her travel book and which she could use in another novel set in West Africa.

From Liverpool Mary took a train to London and returned to her rented apartment in Kensington.

She spent the next six months at her desk writing the travel book commissioned by Werner Laurie and an African novel, *Every Man's Desire* and had several short stories set in Africa accepted by English magazines.

A Woman in Africa won Mary Gaunt a great deal of praise for a gruelling journey under harsh conditions. The literary critic of *The Telegraph* called her African travel narrative 'a remarkable book of energy and vision'.

The National Geographical Journal praised Mary Gaunt's 'lively style and her criticism of British methods of administration'. The book sold extremely well in Britain and had American, Australian and a German editions. Her readers were fascinated by Mary's courage and determination: as a result of the book's success she was invited to speak to the Scottish Geographical Society in Edinburgh about various ethnological aspects of her African tour and write an article for their journal.

The Uncounted Cost had became a best seller after being banned. This well written feminist novel about different sexual standards for men and women n had become a *success de scandale*, banned by subscription and public libraries. Now *Every Man's Desire* dared to relate what so often happened in British colonies where many colonial officers lived with an African cook or housekeeper as their mistress. This was often ignored by the white community who pretended it was not happening or deplored since the white man concerned was 'letting down the side' in doing something inherently immoral as black women were seen as beyond the pale.

Having met African women and liked many of them Mary wanted to show the human feelings incurred in such a relationship and to warn European wives that if they refused to accompany their husbands on long postings this was a likely course of events.

With good royalties from her African books waiting for her little house in Eltham to be completed, Mary meanwhile sought more comfortable accommodation in a quiet square off the Brompton Road, near Harrods.

Plagued by asthma and chest problems and tendency to bronchitis, she now had sufficient funds to enable her to escape from London each year during the coldest months of winter — January and February — to a small hotel in Nice and keep up the payments to the builder who had by now laid the foundations of her new house in Kent.

Mary was still hoping to visit China which she felt could be an excellent source of material for second travel book and hopefully a novel.

Letters to Mary from the newly promoted Captain Ernest Gaunt, briefly Naval Administrator in charge of the Chinese port of Luo-Kung-Tao Lng before being appointed captain of the battleship *Majestic*, warned Mary that the xenophobic Elder Bretheren sect were also aiming to kill all foreigners in China. There were other groups who wished to depose the Manchu and turn China into a socialist republic.[1] Civil war in China was a strong possibility.

As always the thought of danger did not discourage Mary. She knew that China would be a fascinating source of material. Her African books had been a success. She had been taken seriously by other explorers, invited to lecture to the members of Scottish Geographical Society and write an article on her travels in their magazine. In the article Mary described how she had gone up the Congo River as far as Matadi, her visit to Kumasi and its jungle villages y to the north where she had been the first white woman to visit the area.[2].

※※

Mary found it infuriating that the London's Royal Geographical Society scorned the idea that women could be explorers and rejected them as members of the society. For a few brief months they had admitted world travellers like Isabella Bird and Emmeline Porcher, but crusty elderly members had complained, so the committee reverted to their previous policy and once again banned women members.

Mary Gaunt, as well as her fellow explorer and travel writer Gertrude Bell, were keen to use the library which was the best travel library in the world and d applied for membership to the Royal Geographical Society, but their requests were rejected. Finding it unreasonable that, due to their gender, their explorations were scorned and they were excluded from the RGS, they campaigned for a change in the rules to permit women explorers and world travellers to become members.

Gertrude Bell, an English-born heiress turned archaeologist and amateur photographer, was six years younger than Mary. Both these clever and adventurous women were united in their determination to be admitted to the prestigious Royal Geographical Society, citing their need to use the world's finest travel library.

Like Mary Gaunt, Gertrude Bell had lost the man she loved under tragic circumstances. She had been in love with a young but penniless junior diplomat, named Henry Cadogan who introduced her to the beauty of Persian poetry. However Gertrude's wealthy self-made father forbade her to marry the man she loved fearing Cadogan was not wealthy enough to maintain his daughter. However . Gertrude was determined to marry young Cadogan g him come what may and was devastated to receive the news when in England that out in Persia Hugh Cadogan's horse had stumbled so that he fell into a stream and drowned. A grief stricken Gertrude Bell channelled her energies into organising her own expeditions into the deserts of the Middle East.

Like Mary Gaunt, Gertrude Bell had been warned that in order to have her porters respect her she must appear a person of great importance and with this in mind he took her table silver, linen and cutlery with her and used it to dine in a silken tent erected by her servants. Because she behaved like a *grand dame* and travelled with an entourage, Gertrude Bell was received with all the honours usually accorded to men by the sheiks across whose tribal lands she journeyed.

Both lady explorers issued commands and made decisions in an era when women were supposed to meekly take orders from men. But under their le carapaces, both Gertrude and Mary Gaunt suffered from terrible loneliness and overcame this by throwing themselves into the excitement of foreign travel meeting new people and seeing new places and writing about them.

Their strong and amusing personalities were reflected in their writings. Both women loved deserts and wild places and their powers of observation and gift for vivid descriptions made their travel narratives of interest to the general reader. They were in advance of the time in their feminist ideals but were also imperialists, in love with the idea of the British Empire. But then so were most English-speaking people of the Edwardian era.[3] Only if accompanied by male friends, who were Fellows of the Royal Geographical Society, were Mary and Gertrude Bell, on sufferance allowed to enter the RGS library.

Mary wanted to follow the route she and Ernest had discussed for years. She hoped to go west from Peking through inner and outer Mongolia and d follow the most southerly of the ancient Silk Roads and cross the Taklamanan or southern Gobi desert deserts through Kashgar and Azerbijan. But since the society's rules insisted a male member must be with her all the time, Mary had not been able to obtain all the information she needed on the Gobi and Taklaman desert and their oases and the fabled hunting palaces of the Manchu emperors near the town of Chengde on the Jehol River.

The fact that Mary Gaunt was intending to explore the Taklamanan and Gobi Deserts and outer Mongolia had been noted by a number of committee members. There was support for accepting her as a Fellow of the Royal Geographical Society along with Gertrude Bell. However, the old objection which had seen the door slammed on women before that it was most unladylike for a lady to lead an expeditions was raised once again and once more won the day.

***

The idea of following the Silk Road from Xian a into Europe intrigued Mary. Ernest Gaunt, who had hoped to accompany her along the Silk Road years earlier, was married man and commanding a battleship thousands of miles away. She must make this dangerous trip alone or not at all

, Guy Gaunt had become involved with British Naval Intelligence and both he and Ernest warned Mary that trouble was brewing in China and that foreigners were not welcome there. Zaitan, the young reformist Guanxu Emperor, unhappily married to the niece of Cixi, the Dragon Empress, had died from a mysterious illness.[4] Twenty four hours later, Empress Cixi also died at a ripe old age from natural causes. However two deaths in the ruling Manchu dynasty within twenty four hours caused political instability and street riots. A Chinese Revolution seemed a distinct possibility but this did not deter Mary Gaunt from making plans for a Chinese tour.

Mary's publishers William Heinemann enjoyed great success with a non-fiction book set in Peking's Forbidden City. The author was Sir Edmund Trelawney Backhouse. His book *China under the Empress Dowager*, (published in 1910) *had a *success de scandale* in

Britain when its titled author, a fluent Chinese speaker returned to London from Peking. Mary read the book and was fascinated. The titled author claimed he had discovered the gossipy journal of a Manchu bannerman or officer residing in the Forbidden City and translated it to learn secrets about Cixi, the 'Dragon Empress.' Mary's publisher, Mr Laurie, was excited by this publication which revealed that the Qing dynasty (part of the Manchu) and the Forbidden City, with its concubines, eunuchs and sex scandals and wished Mary to write a story about the Forbidden City and its emperors and empresses.

Mary's brother Lance, now married to Violet Morrison, sister of Ernest's friend from the Boxer Rebellion, Dr George Morrison was enjoying life in Singapore, where he had established a thriving legal practice. He and Violet were planning to buy a country house in Sussex to use as a base when taking long leave and for their children who y could use it in the holidays when at English boarding schools.

Lance was planning a family reunion in London, to be attended by Morrisons and Gaunts. Clive Gaunt, whose health was poor, and regarded by his siblings as a confirmed bachelor and working as Assistant Government Advocate in Rangoon surprised all of them when he announced he was courting Violet's younger sister, Hilda Morrison initially by letter and had followed up a promising start with a visit to Hilda in Geelong.[5]

Lance's brother-in-law and Ernest's friend, the famous, Dr George Morrison, scholar, explorer, author and former *Times* correspondent in Peking as a young man had walked through south-western China, where he had been menaced by brigands and written a book on his experiences.[6] Mary longed to meet him. He was reckoned to be the greatest expert on China in the western world and could give her invaluable advice.

Events moved swiftly. George Morrison, now fifty years old and also reckoned to be a confirmed bachelor had decided to marry his secretary-cum-personal assistant, twenty-three-year old Jennie Wark Robin whose parents, prosperous New Zealanders, lived to the south of London. Earlier that year Morrison had resigned from *The Times* to take up the post of advisor to General Yuan Shi-kai, the President of the new Chinese Republic. George Morrison had played what many regarded as a pivotal role in dawn of the fledgling Chinese republic and it was whispered that he was coming to London not only to get married and meet his in-laws but to arrange a bank loan for the new Chinese People's Republic at the request of the newly appointed former general now President Yuan Shih-kai.

Lance's mother-in-law, widowed Mrs Rebecca Morrison, widow of a former headmaster of Geelong Grammar had been relieved when her son, (known for liaisons with several ladies of dubious morals) told her he was marrying a beautiful and unspoiled girl who was a virgin. Mrs Morrison's inquiries confirmed that Miss Robin's reputation was impeccable. She was well educated had a sweet nature and was extremely attractive.

Mrs Morrison was due to arrive in London for the wedding with her youngest daughter Hilda who was expected to announce her engagement to Clive Gaunt. Lance and Violet Gaunt would arrive by boat from Singapore for the weddings of Dr George Morrison and Miss Jennie Robin in South Croydon on 26 August 1912 with a brief honeymoon at Hindhead in Surrey. The Gaunt-Morrrson family reunion would take place ten days later in a London hotel.[7]

At the family reunion Mary met the newly weds. George Morrison was a tall handsome man with a beard and temples were flecked with grey. Mary was impressed by Morrison but realised he had a strong ego and a very good opinion of his own capabilities.

His wedding to an attractive and intelligent young woman half his age provided her with a salutary lesson. Widowed for so many years and lonely she had hoped that one day she might find someone she could love and admire and spend the rest of her life with.

Seeing George Morrison, a man of her own age besotted by a beautiful young wife, almost young enough to be his daughter brought home the fact that intelligent interesting men in her age group were not looking for companionate marriages with women of their own age. They wanted to marry attractive t young wives decades younger than themselves. She would only marry a man she could love and admire and would be alone for the rest of her life.

Learning that his new relative by marriage, Mary Gaunt had written a book on West Africa and was hoping to come to China and write a book on it George Morrison marriage, invited her to stay with them in Peking. Mary was thrilled and accepted the invitation on the spot.

When the Morrisons gave Mary their address, she learned that the street where George lived was named Morrison Street in his honour.[8] They talkd briefly of the possibility of Mary exploring the great complex of palaces and lakes on the Jehol River near Chengde and going from outer Mongolia through the southern Gobi deserts.[9]

George Morrison advised Mary that China had few roads but in some areas now had excellent railways. Walking was hard on such stony and uneven ground and impossible for anyone not an athlete. In areas where there were no roads or railways, it would be necessary to travel by mule cart or in a mule litter — a kind of sedan chair slung on four poles between two mules. The other alternative was to hire a palanquin, a mode of transport used by female Chinese and Manchu noblewomen.

Should Mary be foolish enough to walk it would lower her standing in the eyes of the coolies who would be needed to carry her food, bedding and other equipment. It was vital for Mary Gaunt to maintain her image as 'a grand lady' to ensure the coolies respected and obeyed her and she must hire a 'tour manager' and an interpreter.

Having travelled in West Africa Mary understood what Morrison was getting at and he also warned that in China should she travel by mule she must *not* ride astride. The Chinese regarded it as indecent for a woman to sit astride a mule or a horse.

Mary's British publisher had heard a great deal about 'Chinese Morrison' and was impressed he had invited Mary to stay at his house. Mr Laurie agreed to commission a travel book on China, illustrated by Mary's own photos. He also wanted her to develop a plot for a novel to be set in China which would appear soon after her travel narrative as published. They agreed on a title for the travel book, *A Woman in China.*

Mary, her publisher and Mr Watt, her agent, were certain her trip in such a fascinating country, which had aroused such interest when Sir Edmund Backhouse's book was published would furnish material for plenty of short stories and novels. Pleased with the large sales of Mary's books on West Africa, Mr Laurie signed a contract for a travel book and a novel to be set in China. Mary wanted to make the female protagonist of her novel a medical missionary and hoped to visit several medical missions, aware sixty missionaries at T'ai Yuan Mission had been murdered in the Boxer Rebellion and there would be some fascinating stories about this to uncover.

Werner Laurie hoped *A Woman in China* would include a visit to the Great Wall and e the tomb of Emperor Yongle (the Napoleon of China), the mountain palaces of Chengde. Mary's novel *The Forbidden Town* about a single white woman in charge of a rubber plantation in Africa ahd been very successful. She was sure she could do the same thing with the story of a European or American woman in China, working on a mission station.

Aware he had been stingy over the advance for her African trip now that Mary was such a success managing director Mr Laurie had no wish to lose her to a rival publisher. He told her agent he would increase the advance against royalties to cover the rail fares and help with the travel costs. By now Mary having spoken with George Morrison was aware a large outlay needed to hire g mules, carts, drivers and a cook for her long overland trips and possibly a tour manager cum interpreter.

Women were just starting to break into the lucrative world of travel writing. Edith Wharton, author of the brilliant novel *The House of Mirth had* produced well written travel books describing motoring through France, her travels in Italian cities and a superb volume on *Italian Villas and Gardens,* illustrated by maps and

Edith's own photographs.¹⁰ Between them Mary Kingsley, Mary Gaunt, Gertrude Bell and Edith Wharton were breaking down male prejudice, making travel writing by perceptive female authors a successful proposition for publishers.

Mary Gaunt's travel books brought her many new readers and the characters she met on her travels inspired incidents in her novels and short stories. The same applied to that other magnificent story teller of the pre airline era, novelist, short story writers writer of six travel books, William Somerset Maugham (who was fourteen years younger than Mary Gaunt but lived in London when she was there.

Maugham relied on his homosexual secretary and lover Gerald Haxton to ferret out fascinating stories of murder, sex and greed among the colonial officials and planters they pair met when travelling to British colonies together. Mary Gaunt ferreted out her own stories and was generally kinder than Somerset Maugham to people whose lives and foibles she incorporated into her popular novels and short stories about colonial life in Africa and China, two places Maugham also wrote about.

In 1913 Mary Gaunt became was the first English speaking author of the twentieth century to China after the revolution and to write travel books and a novel set in China. In 1919 Somerset Maugham produced a book of travel notes on China and *The Painted Veil*, one of his Maugham's most popular novels. Literature in English on China is scarce. Not until 1938 would another 'literary' travel book on China in English appear when *Journey to a War* was written in 1938 by Christopher Isherwood and W.H. Auden which covered the effects of the Sino-Japanese Mary while English journalist and broadcaster Edward Ward (Viscount Bangor) wrote two interesting books about his time in China working as Head of Reuters Service,, , No One Boy and Chinese Crackers.

Mary's travel books and novels set in British colonies found plenty of readers and gave her good income. Like Somerset Maugham who was fourteen years younger and had still to write his best novels set in Malaya and Singapore where planters and medical officerfs returning to England 'on leave' often made hasty and disastrous marriages with sad results.

In their subsequent careers as novelist specialising in travel Mary Gaunt and Somerset Maugham would both write about a problem that afflicted their era, men who went out to the colonies and either took wives with them who were deeply unhappy or died of dangerous fevers or those who left wives at home and took native mistresses and the consequences. Both these talented d 'natural' writers described in clear and concise prose the hypocrisy of colonial life where men who had left their wives at home or those bored by their wives took native mistresses whose existence the British community ignored. When the European left for 'home' the mistress was left behind, usually with several half European children acknowledged by neither side to fend for herself and her children as best she could in a harsh world.

However not just colonial society but British society was hypocritical in th Edwardian era. Aware the 'sexual double standard' gave unlimited sexual licence bachelors to sew their 'wild oats,' in a society where Edward VII, Head of the Anglican church and Defender of the Faith, was grossly unfaithful to his wife, upper class society regarded *any* girl who lost her virginity before marriage as a 'fallen woman'. Mary felt this was very wrong and on the long boat journey back to England started plotting a novel called the e *The Uncounted Cost* about a man who goes to work in Africa and does not take his wife there for fear of tropic fevers and the consequences of this, to highlight the unfairness of the 'double sexual standard.'

. *The Uncounted Cost* concerned an 'old' money' family who have lost their fortune and urge the attractive eldest daughter to make a wealthy admirer who she loves to commit himself to marry her, in the hopes he will help them restore their fortune. The wealthy admirer agrees to become engaged before he departs for Africa *provided* the girl ;gives herself' to him before marriage. To help her parents the virginal heroine does so in return for an engagement rather than the desired *wedding* ring.

In the era of the 'double standard' the wealthy young man departs on family business to Africa. After two years apart (with presumably an African mistress or two, he , returns to London, rejects the girl who has given him her virginity w regarding her as 'spoiled goods' and marries a virginal bride.

The *denouement* of Edith Wharton's *The Uncounted Cost* is as tragic for this girl as the suicide of Lily Bart in Edith Wharton's *House of Mirth* or some of those tragic marriages in the colonial novels that Somerset Maugham would writer in future years r dealing with the hypocrisy of colonial society in its attitudes to sex.

. Mary Gaunt's *The Uncounted Cost* praised by the Manchester Courier, forerunner of the Guardian as a clever serious novel' and by The Times literary critic shocked highly conventional readers by its frankness, This daring novel set in England and Africa was banned in 1910 by British circulating libraries which had the effect of making its sales soar and ran to three separate British editions, an American edition published by Edward Clode who in the same year published Mary's detective novel, *The Mummy Moves* to huge success in New York and *The Uncounted Cost* would have a special colonial edition printed and shipped to readers in Australia and New Zealand.

The versatile Mary Gaunt had found fame and fortune in three different genres. From now until 1915 when paper rationing prevented books being published and from 1919 for another decade she would keep her position as a top selling author until by the 1930s younger women writers took over her position.

That other 'outsider' Somerset Maugham, still , guarding the dark secret of his bisexuality had his first great success as a popular novelist in 1915 with *Of Hunan Bondage,* a novel that had as its hero Philip Carey, disabled by a club foot just as Maugham felt disabled by his stammer. *The novel often regarded as* n Maugham's masterpiece drew on his unhappy marriage of convenience to Syrie Barnado Welcome, designed to give the child Maugham fathered with Syrie a father and a home. The marriage to a woman who cared nothing for his books would cause Maugham as much grief as had Mary's marriage to a man with syphilis. Both of them buried their secrets and sorrows in writing. Both of them would visit China and write important novels about the British there. In a strange co-incidence Maugham and Gaunt, both cynical about God and organised religion chose to write about foreigners like Dr Rosalie Gascoigne (Mary's alter ego) and Dr Fane (modelled on Maugham's rather dour hard working elder brother) who went to China to do missionary and medical work and the isolation that entailed in times of crisis.

The success these great storytellers s achieved in mid life took place against a background of envy from the British 'literati,' most of whom failed to earn very much from literary novels, most of which remain unread today while Mary Gaunt's *A Woman in China* and *Broken Journey* each fetch hundreds of dollars on the second hand market.

CHAPTER 11

Through Tsarist Russia to Peking

Mary intended to spend between a year and eighteen months using Peking as her base visiting places of interest before returning via British and American mission stations in Outer Mongolia along the Silk Road into Europe. A brief stay with the Morrisons who knew everyone who was *anyone* in Peking would of course be a wonderful introduction to China and Chinese culture.

Unaware of the chaotic state of the Chinese postal service, Mary wrote to George and Jennie Morrison advising them her train would arrive in Peking in the afternoon of 11 February 1913, hoping someone from their household staff could meet her, The inefficiency of the antiquated Chinese postal service meant that Mary's letter was delayed and she would arrive a couple of weeks before her letter but she had no idea of this at the time.

Ironically, not until after Mary Gaunt had left London to explore some of the wilder parts of China, did the committee of the Royal Geographical Society finally relax their rules banning women and offer her membership.

※

Leaving London on the last day of January 1913 in a Dickensian fog, thick as pea soup, Mary began her twelve day train journey across Tsarist Russia via Irutsk to Peking,

Before the days of air travel and lightweight luggage it was impossible for a lady traveller expecting to be entertained in 'polite society', to travel light. So many items of female apparel as well as jewels were needed for dining at embassies, legations or government houses.

Once again Mary was laden down with heavy portmanteaux, containing ankle length elegant dresses (modesty now allowed a glimpse of ankle to be shown) should she be invited to dine in the British or foreign legations in Peking or should the Morrisons give dinner parties. She also had all the impedimenta of the professional explorer, glass plate camera and tripod, medical supplies and this time a rubber bath rather than a folding canvas one.

Mary had bought a brand new Underwood typewriter, a portable rather than a desk model. She also took her little Smith and Wesson pistol. But after her African experience did not take crates of tinned meat which she found she disliked and was determined this time to rely on food purchased locally. She took her tent although George Morrison had warned her that camping in China was extremely dangerous. The Chinese countryside was riddled with brigands who would rob rape or even murder her for a relatively small sum.

Early in 1913, Mary crossed the English Channel by ferry and caught a train and paid the supplement for a sleeping car. The express train sped through s northern Europe and across the vast plains or steppes of Tsarist Russia covered in snow. As the train slowed on its approach to Moscow, like most Australians impressed deeply impressed by so much snow Mary described how .

> Lights shone clear in the keen, cold, windless air and the sleighs drawn by sturdy little horses glided over the white snow as silently as if they had been moving shadows. When morning came it was snowing. Softly, softly, fell the flakes and the city was... white everywhere, and when the sun came out dazzling, sparkling white, only the cupolas of the 1,600 churches of Moscow, the heart of holy Russia were golden or bright blue, or dark green, for the snow that hid the brilliant roofs could not lie on their rounded surfaces. Above the cupolas are crosses, and

from those crosses hang long chains and in the silence rang out the musical clang of some deep-toned bell. But it is the silence that impresses. The bells were but incidental, trifling the silence is eternal. The snow fell with a hush, there was no rush nor roar nor crash of storm, but every snowflake counted. The little sledges were half buried in it, the drivers in their fur-edged caps and blue coats girt in at the waist with a red sash or silver embroidered band, shook snow out of their eyes and out of their great beards and brushed it from their shoulders ; in every crevice of the old grey walls of the Kremlin snow piled up.

A dream city ! A city of silence!! The snow deadened all sound save the insistent bells that rang to the glory of God, and the cawing of the black and grey crows that were everywhere....They flew round the churches, darting down the spotless roads, gathering in little conclaves, raising their raucous voices as if in protest against the all-embracing silence.

Cold, was there ever such cold? The air crackled with it. It cut like a knife.... At every street corner as I drove to the railway station were piles of fir logs, and little braziers were burning, glowing red spots of brightness where the miserable homeless ones might warm their hands....I shall always be glad, that I crossed the Siberian plain in the heart of winter, and saw it beneath a mantle of snow.

Mary changed trains in Moscow with little time to spare so saw little of the city. Her second train took her across the Central Siberian plateau before entering vast forests of conifers, birch and larch. From a corner seat Mary looked out of the window and watched the vast snow covered plains and steppes of Siberia flash past the windows of the train.

Aware she would have to support herself for eighteen months she was dismayed to discover what her travel agent had failed to point out — there was no dining car or proper washing facilities in second class. At the end of each coach a samovar bubbled away on a wood stove to provide hot water for tea or coffee and the conductor was responsible for stoking the wood stove and supplying more wood.

At one point on the journey an inspector appeared demanding a levy from each passengers to pay for more coal for the engine and wood for the stove. Meekly they all paid up aware this was a Russian custom.

The train stopped briefly at the small town of Ekaterinburg a name unfamiliar to Mary. Within a few years it would be infamous as the place where Tsar Nicholas and his family were imprisoned and shot. But all that lay ahead. Now in 1913 as Mary crossed the vast Russian steppes, the Tsar of Russia seemed very safe on the imperial throne and the world still ruled by kings and emperors soon to vanish in the coming carnage of the first World War though Mary did not realise the fragility of the world of emperors around her.

Lacking a restaurant car, from elderly station vendors at Omsk and Novobirsk in Siberia, Mary bought crisp loaves of bread containing savoury fillings. She lived off loaves like these for the next four days, plus two small packets of Huntly and Palmers' biscuits she was glad she had brought with her. She was able to buy glasses in metal holders filled with hot tea, the sale of which provided a supplementary income to the sleeping car attendants.

Four days after leaving Moscow the train reached Irkutsk, a river city known as 'the pearl of Siberia'. Mary was fascinated by brightly painted Russian Orthodox churches with gilded onion domes, houses made from split logs, placed sideways. Many of these houses had delicately carved balconies, unlike anything she had seen in Europe or Australia. Around the cobalt blue waters of Lake Baikal, the world's deepest lake were more wooden mansions used as holiday homes by wealthy families and decorated with traditional Russian fretwork patterns on their balconies and bargeboards.

After leaving the lake the train gathered speed and raced through vast forests of tall pines. On crowded station platforms she saw Siberian peasants in ankle length overcoats and big fur hats with ear flaps, surrounded by skeletally thin children who begged the passengers for food.

In childhood I had read of the sufferings of those who had been sent to Siberia. As I rushed through it by train I saw a land of exiles in poverty From the plains of Eastern Russia in the west to the frozen hills round Harbin is a great plain thousands of miles in extent. Overhead, far, far away, is the arch of deep blue sky, clear, bright, enticing, with no threat in its translucent depths...Below is the snow-clad plain, stretching far as the eye can see, bathed in the brilliant sunshine with the desert and the Urals in the south stretching northward to the frozen sea.

The next morning all trace of hills covered with forests of fir and leafless larch, dark against the white background were gone. On station platforms stood men and women, Cossacks, Tartars,, Christians, Buddhists and Mohammedans muffled against the cold which was often 30 degrees below freezing-point. The men wore long-skirted coats and wore long coats and skirts, and high boots, so that it was difficult to tell one from the other save that on their heads the men wore fur caps with earflaps while the women muffled their faces with n ragged shawls.[1]

At Harbin, a city of many Chinese as well as Russians passengers bound for Peking had to change trains and changed again at Mukden, (now known as Shenyang) on the Chinese-Russian border.

A young pink faced Englishman in the seat facing Mary helped her stow her luggage in the rack and said he worked at the British Legation at Peking. He expressed surprise she was travelling alone and added 'China can be dangerous for foreigners on their own, but don't worry! The Chinese admire plump people and respect the old' But realising how tactless he had been the young Englishman blushed even pinker to the roots of his hair.

Aged fifty Mary looked years younger, although her blonde hair was streaked with silver. She prided herself on being full of energy so was surprised to hear herself described as 'old' but said nothing, aware the young Englishman had tried rather clumsily to be kind to her. They chatted away and he promised to accompany her to the Great Wall of China.

As the train approached Peking Mary caught her first sight of its high walls that surrounded this ancient imperial city.

The train slowed down as it prepared to enter the Ch'ien-men Station. The young Englishman pointed out the toweringly high Chien' men Gate. He told Mary this famous archway had been badly damaged in the Boxer Rebellion and was still undergoing repairs.

The city of Peking was shrouded in mist the colour of brick dust. Having left London in a greenish-grey fog Mary was surprised to see such a difference in colour between fog in London and Peking.

The young British Legation official, lifted Mary's baggage down from the rack and explained the reddish haze was topsoil, blown all the way from the Loess Plateau and the Gobi Desert to Peking — a frequent occurrence. The sun made what was really yellowish dust look much redder than it was.

Passengers were met by relatives, friends or servants. Alone on the platform, covered in dust and plagued by flies, Mary looked in vain for one of the Morrisonson's servants, carrying a placard bearing her name.

The young Legation official had been met by a legation car. Mary's heart sunk as she realised there was no one to meet her. She had no idea her letter informing the Morrisons of the date of her arrival had been delayed. She was alone and could not speak a single word of Chinese and had arrived in a country where very few people spoke English.

Miming what she wanted, Mary managed to hire two ragged men with a handcart to transport her baggage and climbed into a rickshaw drawn by burly Chinaman with his hair in a long pigtail. Feeling it would be rude to go to a hotel as her letter had given the date and time of her arrival Mary told the rickshaw man to take her to 'the house of Doctor George Morrison on Morrison Street.' To Mary's relief the rickshaw man seemed to understand her and set off at a good pace over a bumpy road with the men bringing her luggage, doing their best to keep up.

Mary bumped along inside the rickshaw through a network of narrow streets that seethed with humanity. She saw men in ragged blue jackets and trousers but few women. The wider roads were filled with laden donkeys, mules and horses, rickshaws drawn by coolies and glass-windowed horse drawn broughams. Everywhere she saw carts with a blue canvas covering with very large wheels, clearly the most common form of transport in Peking other than the rickshaws.

They passed under arched gates that to Mary resembled giant dovecotes with curling eves and she caught a swift glimpse of high red walls. With a thrill of excitement she realised these must be the walls of the Forbidden City.

The rickshaw man turned down Morrison Street, a wide thoroughfare lined with a variety of small shops and residential dwellings. On the ground outside many of the larger shops, whose names were written in black Chinese characters on a scarlet ground, were camels resting in the dust beside the dirt road. Mary gazed at the camels, noticing that each one had a cord round its head or protruding from a nostril linking it to the next one. Camels had been used for thousands of years to bring fruit and grain from the interior.[2]

Gradually the dwellings became larger and they stopped at an impressive looking house with a gate guarded by a pair of stone lions with fierce expressions. The rickshaw driver announced they had arrived at the house of Dr Morrison.

Mary climbed out of the rickshaw and rang the bell, worried about her welcome, afraid she was not expected. The double doors studded with brass were opened by a Chinese servant who told her that Dr and Mrs Morrison were away.

Mary felt embarrassed. She explained she had been invited to stay at the Morrisons, fully aware she was dishevelled, grubby and dusty. The Morrison's manservant did not have the traditional Manchu pigtail but a mop of short black hair. He was extremely polite, introduced himself as 'Number One Boy' and invited her inside for a cup of tea, insisted on paying the rickshaw driver and the luggage carriers and leaving her luggage piled high in the courtyard.

George and Jenny Morrison's house was attractively furnished with red, black and gold lacquered furniture, fine antiques and jade ornaments. The house which consisted of a series of single storey pavilions was connected to the electricity grid, which was still usual in most Peking houses Mary would learn.

The door bell rung several times and each time No One boy received letters brought by message carriers and gave them to Number Two or Number Three boy to take to George Morrison's home office.

The door bell rung for the fourth time. Number One Boy ran to answer it. This time the caller was a well-dressed English lady, wife of an official in the British Legation, expecting to have tea with Jennie Morrison. Mary was very embarrassed to see Jennie's friend and explained the reasons for her dusty, dishevelled appearance.

Over cups of jasmine flower tea, the British Legation wife told Mary that Number One boy's pigtail had been cut off by members of the Republican Party. They regarded wearing the pigtail as a sign of subservience to the previous Manchu rulers who had made the Chinese shave their foreheads and wear the traditional Manchu pigtail on pain of death. Now in the new republic those reformists who supported Dr Sun Yat Seng were keen to 'modernise' China and stamp out all relics of the Manchu way of life.

The English lady told Mary that all Europeans in Peking had at least five boys, usually all related to undertake all household tasks. The news everyone was discussing was that Empress Long Yu, a widow in her early forties, had had died only that morning. There had been no previous announcement she was ill and the suddenness of her death bore an unnerving resemblance to the death of Long Yu's husband the young Emperor Zaitan. It was rumoured the young emperor had been poisoned on the orders of the e murderous Dowager-Empress Cixi.[3] But why would anyone murder poor Long Yu *after* she had abdicated? She had no power left and her only interests lay in clothes and attending official ceremonies.

While waiting for Jennie to return, the elegant English lady, whose husband worked in the British legation, informed Mary about recent events in Peking. As she was launched into what seemed to be a murderous world of Imperial politics and the story of the deceased and unloved Empress Long Yu, Mary's head began to whirl. Although she tried to concentrate, all she could think of was a nice hot bath and washing her hair, which was thick with dust, making her dread meeting the Morrisons.

Number One Boy realised her predicament and left the room. A few minutes later he reappeared and said 'Barf ready, Missie Gaunt. He showed Mary to a guest bedroom with a bathroom attached. While she was taking a bath and washing her hair, Jennie Morrison returned home. She, saw Mary's dust-covered luggage and equipment in the front courtyard and was told an unexpected guest had arrived.

As Mary emerged from her room, wearing clean clothes and feeling better, Jennie greeted her warmly. Since the Chinese post was so unreliable the Morrisons had not received Mary's letter announcing her arrival.

After discussing family news the talk turned to George Morrison's job as policy advisor to the fledgling Republican government of Yuan Shikai, which had not turned out as expected. The loan Morrison had negotiated for the Republican Government in August of last year had been altered in favour of a larger one from five European countries. The Chinese Republican government was now split into two factions, one of them led by President Yuan and the other by the reformist leader Sun Yat Sen and his young and very popular disciple, Sung-Chao-Jen.

The Morrisons proved to be kind and generous hosts although George was clearly under a great deal of stress. Dinner table conversations revealed his worries that he was no longer being consulted by, President Yuan who he feared was entangled in intrigues against the former provisional president Dr Sun Yat Sen with his ambitious plan of reform. It was feared Yuan might use some of the loan money from foreign governments to buy arms and quash any attempts for reformist policies which he considered dangerous.

It was clear to Mary that President Yuan's 'republican' government was not proceeding with reforms as fast as George Morrison or Dr Sun Yat Sen would have liked. Despite worries about where China was heading and the possibilities of a civil war George Morrison still found the time to be a kind and generous host. Not that Morrison, traditionalist in his view of women, entirely approved of female explorers and in fact had cordially disliked Gertrude Bell when he met her. However he had a strong sense of family, Mary was his sister-in-law by marriage and the sister of his good friend from Boxer Rebellion days, Captain Ernest Gaunt and he went out of his way to help Mary Gaunt as much as possible.

Morrison's kind intervention with the office of stout bull-necked he President Yuan, Mary became the first foreigner for almost a century allowed to visit the beautiful mountain resort of Jehol, near Chengde.[4]

Mary was fascinated by the workings of Morrison household, which was run very efficiently by Jennie Morrison with the aid of six houseboys. She learned that in the Far East the term 'boy' was applied to all domestic servants, young or old. All households of any social standing in Peking had at least three or more 'boys' who took a commission or 'squeeze' on everything the household purchased from local shopkeepers and through a network of relatives were excellent at borrowing additional china and cutlery from another household where the relatives were working whenever a large party or celebration was to be held by their employers.

In addition, the Morrisons employed a Chinese cook, a cook, a gardener and numerous coolies. The coolies, rather like scullions in a mediaeval manor house, looked after the fires, as though Peking was hot and humid in summer it was extremely cold in winter when snow lay on the ground. Coolies scrubbed floors, washed dishes, peeled vegetables and performed the menial household duties and carried their employer's wife around in a sedan chair or palanquin if she did not wish to walk. If she went out shopping a servant walked a few paces behind her to carry back any packages she might buy.

A really good Number One boy was supposed to be able to procure anything from a table napkin to a jade statue. He could care for anything from a canary to a lady friend and was responsible for the smooth running of the home by Chinese staff under him. A. Number One Boy had to speak fluent English. engage and dismiss other servants and teach them how to perform their duties for their foreign employers. Mary was told that many houseboys were plausible rogues, efficient at their work but expertly adding commissions, called 'squeeze'; to all the house hold bills.

However some were totally honest and devoted to their employers and like the Chinese *amahs* who cared for babies they wept bitterly when it was time for their foreign employers and their children to depart for home.

George Morrison showed Mary the magnificent library which he had installed in its own a fireproof pavilion. What was now famous as 'The Morrison Library' consisted of many thousands of printed Chinese books, maps, ancient manuscripts and an important collection of books on China in foreign languages. Morrison had been collecting and indexing these books for years intending his library to serve as superannuation when he would finally sell the complete collection.[5]

Mary was surprised to learn that the Heinemann best seller on Peking at the time of the Boxer Rebellion written by Sir Edmund Backhouse, who had worked as a translator of Chinese manuscripts into English for George Morrison contained a great deal of information that the author had invented including the alleged journal of the Manchu bannerman or officer in the Forbidden City. While many descriptions of the interior of Peking's royal palace complex were correct much of it was invented by Edmund Backhouse, who in spite of his ancient title was a disreputable character, capable of any amount of deception in order to make money which as a bachelor he lavished on the many small boys encountered in the stews of Peking.[6] Hearing about the falsehoods in Backhouse's book made Mary all the more determined to see the Forbidden City for herself and write about it.

Mary was thrilled to be able to work amid this collection of books on China. She was delighted to find a second leather bound copy of the Chinese travels of Lord George McCartney which she had started reading in the library of London's Royal Geographical Society but been unable to finish.

Now she could finish it at her leisure. She was fascinated by the account of the 1793 visit of Ambassador McCartney to the Imperial Park and Hunting Palaces of the Manchu. The descriptions of the beauty of these gardens and pavilions made Mary determined to go there, even though George Morrison had warned that the steep mountain track was badly overgrown and would take at least five days to reach it in a mule cart.

Although he was extremely busy with people coming and going all day, George Morrison kindly showed Mary maps that would help to plot her route across the mountains to Jehol. He made a formal request to President Yuan's office for permission for Mrs Mary Miller to visit the Imperial Park at Jehol in the prefecture of Chengde, aware the president was a good friend of the governor of Chengde province.

Aware that Mary hoped to leave China via the walled city of Xian and the northerly Silk Route, George Morrison warned her to beware of a war lord named Pai Ling ('White Wolf') who dominated the province of Shensi (Shaanxi). The war lord's henchmen had already captured several walled cities, robbed the banks and ordered the torture and beheading of all those dared to who resist them.

White Wolf's thugs routinely robed and raped women prisoners before killing them and had been known to hack off their breasts for amusement. Morrison warned Mary her to keep the last bullet in her revolver to shoot herself if it appeared she might be captured by White Wolf's thugs. Not only did they rape women they had cut off the hands of men who resisted them and then emasculated them.

These stories of atrocities committed by White Wolf's men gave Mary nightmares. But she was still determined to pursue the dream she and Ernest had shared. She would hire or purchase mule carts and follow the northerly Silk Route to the imperial city of Xian and the Taklamanan or southern Gobi desert, visit the Great Market at Kashgar, and proceed to Constantinople, gateway to Western Europe.

Mary had made her travel plans without taking into account the possibility of world war. Although British press baron , Lord Northcliffe had been predicting war with the Kaiser's Germany in his newspapers warning that the Kaiser was arming Germany for war with Britain, and France, British diplomats in the Peking Legation ignored the possibility. Mary had witnessed the rivalry in Africa between Britain and Germany in the scramble to grab African territories rich in minerals and diamonds in which Britain had done better than Germany. But since the royal houses of Germany and Britain were related, all of them cousins it seemed unlikely there would be a war in Europe at this juncture.

On the third day after Mary's arrival, President Yuan announced there would be an official lying-in-state of the deceased empress next week inside the Forbidden City. For centuries the walled complex, now the home-cum- prison of the former 'baby emperor', Pi Yu, had been out of bounds to the Chinese as well as foreigners. Anyone rash enough to enter the Forbidden City was automatically beheaded so few people had any idea of its splendours.

An announcement from President Yuan changed everything. All those who wished to pay their respects to the mummified empress could do so, provided they obtained an official pass granting them admission to the Forbidden City. This vast walled complex sprawled over three square miles and comprised paved courtyards, gardens, halls of audience, temples for Taoist and

Buddhist gods, ornamental ponds and lakes. Inside were fifty separate palaces or pavilions, many dating from the days of Emperor Yongle, built as homes for emperors, empresses, princes, courtiers, concubines, eunuchs and female palace servants no uncastrated man being allowed to live there. At various periods as many as 9,000 people had lived inside the Forbidden City and its high walls were painted vermilion red, a colour denoting nobility. In the imperial past whenever the emperor left the Forbidden City all the people outside the gate had been removed by the imperial guard , so no commoner could see the Son of Heaven born aloft in a palanquin lined with yellow silk with scarlet trimmings.

Mary hoped fervently she would receive a permit to visit the imperial lying in state. The ceremony and her account of the interior of the Forbidden City would be one of the highlights of her book.

Jennie Morrison introduced Mary to senior British Legation officials who promised the Legation would make an official request for her as the holder of a British passport to attend the lying-in state of the late Empress Long Yu. All Mary could do was wait.

She planned to make Peking her base for the next ten or eleven months but could hardly expect the Morrisons on such a slender acquaintance to act as her hosts for a almost year. Mary knew she must find secure accommodation as the Chinese city g was considered a dangerous place for foreigners to live due to the high number of robberies with violence. A small hotel or *pensione* inside the walled Legation Quarter would be better but it must have the space to store all the baggage she needed for her expeditions outside Peking.

One of Jennie Morrison's friend managed to secure Mary a pleasant room at the Hotel Wagons-Lits *inside* the high walled Legation Compound, The hotel staff spoke excellent English and it had a large storage area which would be ideal for Mary's luggage and all the equipment needed for her tour to Jehol.

Mary liked the Hotel Wagons Lits and described it as spotlessly clean and its well trained staff spoke English. Life in the walled Legation Compound with its wide streets was pleasant unlike life in the Chinese and Tartar cities of old Peking which were overcrowded.

From dinner parties she attended at the British Legation Mary learned that after Empress Long Yu had abdicated in the Xuhan Revolution of 1911, Sun Yat Sen had been appointed as Provisional President. But then Morrison's friend, the former general Yuan Shikai took over as president of the new republic, his supporters believing Yuan would be a stable figurehead for the new republic which was heavily in debt due to its foreign loans to build railways since there were so few roads.

Several British legation members remembered Ernest Gaunt when he was working as Naval Attaché and they gave dinner parties for Mary and their wives showed her around. Peking. Since the Boxer Rebellion, very tight security was maintained at the Legation Quarter which had been completely rebuilt. British and American sentries patrolled the walled area and banned the entry of any Chinese without a special pass.[7] Mary saw how British and American sentries patrolled the towering Chien Men Gate, now used as a watch tower.

Her new friends escorted Mary through Peking's crowded streets where peddlers sold sweets, toys and rice cakes and acrobats and jugglers performed. The smell of unwashed bodies, garlic and tobacco was overpowering. Disfiguring diseases were like smallpox and goitre were prevalent and the faces of many Chinese women had been left badly pockmarked.

Small wooden carts drawn by mules or sweating coolies tangled with each other in the unpaved roadway, donkeys staggered past her under huge loads, doe-eyed camels from Mongolia were tied to posts in dust streets. When a mandarin born aloft in a sedan chair wanted to get through so much dense and noisy traffic , his attendants cleared a passage for him using long bamboo rods and yelling at passers by.

It was a relief for Mary to escape from crowded noisy streets into the picturesque alleyways known as *hutongs*. Each *hutong* was bordered by the courtyard residences of those whose ancestors had lived there for many generations in single storey dwellings consisting of separate pavilions grouped around one or two courtyards. The houses had elaborate front doors, windows of delicate lattice-work and tiled roofs. Through half open doorways Mary caught a tantalising glimpse of tiled courtyards, ponds containing goldfish and ornamental trees in colourful ceramic pots.

Some *hutongs* were reserved for specific trades, one held a large family who for centuries had made arrows for the Chinese army. A large *hutong* with a beautiful courtyard was reserved for retired eunuchs from the Forbidden City and a larger *hutong* had once housed ageing concubines who were pensioned off. These had been the very lucky ones. As emperors had hundreds of concubines to feed and maintain in old age, any concubines who had not born children to the emperor, were strangled by the black robed eunuchs while Emperor Yongle suspecting that some of his 2,000 concubines had engaged in what was euphemistically known as 'vegetable sex' with eunuchs, so he ordered many of them to be killed since his word was law.[8].

The capital city Mary Gaunt in 1913 known as Peking had been built on the orders of Emperor Yongle's who had originally named it Beijing. The area had been inhabited by since the Stone Age but the first settlement of any size was a town called Khanbalic founded in 1267 by the great ruler Kubla Khan.

In the fifteenth century the newly created Emperor Yongle, who had usurped the imperial throne, moved his capital from the former capital of Nanking. As a prince of the Ming dynasty Yongle had ousted a younger relative and, having many enemies, wanted to set up a new capital in an area where his supporters were numerous. The drawback to this choice was that the city Yongle called Beijing was freezing cold in winter and hot in summer. Construction was difficult, canals had to be dug to bring building materials. The Forbidden City, home of the emperor, his court and his 2,000 concubines took decades to complete, largely by slave labour as well as trained workers. Emperor Yongle had arranged that the Forbidden City, the largest royal palace complex in the world, was divided from the Chinese quarter and the Tartar city by high walls.

Ascending the high walls of the newly rebuilt Legation Compound which had been been badly damaged in the Boxer Rebellion, Mary looked across at the yellow tiled roofs of the Forbidden City. Through binoculars she could see the dragons, phoenixes and winged horses at the end of the roof ridge. These carved stone or marble animals had been put there in the belief they would protect the pavilions from being struck by lightning, often a vain hope.

Not only was Peking dusty but Mary soon discovered it had even more e flies than the Australian outback. From the top of the walls of the Legation Quarter, the wealthier parts of Peking looked very green, due to so many with flowering trees and exotic shrubs. Through the foliage shone the golden yellow glazed roofs of the tiles of the Forbidden City. This was the imperial colour which signified nobility. Pavilions designed to house royal princes were green: the roof of the imperial library was black in the vain hope that this colour would prevent fire from destroying it.

Mary thought the layout of the imperial city of Peking eccentric. All the shops were, grouped together by their various trades. The Street of the Hammer Makers was the *only* place where hammers were sold. At considerable inconvenience to buyers they had to walk for a mile to reach the Street of the Nail Makers, the only area in Peking where the nails were made and sold.

Peking's best antique shops were situated in the Tartar or Manchu city which lay to the north of the Forbidden City. The Chinese or Han city lay to the south divided by high walls from the Forbidden City. Mary's English friends warned her to be very careful before purchasing antiques in Peking. Many of the *alleged* Ming vases and T'ang horses were clever forgeries which had been buried underground for a few years to give minute cracks in their surface glaze. This created the false impression the pieces were centuries old. T'ang horses were good value as the Chinese disliked the idea of being surrounded by funerary objects. While Westerners prized T'ang horses the Chinese did not like them in their homes fearing it brought bad luck. Should Mary wish to buy jade she should take an expert with her or she might be cheated.

Mary replied that her budget did not allow for luxuries like Ming vases, jade or carved ivories. She already owned a small Ming bowl brought back to Australia by her grandfather. What she wanted most was to see the tomb of the Emperor Yongle, the most important Ming Emperor and visit what she had been told was a place few had written about and one of the great splendours of China, the great mountain palaces, gardens and temples of what was known as Cheng the Fu, [now the Imperial Park and Mountain Resort of Chengde, as shown on the page on page....].

Mary was told that it took four or five days to follow the rough road from Peking to Chengde — an area where the railway had not yet reached — by litter or palanquin. Then came a short but bruising journey to the Imperial Park in bumpy mule cart or in a litter. However litters swayed a great deal when carried over rough ground and could cause motion sickness. The train line was not yet completed and a journey over pot-holed ground littered with stones in mule cart lacking springs, was extremely uncomfortable. Passengers had been known to fall out and break legs or arms when the flimsy mule carts overturned.

Mary replied calmly that she made difficult and dangerous journeys in West Africa and was not afraid to do so again.

CHAPTER 12

Inside the Forbidden City

Mary learned a great deal more about the Ming and Manchu dynasties from the conversations around her host's dinner table. Having spent years as the Peking correspondent for *The Times*, George Morrison was an expert on Chinese politics and culture and Mary felt privileged as his house guest and learned a great deal about the fledgling republic and its problems.

The little blue and white Ming bowl given to Mary by her grandmother meant she was fascinated by the story of the Ming emperor, Yongle, who had ordered the construction of Peking's Forbidden City. As a prince of the royal house and a young and successful general Yongle seized the imperial throne from a weakling nephew and executed many of the previous emperor's supporters. Appointing himself emperor, Yongle had shown an extraordinary blend of beneficence of cruelty.

Mary also learned about the rise to power of Cixi, the former concubine who having conceived a son by an elderly and half demented emperor had by guile and a strong personality become the most powerful woman in China. Mary was absolutely determined to see the Forbidden City, former home of Cixi and her niece, Long Yu and now the residence of little Pi-Yu, the deposed six year old emperor. She also wished to visit , the tomb of Emperor Yongle, and the Imperial Mountain Resort of Chengde, which Morrison told her were called The Palaces for Fleeing from Peking's Summer Head.

Mary was told that the beautiful complex of palaces, temples and gardens built in a wide variety of styles by various Manchu emperors had not been entered by a westerner for almost two centuries. She believed that the more difficult a place was to reach the more inspiring was the visit and was also determined to go there although warned the journey there would be uncomfortable and could be dangerous for a woman alone.

George Morrison and his fellow Australian, William (Billy) Donald, former managing director of *The China Mail* were old friends and he was one of the few people Morrison trusted and spoke freely to. Whenever Billy Donald dined with them Mary heard the men discuss the problems facing President Yuan as head of the cash-strapped National Republic of China. The the treasury had been drained before Yuan took office due to the extravagance of Manchu emperors and minor princes whose extravagant building schemes had left the country almost bankrupt. President Yuan's government had borrowed large amounts of foreign money to build railways since there were so few surfaced roads in China but his foreign investments was resented by the Chinese people who were taxed more highly and this policy was causing unrest.

Mary learned a great deal about President Yuan, who had employed George Morrison as his trusted political advisor and consulted him when changing sides from supporter of the Manchu to the foxy former general who had persuaded the recently deceased empress to abdicate.' Y

Mary learned that President Yuan had terrified the deceased Long Yu by warning her if she did not abdicate millions of her subjects would die in the civil war which would follow the anti-Manchu riots in Wuchan province. If she remained in power the blood of millions would be on her hands. Naively believing Yuan for years in the service of the Manchu had her best interests at heart the dithering and politically naïve Long Yu had believed him and failed to see his advice was not based on what was good for the Chinese people or the dynasty he had served but on his own naked ambition. Empress Long Yu had signed the abdication papers on behalf of baby Pi Yu and so shortly before Mary arrived in Peking, centuries of imperial Manchu rule had ended and China was now a young republic with a government bitterly divided over policies.

The very popular Dr Sun Yat Sen, head of China's Revolutionary Alliance who had spent years in exile in fear of his life had initially been appointed as provisional President of the fledgling republic. But Sun Yat Sen did not last long as the still powerful provincial governors. (most of whom were former generals) felt that China must be headed by a more conservative figure. Accordingly they replaced the would be reformrer, Dr Sun Yat Sen as with their old colleague, the former General Yuan Shikai, the man who had secured the abdication of Empress Long Yu.

Mary had arrived in Peking in February 1913, by which time the autocratic President Yuan was at loggerheads with reform-orientated members of the government led by Dr Sun Yat Sen and his younger colleague, Sung Chao Jen.

President Yuan was alarmed when the younger politicians gained a majority votes in the National Assembly. He decided it was time to silence e Sung Chao-Jen, who had suggested Yuan wished to make himself into an emperor (a statement which would later be proved correct although as yet George Morrison was not aware of this).

By 1913 following a peaceful revolution which led to the fall of the Quing dynasty China was embarking on a new stage in its history. For centuries the Quing emperors, originally from Manchuria, had ruthlessly imposed their will on the Chinese people, insisting all Chinese men shave the front of their heads and wear the Manchu pigtail as a sign of subservience to the Dragon Throne. Now Chinese men with pigtails were seized by revolutionary groups in the street, had their pigtails cut off and their heads shaved.

Mary, keen to attend the funeral celebrations of the recently deceased Empress Long Yu, was interested in a woman who she understood had led a sad life, a plain slender girl forced in an unhappy dynastic marriage arranged by her aunt, the Dowager-Empress. The only son of Cixi, the ruthless Dowager Empress had died aged eighteen from smallpox. So the widowed Dragon Empress, aware China must have a male ruler, in her role as regent proclaimed her young nephew Prince Zaitan to be the next emperor with the title of Guangxu Emperor. She insisted he marry her nice, Long Yu who was a three years older than the young man who protested that his proposed bride unattractive but Cixi refused to listen.[1] Their union was unhappy and childless. Emperor Zaitan regarded his wife as a spy manipulated by her cunning Aunt Cixi, refused to visit his wife's bed, saw her only on ceremonial occasions and lived with the beautiful Pearl Concubine in another part of the Forbidden City.

As a barren empress was regarded as a disgrace to her sex, Long Yu's husband derived satisfaction from refusing to give the wife who had been forced on him what she and Cixi craved most — a legal heir to the Dragon Throne.

As the young Emperor Zaitan matured he asserted his authority and instituted his 'Hundred Days of Reform'. The Dragon Empress, alarmed by any talk of reform, reasserted her authority and had her nephew placed under house arrest in the Forbidden City. Aware she did not have long to live, it was rumoured Dowager Empress Cixi had, decided the only way to prevent reform was to have the young emperor poisoned with arsenic. It has been conjectured the Empress Cixi, no stranger to poisons in the past, bribed the food taster to add arsenic to the young emperor's meals. Decades later huge levels of arsenic would be found in his body.

Zaitan, the Guangxu emperor died in 1908. Convinced she had secured the Dragon Throne for her young great nephew Pu Yi, 'the baby emperor' and that Zaitan's reforms could not take place, the frail Empress Cixi died of old age, the day after Zaitan's untimely demise.

Two imperial deaths within such a short space of time weakened the power of the Qing and led to fighting between those loyal to the Manchu dynasty and the 'baby emperor' Pi Yu and all those who wanted China to become a republic led by the charismatic Dr Sun Yat Sen.

Empress Long Yu had instructed General Yuan Shi Kai to negotiate a peace settlement with the revolutionaries. However he cleverly persuaded her that civil war was inevitable if she did not abdicate and allow China become a republic.

In tears, the new Dowager Empress Long Yu signed abdication documents on behalf of Pi Yu, 'the baby emperor,' and she was to receive a handsome annual allowance on the understanding that she and little Pu-yi remained within the walls of the Forbidden City. Mary Gaunt had arrived in Peking the day the empress died, her age given out as forty-seven. Rumours abounded in diplomatic circles that Empress Long Yu had been so depressed at signing away her empire she ended her own life thus allowing a People's Republic to be set u without a civil war.

***

George Morrison had been appointed political advisor to President Yuan Shi-kai's Republican government in 1912, a position which had failed to turn out as hoped.

Over dinner at his home, George Morrison and his Australian friend, Billy Donald discussed politics and other topics of interest from which Mary learned a great deal. There was concern about China's increasing debt to the western powers to build railways, the Republic's financial problems and the possibility of civil war between President Yuan's followers who were reactionary and the left wing followers of Dr Sun Yat sen.

Would President Yuan, a former employee of the Qing dynasty, spend large sums on a costly imperial funeral for the late empress at a time when so many Chinese people were starving? And if President did hold a costly funeral, how would Dr Sun Yat Sen and his republican friends in the National Assembly react?

When President Yuan Shih Kai announced that the late empress would be given a lying-in-state ceremony inside the Forbidden City followed by a large funeral procession through the streets of Peking, Dr Sun Yat sen and his followers were outraged as they felt it was morally wrong to spend vast amounts on a dead empress while millions of Chinese workers were starving. Dr Sun

Yat Sen and his second in command,, Sung Chaio Sen, told the National Assembly the fledgling republic should spend their money on social reforms. Sung Chaio Sen dared to suggest that President Yuan was attempting to turn himself into an emperor — Yuan affected outrage but the suggestion was in fact true.

The fledgling republic had such severe divisions Morrison feared that the money President Yuan was borrowing from the West would be used to buy arms to fight his opponents in a civil war. But Mary was fearless and refused to leave China determined to see as much as possible of a country she found strange but fascinating even if there was a danger of a civil war erupting.

Mary hoped that her new friends at the British Legation could obtain an invitation to the lying-in-state of the empress so she would be one of very few foreigners to enter the walled Forbidden City.

George Morrison promised to talk to the president's office secure her entry to the great Imperial Park and summer resort of the Manchu near Chengde. No foreigner had been admitted to see these splendours for over a century. Mary knew that eye witness account of these areas would make the book she was writing on China of great interest in the west.

From reading books in Morrison's vast library Mary now realised that Peking's Forbidden City, constructed by order of Emperor Yongle in the fifteenth century was much larger than any single palace in Europe. Over one a million labourers and craftsmen had toiled for a decade to build Yongle's new capital at Peking, which he liked as it was far from the former capital of Nanjing where Prince Yongle had usurped the throne from a weak nephew. The area around Peking was bleak and barren so Emperor Yongle's workmen had to construct canals to bring in the building materials and build as vast complex of palaces, temples, pavilions, courtyards and gardens.

No foreigner had been admitted to The Forbidden City for decades. Palatial living quarters were provided for the emperor, relatives of the emperors and their wives, as many as to 2,000 concubines and space for armies of female servants for whom hundreds more pavilions were provided.

The central motif in the décor was the imperial five clawed dragon which represented imperial characteristics like nobility, heroism as well as the divinity of the emperor. Emperors had been worshipped as the Sons of Heaven by the Chinesee who believed they ruled by divine right. But in 1912, with staggering swiftness these beliefs had been swept away as China entered a new era. Mary wondered if the new Chinese Republic would become more approachable to the west or would its leaders continue to distrust western thought and ideas?

Fascinated by the size of the imperial complex, City Mary and two British Legation wives, were friends of Jennie Morrison, peered down at the red tiled roofs of the Forbidden City t from the flat topped walls of the Legation Compound, now fully restored since the extensive damage done to it in the Boxer Rebellion. Using binoculars they could see the marble dragons perched on the roof of large buildings such as the Hall of Supreme Harmony while , hundreds more marble dragons formed waterspouts on roofs and eaves. Apparently thousands more imperial dragons were carved on screens and interior walls of the many temples and pavilions.

Mary prayed that British Legation officials would be able to secure her a ticket for the lying in state of Dowager Empress Long Yu which would be a memorable event to record in her travel book.

Early in March 1913, Mary received an official pass in the form of a paper chrysanthemum which provided admittance to the Forbidden City. As there was a cold wind Mary wore her fur coat and pinned the paper flower to her lapel. She recorded that the Forbidden City

> ...was thrown open for three days to all who could produce a black paper chrysanthemum with five leaves, red, yellow, blue,

black, and white, fastened to a tab of white paper with a mourning edge and an inscription in Chinese characters. The foreigners had theirs from their Legations, and the Chinese from their guilds. And those Chinese — there are many of them — who are so unlucky as to belong to no guild, Chinese of the humbler sort, were shut out, and for them there was erected on the great marble bridge in front of the southern entrance, a pavilion of gorgeous orange silk enclosing an altar with offerings that stood before a picture of the dead Empress, so that all might pay their respects.

I pinned my badge to the front of my fur coat, for it was keen and cold in spite of the brilliant sunshine, and went off to the wrong entrance, the eastern gate, where only princes and notables were admitted. I thought it strange there should be no sign of a foreigner, but foreigners in Peking can be but as one in a hundred or less, so undismayed, I walked straight up to the gate, and immediately a row of palace servants clad in their white robes of mourning, clustered before the sacred place. They talked and explained vehemently, and with perfect courtesy, but they were very agitated, and though I could not understand one word they said, one thing was certain, admitted I could not be there. So I turned to the southern gate and there it seemed all Peking was streaming in…

All must walk, old and young, great and lowly, representatives of the mighty nations of the world and tottering Chinese ladies swaying like 'lilies in the wind' upon their maimed feet — only one man, a Mongol Prince, an Incarnation of a Buddha, a living Buddha, was borne in a sedan chair. But every other mortal had to walk.[2]

Mary followed a vast paved walkway that runs alongside a canal with marble-lined banks. On the main bridge across the canal stood an orange silk pavilion for the poorer classes, but Mary and ten thousands of other wearers of a black chrysanthemum entered the first courtyard through one of the huge archways. Normally the brass studded doors in the archways were kept shut, but for this special occasion they had been unlocked. Soldiers of the New

Republic in full-marching order, guarded the entrances to the Imperial City.

A causeway of hewn stones, worn by the passing of many feet, ran across the first courtyard. On both sides of the vast courtyard were low dilapidated buildings with fronts of lattice-work. Some of these buildings were guard-houses, others had been the quarters of the six thousand eunuchs who had attended upon their rulers.

There were more tunnel-like archways that gave access to an even larger courtyard, at least four-hundred metres across. Eventually Mary and over a thousand other mourners came to a third courtyard where lay the mummified body of the late empress.

> The third courtyard was spacious as Trafalgar Square, and round three sides was a wide raised platform of stone reached by broad and easy ramps, and all across it ran a canal held in by marble banks, crossed by graceful bridges, and every one of the uprights, made of white marble, was crowned by a figure that I took for the representation of a flame ; but those, who know, tell me it is meant to represent a cloud, and is part of the dragon symbolism… Two colossal bronze monsters with grinning countenances and curly manes, conventional lions, mounted on dragon-carved pedestals, stand before the entrance to the fourth temple or hall of audience, and here was what the crowd had come to see… here was the altar to the dead.
>
> The altar on the northern platform was hidden behind a trellis-work of gaily coloured paper, and there were offerings upon it of fruit and cakes in great profusion, all set out before a portrait of the late Empress. On either side were two choirs of priests, Buddhists and Taoists in gorgeous robes of red and orange. What faith the dead Empress held I do not know, but the average Chinese, while he is the prince of materialists, believing nothing he cannot see and explain, has also a keen eye to the main chance, and on his death-bed is apt to summon priests of all faiths so as to let no chance of a comfortable future slip ; but possibly it was more from motives of policy than from any idea of

aiding the dead woman that these representatives of the two great faiths of China were summoned.

On the right, behind a trellis-work of bright paper, one choir sat in a circle, beating gongs, striking their bells and intoning, and on the left, behind a like trellis-work, the other choir knelt before low desks and solemnly intoned. Their Mongolian faces were impassive, they looked neither to the right nor the left, but kept time to the ceaseless beat of their leader's stick upon a globe of wood split across the middle like a gaping mouth called *mu yu*-or wooden fish. What were they repeating? Prayers for the dead? Eulogies on the Empress who had passed away? Probably they were intoning Scriptures in Tibetan, a tongue come down to them through the ages and sanctified by thousands of ceaseless repetitions.[3]

Looking around, Mary could not see one sad face among the hundreds patiently waiting in line to view the bier of the Empress Long Yu. She was puzzled by this until she remembered that from the moment of Long Yu's enforced marriage she had never been allowed to emerge from the Forbidden City, so virtually none of her former subjects knew what she looked like.

Hundreds of people came up the steps and bowed in front of the dead Empress. Before joining the crowd in the great courtyard again, everybody had to walk passed a row of brightly clad priests. Mary described how

> To the sound of Eastern music the yellow-clad Buddhist high-priest went to make his reverence. He was taken op the steps in his yellow sedan chair, carried by four bearers in dark blue gowns with Tartar caps on their heads.[4]

The high-priest was followed by a band of Chinese children from an American mission school, who most, inappropriately, sang at the top of their voices *'Down by the Swanee River'* and *'Auld Lang Syne!'*

It was a strange experience for Mary to take part in a ceremony mingling of ancient Chinese traditions with foreign customs. The Chinese attending the ceremony looked cheerful and keen to enjoy themselves. Bands played high pitched Eastern music and airs from the European operettas. There were tents with seats and tables and refreshments were served: tea, oranges, crystallised ginger and cakes of all kinds. People walked around, looking at everything, peeping through every crevice in the hope of seeing some part of the palace that was not open to them. They chatted, laughed and greeted each other as they would have done at a garden-party in Europe.

The young people of the new Chinese Republic looked ordinary enough in European clothes, but the older members of the population still wore their hair in a long queue (pigtail) and were dressed in expensive silk jackets and brocaded coats over black trousers. Manchu ladies wore high black head-dresses, brilliant silken coats in, blue, pink or grey. Chinese ladies wore more sombre colours and no make up and tottered along on tiny, bound feet that reminded Mary of the hoofs of a deer. The more fashionable, unmarried girls wore short coats with high collars covering their chins, and tight-fitting trousers, often of brightly coloured silk. The older Chinese women wore long jackets and skirts, and the poorer people wore long coats of cotton, generally blue, with trousers tightly girt in at the ankles, and their maimed feet in tiny little embroidered shoes.

Chinese woman plastered their hair with a gell that made it smooth and shiny andn placed flowers and jewelled pins in it. Aaristocratic Manchu women had elaborate headdresses of dark fabric over a small wooden frame, combined with flowers and beads so heavy the women could scarcely move their heads.

In the street Mary had seen women with black embroidered bands round the front of their heads and was told that this denoted that the wearer was a Roman Catholic.

For centuries Chinese men had not approved women going about in public and supported foot binding designed to limit women's ability to leave their homes. Mary realised that the fact the Republic was against this practice marked a radical change in Chinese male dominated society. A few years earlier a woman walking alone through the narrow streets of Peking would never have been seen but this was just starting to occur. Mary regarded the old Quing empire as barbaric for the oppressive way Chinese men treated women and denied them the right to learn to read and write. She hoped that the new republic would change women's lives completely.

Mary started plotting a novel to be titled *A Wind from the Wilderness* was based on her observations of Chinese society in the sixteen months she spent in Peking. She was in fact the first female Western novelist to write with outrage about 'the position of women in China'.

Later the American born author, Pearl S. Buck, daughter of American missionaries in China who Mary did not meet as Pearl Buck was attending Randolph Macon Woman's College in America during the sixteen months Mary was in Peking. Pearl Buck would eventually make her name with novel about Chinese peasants *The Good Earth* published in 1931 while Mary's Chinese novel, The *Wind from the Wilderness* was published in 1919 at the end of World War One and her account of women with bound feet in virtual slavery to their husbands had a great impact in Britain.

In her Chinese novel and in her travel book Mary Gaunt described with outrage the blighted lives of Chinese women crippled by bound feet. She also wrote about the sad life of the eunuchs whose genitals had been removed so they could never sire a child when guarding the emperor's wives and concubines and other imperial duties.

> There were numbers of palace eunuchs, keepers of the women who, apparently, may now show their faces to all men, and they were clad all in the mourning white, with here and there one, for some reason or other I cannot fathom, in black. The demand for eunuchs was great when the Emperor dwelt, the one man, in the Forbidden City surrounded by his women, and they say that very often the number employed rose to ten thousand. Constantly, as some in the ranks grew old, fell sick, or died, they had to be replaced, and, so conservative is China, the recruits were generally drawn from certain villages whose business it was to

supply the palace eunuchs. Often, of course, the operation was performed in their infancy, but often, very often, a man was allowed to grow up, marry and have children, before he was made ready for the palace.

'Impossible,' I said, 'he would not consent then. Never.'

And my informant laughed pitifully. 'Ah,' said she, 'you don't know the struggle in China. Anything for a livelihood.'

There were coolies, too, in the ordinary blue cotton busy about the work that the entertaining of such a multitude necessarily entails, and everyone looked cheerful and happy, as, after all, why should they not, for death is the common lot, and must come to all of us, and they had seen and heard of the dead Empress about as much as the dweller in Chicago had.

Against the walls the coolies kept putting up long scrolls covered with Chinese characters in praise of the virtues of the Empress in they same way we would send funeral wreaths, to honour the dead. Soon a strong wind arose and tore at them: the scrolls fluttered out from the walls like long streamers, and as the wind grew wilder, some were torn down altogether.[5]

CHAPTER 13

A political assassination

The funeral procession of the embalmed body of the Empress Long Yu was originally planned to take place shortly after the lying-in-state ceremony Mary Gaunt witnessed.

However on 20 March 1913, the left wing politician Chaio Sen had been assassinated at Shanghai railway station and the murder of this handsome and popular politician shocked the entire Chinese nation. The assassination of Sun-Yat-sen's young and brilliant second in command had such profound political ramifications that delayed the arrangements for Empress Long Yu's funeral procession.

Chaio Sen had publicly claimed that President Yuan was a Machiavellian figure with secret plans to seize power and form his own imperial dynasty. This was be proved true in 1915. Young Chaio-Sen's speech was far too close to the truth for the ambitious general turned president. Unknown to George Morrison, President Yuan, the former general who had secured George's his appointment as political advisor but was no longer confiding in him, had contributed money to have the young politician shot as Chaio-Sen was about to board a train at Shanghai.

. George Morrison was horrified when telegrams were produced in front of members of the National Assembly linking President Yuan with Sung's assassination. An outraged Sun Yat-sen claimed he had evidence that President Yuann had authorised the payment of money to the assassin to kill his friend and political associate.

In *A Woman in China,* Mary wrote that 'the National Assembly was in an uproar, the president openly was being accused of murder and of ruling like a dictator'.[1] It spelt ruin to any hopes of a well run republic bent on reform.

George Morrison, as a policy advisor to President Yuan, became increasingly gloomy convinced there was a good chance it would lead to civil war between the two factions.

The loan Morrison had secured from the British government had been cancelled in favour of a larger loan from four other European nations. Morrison was worried that the new and very unpopular high interest loan would be used by President Yuan to buy arms. It was becoming clear fighting would soon erupt between the left and right factions of the republican government.

George Morrison was asked to serve on the board of inquiry into the death of the murdered politician but felt it wiser to decline, claiming tactfully that, 'as an employee of the Chinese Republican Government this appointment would be inappropriate'.[2]

Mary described how President Yuan's northern Chinese allies and Sun Yat Sen's south were at each other's throats. British legation staff told her that Peking resembled a volcano waiting to explode. The thought of civil war was scarcely reassuring for a new arrival hoping to explore China by rail or to hire mule carts and travel over remote tracks where as yet proper roads did not exsist.[3]

George Morrison was so upset by the crisis that he thought of resigning his position as advisor, and taking his young and pregnant wife to London or returning to Australia.[4] He was moody and unhappy and felt that accepting the well-paid job of advisor to President Yuan had been a great mistake. He had no power to influence events and President Yuan no longer seemed to consultg him on anything.[5]

***

George Morrison was a brilliant man who enjoyed dominating

A POLITICAL ASSASSINATION

conversations. He was at ease in male company but found dealing with women unless plaint and beautiful difficult. Morrison's diaries are larded with disparaging criticisms of the opposite sex unless the women were young, pliant and beautiful.

In 1903 Morrison had met Mary's friend, the highly intelligent Gertrude Bell and had been disparaging about Bell, an astute woman with a good understanding of Middle Eastern politics and disliked Gertrude claiming she talked too much. 'My God, she'd talk the leg of an iron pot and has the cheek of the devil,' Morrison wrote in a letter to J.O. Bland, his replacement as correspondent for *The Times* in Shanghai.[6]

Since Mary was as talkative and strong minded as Gertrude Bell, she was probably not his idea of the ideal house guest at a time when he was under great stress with a pregnant young wife and worried as to what the future held in Peking for both of them.

Mary did not reveal much of life at a tense time in the Morrison household in *A Woman in China*. She merely stated that after a fortnight's stay at Morrison Street she moved to a hotel inside the Legation Compound no doubt aware that the Morrisons, however hospitable and kind, could hardly be expected to house and feed her for over a year while she was in Peking on and off but did appreciate how kind they had been to her and that Morrison's contacts had enabled her to visit the Forbidden City and the Imperial Hunting Palaces at Chengde, also banned for decades to all foreigners.[7]

Laden down with baggage, Mary, undeterred by talk of civil war continued with her travel plans. She had to baggage for her expedition to Chengde and across inner Mongolia towards the Gobi Desert.

Accordingly she she rented a bedroom, sitting room and additional storage space underneath the Hotel Wagon Lits, a comfortable hotel inside the Legation Compound frequented by diplomats and consular staff.

Photographs taken in 1913 show the Legation Compound with

broad tree- lined streets and palatial residences built by the various legations. The buildings had all been badly damaged by shellfire from the Chinese Imperial army, sent to help Boxers. After the Boxer rebellion ended in defeat, the Chinese had paid large fines to various countries so the foreign legations (smaller versions of embassies) could be rebuilt.

Safely installed in her hotel Mary climbed the steep steps that led to the walkway on the top of the flat walls of the Legation Compound to survey the city. Mary saw Peking was divided into distinct areas, cut off from each other by high walls with a Chinese city for ethnic Chinese, a Tartar City (where George Morrison lived) containing palaces of Manchu princes, libraries and government buildings.

Adjoining the Tartar City, surrounded by vermilion painted walls was the Forbidden City. To the south s lay the large Legation Compound with its flat walls patrolled by sentries which made an excellent observation point for Mary.

Peking's dry season was almost over. But the cloud of reddish-yellow dust, that had greeted Mary Gaunt on her arrival at the railway station , still hung over the city. Mary tried to imagine the Legation Compound as it was twelve years ago during the Boxer Rebellion when her brother, as Lieutenant Ernest Gaunt RN had marched his band of marines through the Imperial Drainage Canal, a grandiose name Peking's main sewer. Marines as well as British and Indian soldiers had gained access to the Legation Compound as the main gates of the city were shut and bolted.

. British and Indian forces braved the stench of raw sewage, entered the city and managed to fight off the Boxers and liberate besieged Legation staff. Many of the foreign legations had been destroyed and others badly damaged by shellfire from imperial troops, sent by Dowager Empress Cixi.

With a writer's eye Mary tried to imagine the scene as it had been in that 55-day siege by the Boxers. The air must have been blue with gunsmoke and corpses piled against the walls of the Legation Compound. Inside the walls clerical staff and diplomats on the edge of starvion after a long siege had defended themselves with ancient canons and been reducded to eating their pet cats and dogs.

In 1913, more than twelve years after the Boxer Rebellion, most of the damage caused by the Boxers and Cixi's troops had been repaired. However a few bullet holes had been allowed to remain in the stables and the main building of the palatial British Legation as reminders.

Mary was shown the bullet holes when was invited to dinner parties given by Britsh Legation staff contacted on her behalf by Enrest, , now Captain Ernest Gaunt and was glad to learnthat Ernest had been an efficient and popular Naval Attache with a brilliant career predicted for him in the navy.

Mary enjoyed an early morning walk along the top of the high r wall of the Legation Compound where she overlooked narrow streets filled with carts drawn by mules or horses.[8] She watched elderly men in blue coats using scoops and pails collect animal dung, while more men with pails of water and shovels tried to dampen down the red dust that filled the streets and described

> ...the dust of Peking is a problem beyond a mere pail and scoop. This spattering of water has about as much effect upon it as a thimbleful of water flung on a raging fiery furnace. Still, in spite of the mud and the dust, the streets are not without charm. They are lined with trees; indeed I think no city of its size was ever better planted. When one has realises how treeless is the greater part of China, this is rather surprising.
>
> Peking, or rather the Tartar City is enclosed in seven miles of pinkish red walls, close on twenty feet here, and in the heart of it, behind more pinkish red walls is the Forbidden City, where dwell the remnant of the Manchu dynasty, the baby emperor and his guardians, women and eunuchs and attendants... Here are specious courtyards, ancient temples and audience halls with yellowish-brown tiled roofs, extensive lakes where wild duck flying north for the summer find a resting place.
>
> [Peking] consists of a network of narrow streets and alleys lined with low buildings with windows of delicate lattice-work and curved tiled roofs... All the clamour of a Chinese city is here;

laden donkeys, mules and horses, rickshaws from Japan, tilted Peking carts with studded wheels.

The Tartar city has nine gates, great archways with iron-studded doors and watch-towers above them... Over every archway is a watch-tower, with tiled roofs rising tier above tier, and portholes filled with the painted muzzles of guns. In the year 1900, when the Boxers looted the Chinese Peking, the Europeans in their Legations trembled for their lives...

To Western eyes the traffic is archaic... it consists of rickshaws with one or Peking carts with blue tilts and a sturdy pony or a handsome mule in the shafts, and the driver seated cross-legged in front. [There are] longer carts with wheels studded, as the Peking carts are, and loaded with timber, with lime, and all manner of merchandise, and drawn by three or four underfed little horses... The rickshaw coolies clang their bells, men on bicycles toot their horns, every donkey, and most horses and mules, have rings of bells round their necks, and everyone shouts at the top of his voice.[9]

※

On 3 April, 1913 Mary obtained a good view of the funeral cortege of Empress Long Yu bound for one of the three railway stations sited side by side, from the top of the Legation Compound's wall.

The procession started from the Eastern Gate of the Forbidden City, advanced slowly down Morrison Street, past George Morrison's home, turned left and passed the spot where Mary was standing.

> It seemed to me strange this ruler of an ancient people, buried with weird and barbaric rites, was to be taken to her last resting-place by the modern railway, that only a very few years ago her people, at the height of their anti-foreign feeling, had wished to oust from the country root and branch. But since the funeral procession was going to the railway station it must pass through the Chien Men, and the curtain wall that ran round the great gate offered an excellent point of vantage from which I, with the rest of the European population, might see all there was to be seen. And for this great occasion, the gate in the south of the curtain

wall, the gate that is always shut because only the highest in the land may pass through, was open, for the highest in the land, the last of the Manchu rulers, was dead.

I looked down into the walled-in space between the four gateway arches, as into an arena, and the whole pageant passed below me. First of all marching with deliberate slowness, that contrives to be dignified if they are only carrying coals, came about twenty camels draped in imperial yellow with tails of sable, also an imperial badge hanging from their necks. The Manchus were a hunting people, and though they have been dwellers in towns for the last two hundred and fifty years the fact was not forgotten now that their last ruler had died. She was going on a journey, a long, long journey; she might want to rest by the way, therefore her camels bore tent-poles and tents of the imperial colour. They held their heads high and went noiselessly along, pad, pad, pad, as their like have gone to and fro from Peking for thousands of years.

There were about fifty white ponies, without saddle or trapping of any kind, each led by a *mafoo* clad in blue like an ordinary coolie. The Peking carts that followed with wheels and tilts of yellow were of a past age, but, after all, does not the King of Great Britain and Ireland on State occasions ride in a most old-world coach. And then I noticed things came in threes. Three carts, three yellow palankeens full of artificial flowers, three sedan chairs also yellow covered, and all around these groups were attendants clad in shimmering rainbow muslin and thick felt hats, from the pointed crown of which projected long yellow feathers.

Slowly, slowly, the procession moved on, broken now and again by bands of soldiers in full marching order. There was a troop of cavalry of the Imperial Guard they told me, but how could it be imperial when their five-coloured lance pennons fluttering gaily in the air, clearly denoted the New Republic? There was a detachment of mounted police in black and yellow the most modern of uniforms, there were more attendants in gaily coloured robes carrying wooden halberds, embroidered fans, banners, and umbrellas, and the yellow palankeens with the artificial flowers were escorted by Buddhist lamas in yellow robes crossed with crimson sashes, each with a stick of smouldering incense in his hand.

In those palankeens were the dead woman's seals, her power, the power that she must now give up. I could see the smoke, and the scent of the incense rose to our nostrils as we stood on the wall forty feet above. Between the various groups, between the yellow lamas who dated from the days of the Buddha long before the Christ, between the khaki-clad troops and the yellow and black police, things of yesterday, came palace attendants tossing into the air white paper discs.

The dead Empress would want money for her journey, and here it was, distributed with a lavish hand. It was only white paper, blank and soiled by the dust of the road, when I picked it up a little later on, but for her it would serve all purposes. The approach of the bier itself was heralded by the striking together of two slabs of wood by a couple of attendants, and before it came, clad all in the white of mourning, the palace eunuchs who had guarded her privacy when in life; a few Court attendants in black, and then between lines of khaki-uniformed modern infantry in marching order, the bier covered with yellow satin, vivid, brilliant, embroidered with red phoenixes that marked her high rank the dragon for the Emperor, the phoenix for his consort.

The two pieces of wood clacked together harshly and the enormous bier moved on. It was mounted on immense yellow poles and borne by eighty men dressed in brilliant robes of variegated muslin, red being the predominating colour. They wore hats with yellow feathers coming out of the crown, and they staggered under their burden, as might the slaves in Nineveh or Babylon have faltered and groaned beneath their burdens, two thousand years ago.

Out of the northern archway came the camels and the horses, the soldiers, the lamas, the eunuchs, out came all the paraphernalia —umbrellas, and fans, palanquins, sedan chairs and banners.

The procession slowly crossed the great courtyard, the arena.; a stop, a long pause, then on again, and the southern gate swallowed them up, again the clack of the strips of wood, and the mighty bier, borne on the shoulders of these slaves. Slowly, slowly, the bier halted and we felt as if it must stay there for ever, as if the eighty men who upheld it must be suffering unspeakable [pain]. Once more came the clack of the strips of wood, and the southern archway in due course swallowed it up, with the halberdiers and the detachment of soldiery who completed the procession.

Near the Chien Men Gate and the railway station, people were crowded together like Chinese flies in summer, and that is saying a great deal. They were cleared away by the soldiers, the bier was lifted on to a car, bands struck up a weird funeral march, soldiers presented arms, the priest-like lamas fell on their knees.

And finally very slowly the train steamed out of the station, and the last of the Manchu Empresses was borne to her final resting place.[10]

CHAPTER 14

The Great Wall of China and Emperor Yongle's tomb

In April 1913, while pear and apple trees were blossoming, Mary Gaunt and the pink faced young official from the British Legation and a friend of his made another journey by train to the small town of Nankou, close to the Nankou Pass. Leaving the train they found no road and over rough stony ground Mary was carried to the Great Wall in a mule litter,

The drought had broken and the first spring rains had arrived Peasant and farmers had planted grains like kaoling and millet and prayed for rain as a proonged drought would mean their families would starve.

In the era before mass tourism there were only two trains a day from Peking to Nankou in contrast to the present when trains and tourist coaches leave at frequent intervals for many different sections of the Great Wall.

Mary and the two young Englishmen and a lone American and his family were the only foreigners on the train heading for Nankou where a well preserved section of the Great Wall could be seen commenced in the year 214 before the birth of Christ, replacing earlier earthworks designed to keep out the nomadic tribes who were the enemies of the Chinese people.

They discussed how the Great Wall had been built with tears, sweat and blood when d thousands of free labourers and slaves had died during its construction. To build the wall they used stone or occasionally blocks of rammed earth known as pisé but almost a third of the wall had been removed to build other structures from peasant's houses to pig pens. The wall extended over 4,800 kilometres, snaking along mountain ridges and descending into deep valleys and in 1913 was in a bad state of remain. Its staggering length and height had failed to prevent the Manchu from invading and imposing centuries of domination on the Han Chinese.

Descending from the mule litter or sling by a small set of steps, Mary, prone to attacks of asthma, struggled up the steep steps that led to the top of the wall. A porter carried her heavy camera and brass tripod. She had great ed difficulty climbing the steps as the treads were widely spaced having been designed and built for soldiers and far too high for her to negotiate with ease. She prayed that all this climbing up and clambering down would not bring on an asthma attack and her prayers were granted.

Soldiers of the fledgling Nationalist Republic in shabby uniforms were camping under the watchtowers. Mary peered inside one of the watch towers imagining it centuries earlier with sentries keeping watch throughout the night for the Mongol hordes who arrived to steal young Chinese women or try to to hold a camel caravan to ransom.

The Great Wall had been designed so that entire companies of Chinese archers could stand on the top,, protected by chest-high slits through which they could use their heavy bows to fire arrows at their enemies. The wall sprawled across hills and valleys, bridging vast gullies, climbing up and dipping down as far as the eye could see. A Chinese guide, retained by a wealthy American visitor (foreign visitors being very rare in 1913, explained in fractured English that over 2,000,000 labourers had died during the building of the wall, described in a Chinese poem as 'built on skeletons.'

Mary saw gaping holes where e peasants had removed stones to use them for building their own homes — just as Roman peasants had done with stones from the Coliseum in the Middle Ages,[1]

A Ming emperor had arranged for track to be dug beside the wall and centuries later mules, donkeys and horses, laden with sacks of grain and hides were still using the same track. Blue-coated coolies trudged along with bamboo poles across their shoulders. Camel trains from outer Mongolia padded past, just as they had done for centuries.

y Mary was exhausted from so much climbing she and her young companions returned to Nankou, where they found inexpensive accommodation at a hotel near the railway station, the only one in the town. The hotel was very clean but consisted of one large room, divided into many smaller ones by large sheets of paper. The least whisper could be heard in every room in the hotel. Mary was so tired that despite the flimsy walls made of paper, slept extremely well.

*
**

The next morning the sunshine was glorious, the air clear and dry as champagne. Having walked on the longest wall in the world, Mary was to visit the tomb of Yongle (Yung Lo), the famous emperor of the Ming dynasty. Ever since Granny Palmer had shown her a blue and white porcelain plate from one of Yongle's dinner services, Mary had wished to visit the emperor's tomb, high in the foothills of the Jundu and Tianshou Mountains.

. From books and maps in George Morrison's library Mary learned that Yongle had stolen the imperial throne rather than inherited it. He had successful warrior prince, with no claim to the throne, and seized power from his feeble minded nephew, Jianwen.[2] It was very convenient for Yongle that Jianwen died in a mysterious fire at his palace in Nanjing, at that time the capital of imperial China so could not make trouble for his uncle, the usurper.[3]

Crowned as Yongle, the Son of Heaven, to eliminate y potential rivals, the new emperor ordered the murder of two thousand of the late emperor's eunuchs and concubines and watched the beheading of nine young princes of the blood royal. He was outraged to learn the concubines had enjoyed 'vegetarian sex' a term which implied vaginal penetration with cucumbers or gourds, performed by the eunuchs paid to guard them.

Regarded by some as 'the Napoleon of China', Yongle was a brilliant military commander and instituted a massive rebuilding of China's Grand Canal to promote trade and allow transport of building materials for the construction of Peking's Imperial City.

Mary read how in 1406 Yongle sent an expedition to conquer Vietnam, making it temporarily a part of China. A scholar as well as a man of action he had commissioned leading scholars to create the great *Yongle Encyclopedia* in an effort to preserve Chinese culture and literature. Unfortunately, due to the high cost of woodblock printing, the encyclopaedia was printed and many manuscript were when the great Hanlin library was torched by the Boxers at the time of the Boxer Rebellion.

As part of his wish to expand Chinese influence, Emperor Yongle sponsored sea-going armadas of sailing ships, the first launched in 1405, almost a century and a half before Sir Francis Drake and other pirate captains of Queen Elizabeth made their extemsove sea voyages. At enormous cost to the Ming empire, Chinese ships visited the Asian coast, Ceylon, the south of India and the Middle East bringing back animals then unknown to the Chinese such as ostriches, zebras and giraffes.

Early in the fifteenth century Yongle order the building of the Forbidden City. No expense was spared in creating one of the world's most magnificent palace complexes, Thinking about her little Ming bowl given her all those years ago by Granny Palmer Mary was interested to learn that Yongle ordered over 25,000 bowls and saucers of hand decorated porcelain from the Imperial Porcelain works.[4]

With so many achievements to commemorate, Mary expected that Emperor Yongle's tomb would be the most splendid of all the Ming tombs. It was situated some 60 kilometres from Peking and there was no proper road for much of the journey.

Mary recalled George Morrison's advice that in order to be obeyed she must behave like a wealthy Chinese lady and be carried to the Ming tombs in a palanquin — a type of sedan chair on poles — born on the shoulders of four burly coolies.

After covering several kilometres over stony ground, Mary's small expedition came to the Holy Way of the Ming Emperors. This paved avenue was guarded by stone lions, camels, elephants and warriors, all larger than life. Mary was carried underneath a massive red painted arch, covered with carved animals and reached a huge natural amphitheatre surrounded by low hills.

'What a magnificent setting to bury a great emperor,' Mary wrote.

Each marble memorial hall to an emperor of the Ming dynasty lay at the foot of a low hill. The hills formed burial mounds for the embalmed corpse of each emperor as well as bodies of s wives and favourite concubines, who had been made to kill themselves while standing on foot stools they had nooses of white silk placed around their neck before the stools were kicked over by eunuchs. After the unfortunate women choked to death they were buried with their emperor to minister to his every need in the afterlife.

Approaching the memorial hall and burial mound of Emperor Yongle, Mary was confronted by a second huge arch tiled in imperial yellow.

Mary's swaying palanquin was set down by the porters in front of an imposing reception hall. Looking as regal as possible and hoping her linen suit was not too creased, Mary, by now stiff from the journey, climbed down from her palanquin. She entered the hall and presented her letter of introduction from President Yuan's office and was allocated the services of an official guide who spoke a little English.

Emperor Yongle's Memorial Hall was entered through a huge wooden door studded with bronze knobs. Mary and her guide walked across a marble pavement into what was known as the Hall of Eminent Favours. She saw a gigantic gilded dragon with five claws, the symbol of imperial power, beside an enormous prancing horse, carved in stone, the Chinese symbol for good fortune.[5]

Mary knew that Emperor Yongle had ruled around the same time as Prince John of Gaunt's eldest son, King Henry IV. She had visited Henry IV's tomb at in England and found it paltry compared to the magnificent tomb of Emperor Yongle.[6] The great emperor's s Memorial Hall had a magnificent carved ceiling supported by the polished trunks of fifty cedars over twenty metres tall. Even after five hundred years the scent of the cedar wood perfumed the air.[7]

Mary had obtained a letter from President Yuan's office, requesting special treatment and showing him the letter asked guide to show her Yongle's burial mound. Mary asked to visit the burial mound and discovered Yongle's coffin lay deep inside a knoll covered with cypress and pine trees sited behind the Hall of Eminent Favours.

The guide somewhat reluctantly unlocked a small wooden door in the burial mound and ushered her inside. The air smelt damp and musty as they walked 'along a paved passage whose stones were worn and slippery. The passage led down to a stone chamber in the heart of the burial mound. Two two more ramps led upwards, one to the right, the other to the left'.[8]

Mary had been hoping to see golden artefacts, and beautiful objects of Ming dynasty porcelain buried with the emperor. But all that was visible was a plain granite tablet with an incised message, which according to the guide tly praised the virtues and achievements of the deceased emperor. She asked the guide if Yongle's treasures had been stolen by tomb robbers, or were they still waiting to be excavated. He looked embarrassed and claimed that in 1644 a group of soldiers from the army of Li Zicheng had ransacked Yongle's tomb. To cover up their misdeeds the soldiers lit a fire which destroyed all the treasures that they had been unable to carry away.

Sic transit gloria mundae thought Mary, by now aware that in China things were rarely what they seemed in a country where 'losing face' was a national preoccupation. She wondered how much of what the guide told her was true.⁹

CHAPTER 15

'Behind every small foot is a jar of tears'

On her return to Peking Mary saw aristocrat Manchu women riding in rickshaws or silk covered palanquins, carried by sturdy coolies. These women wore high head-dresses that reminded Mary of black bats' wings ornamented with jewels and flowers, their hair wound round a strip of metal or ivory attached to the back of the head and long brightly coloured silken robes. With their distinctive head-dresses, Manchu women stood out from the Han Chinese women with their pale skins devoid of make up as the Manchu ladies wore rouge, blue or green eye shadow and lip paint. Mary was assured that in contrast to Chinese women, Manchu ladies had never bound *their* feet.

The unfortunate Chinese women hobbled around on feet that had been bound in childhood in tiny silk shoes, those of wealthier women being exquisitely embroidered. Mary described their faces as 'impassive, with a fixed smile that gave no indication of the pain that foot binding caused.'

She felt deeply sorry for these women and angry at what had been done to them. In all three of her books on China Mary denounced the fact Chinese men had enslaved women through foot binding and denying them an education. Although foot binding had been banned by Zaitan, the Guangxu Emperor, and banned again by the new Republican Government, many rural families chose to ignore the ban and continued binding the feet of five and six year old girls to stop their growth. The practice began in the tenth century when it was a carried out on girls aged from four to six intended to become concubines and entertainers. Gradually the binding of feet spread until it was adopted by most Chinese families on their daughters.

Chinese women, wearing clothes in far more sombre colours than the Manchu women, hobbled about in embroidered silk shoes that measured between 10 and 15 cm. Mary was told that Chinese husbands were proud of their wives' tiny feet and found their swaying gait erotic. Some unfortunate Chinese women found walking so painful they rarely ventured outside the home so that the only males they saw were their husbands, fathers and brothers.

A Chinese speaking friend from the British Legation acted as interpreter for Mary when she interviewed women with 'lotus' feet. Mary was told that the pain and the tears began when little girls were between five and six years old. To soften the little girl's feet, the mother first soaked them in a mixture of herbs and water before the toes were bound tightly under the foot with bandages. These long bandages were re-wrapped and tightened every day so the pressure caused the delicate bones to break.

After binding their little daughters' feet, mothers made them walk up and down a room until the bones of their toes broke — then their feet were bound even more tightly. This constant walking on bound feet would eventually break the bones of the centre of the foot. The toes were then bound back even more tightly, with the result that the big toe was curled against the heel. This meant that these unfortunate girls would have to walk in pain throughout their lives Eventually the arch of the foot was forced to assume the desired 'golden lotus' shape.

After girls reached the age of seven they were seldom allowed to go out. They were confined to the women's quarters on the upper floor of the house until they were married off — usually before the age of seventeen — to a man they had never seen. Once a girls was married she went to live in special women's rooms in her husband's house or in the home of her in-laws, and endured a life of total servitude.

In her excursions to rural areas Mary heard children crying

and was told the crying came from girls weeping as their foot bandages had been tightened. The only way these poor little girls could gain any relief was to sit on the edge of the stone *k'ang* (the heating platform) in their homes. They pressed their calves against the edge of the *k'ang to* stop the flow of blood and numb the pain from their feet as a brief respite.[1]

Chinese girls were taught they must never complain in order to prepare them for childbirth. They were raised with the idea they must obey first their parents and then their husbands without question. What angered Mary was the fact that apart from a few educated and enlightened city families most rural families were continuing this brutal practice designed for the pleasure of men. All the outrage she had felt at the treatment of women in her schooldays, when girls were told they were weak feeble creatures subservient to men emerged again at the sight of what men had done to Chinese women.

> The pity and the horror of it never failed to strike me. If the missionaries do but one good work, they do it in prevailing on the women to unbind their feet, in preventing unlucky little girls from going through years of agony. There is no mistaking the gait of a woman with bound feet, she walks as if her legs were made of wood. Her feet are tiny, shaped like small hoofs, about four inches long encased in embroidered slippers… Four doctors who came into contact with these women told me their sufferings were great and after the process was finished the feet were often sore and ulcerated and the least exertion makes them ache.[2]

On her visits to different parts of China, Mary talked to many doctors working in British and American mission hospitals. They confirmed that foot binding in childhood often led to sores and gangrene in the women's feet — when that happened one or even both feet had to be amputated in order to save the woman's life. Women, whose feet had been bound, often developed hip and spinal problems, due to the fact that tiny feet, only 10 cm long, had to bear the full weight of an adult body. One mission doctor told

Mary that as a result of those problems many of these women had difficulty giving birth.³

Chinese mothers knew that, unless their daughters' feet were broken and bound, their chance of marriage were poor and in a country where poverty was endemic and children could be sold into slavery during a drought, an early marriage was the best chance of survival for many girls from large families. It made Mary even more convinced that education was the only thing that could save women from male oppression. A female mission doctor interviewed by Mary told her she had known mothers who had broken the central bone of their daughter's feet with a meat cleaver before binding them. They had done this not out of cruelty but in desperation so the daughter could find a husband to feed and support her once her parents were dead.⁴

At one occasion Mary was present when a male mission doctor examined the leg of a woman with bound feet. She described

> ...the whole limb from the big toe to the knee was hard and immovable as stone. If you press ordinary flesh anywhere it pits, yields a little, but a woman with a bound foot has a leg that is thin, perished, hard as marble. Once having seen a foot unbound, it is a wonder to me that any woman should walk at all. And yet they do. They hold out their arms and walk, balancing themselves and to do this use a stick. Sometimes they walk on their heels, sometimes they try the toe, but once I realised what those bandages concealed it was a dreadful thing to see a Chinese woman walking. In spite of the hardness of the flesh, or probably because of it, they get corns on the spot upon which they balance, and sores, eat into the foot.
>
> But the evil does not stop at the foot. In Shansi it seemed to me every woman's face was marked by suffering. I often got a glimpse of one peering out of a cart or litter at the foreigner, and that face invariably was patient, pallid and worn, for foot-binding brings no end of evils in its train. The mission doctor at Fen Chou Fu declared that nine-tenths of the women who came to him for treatment suffered from tuberculosis in some form or another,

and in a climate that in the winter must rival in dryness Davos Platz [in Switzerland]. A few women, develop spinal curvature low down in the back, and often because of the displacement of the organs they die in child-birth.

A missionary in one of the little towns where I sheltered, a trained nurse told me that when a woman suffered from *osteomalacia* she could never give birth to a child. At times this nurse had been called to see a young woman about to give birth but could do nothing to help her and could only stand by and see her die in agony.[5]

Mary took up the fight against foot binding. To highlight the horrors of this custom she made the heroine of her novel set in China, *The Wind from the Wilderness* a brave young mission doctor called Rosalie Gascoigne who leads a crusade against foot binding which still continues in the remote village near the mission.[6]

CHAPTER 16

Chende and the hunting palace of the Manchu

Early in May 1913, Mary undertook an uncomfortable and hazardous expedition to visit the hunting resort of Manchu emperors on the Jehol River. The imperial summer resort of Jehol was near the town of Cheng Te Fu (Chengde). Jehol was now forbidden territory and Mary needed President Yuan's permission to visit and through the intervention of George Morrison the President of the Chinese republic gave Mrs Mary Miller, the name on her passport, a letter of introduction to his friend, the Military Governor of Hebei Province which she had to present.

A photograph taken in front of the Hotel Wagon Lits (plate xxx) shows Mary in a sun hat and long flowing skirts inspecting two mule carts and their drivers as her small expedition was about to leave for Chengde and Jehol.

The 'Peking carts' as they were called were flimsy and unstable. An American traveller named Isabella Bird broke an arm when the Peking cart in which she was travelling overturned.

The leading cart held Mary and Tuan, her Chinese tour leader-cum-cook, including his motley collection of iron cooking pots and meat cleavers. The second cart held the luggage including Mary's portable rubber bath which replaced the old canvas one she took with her around West Africa. She also took a small charcoal burning stove, bags of rice, tea and flour, her camp bed and sleeping bag, so she would be reasonably comfortable at the primitive Chinese inns where she had to stay because camping out in the wilds of China was far too dangerous due to the large number of robbers and bandits.

Today Cheng Te Fu (Chengde) can be reached in a single day by luxury coach from Beijing, (the former Peking). But in 1913 , travel to this isolated area over a stony track and across a mountain pass was extremely difficult. Groups of thugs murdered and robbed travellers at the head of the pass so the office of President Yuan issued orders that Mrs Mary Miller) be escorted by soldiers over the pass and to prevent attacks by robbers armed soldiers were to guard Mary while she slept in her tent or in the Peking cart.

***

Leaving Peking by one of the enormous gates, set into the outer walls of the city, those flimsy Peking carts jolted and bounced over broken paving for several kilometres. Although called a cart in reality it was a n wooden tray, devoid of all seating or springs, covered by a faded blue cotton canopy supported by a bamboo frame. Mary feared her cart might split in half or overturn and she was proved correct.

The road consisting of large stone pavers had been laid down by slave labour centuries earlier. Some of the pavers had been stolen leaving giant potholes into which the wheels of the Peking carts dropped with a judder and a crash. Each jolt reverberated along Mary's spine and soon her lower back was bruised and very sore.

George Morrison had told Mary that wealthy Chinese never stayed at the inns reserved for mule drivers — instead they hired disused temples from priests. Mary felt that hiring a complete temple is was beyond her slender resources and resigned herself to staying at smelly and very primitive mule-drivers' inns.

Tuan, Mary's tour leader, had with excellent references, but when she knew him better e suspected that they had been forged. Tuan turned out to be a glib rogue, who on Mary's behalf employed two drivers, four porters and Mr Wang, the interpreter and took 'squeeze' or secret commissions from all of them.

Mr Wang's knowledge of English proved to be minimal and he saw ded Mary as an easy target who would give him free English lessons as well as paying him a wage. Mary was furious that Tuan had deceived her about Mr Wang's language capabilities. However interpreters were hard to come by so it was too late to sack Mr Wang and find someone better qualified. Mary had taken only a modest supply of tinned food on her expedition to Jehol, far less than she had taken on her African journeys.

She had begun reading George Staunton's account of the fearsome journey of British Ambassador Lord Macartney to Jehol in 1793. The British Ambassaor sent by George III travelled there to obtain important trade concessions from the Qianlong Emperor having failed to gain an audience with the Son of Heaven at the Forbidden City.

Unfortunately, Mary had been unable to finish the account of Lord Macartney's historic visit, a copy of which was held in the library of the Royal Geographical Society in London as since women could not be members she could only visit the library if invited by a male member.[1] Keen to finish reading George Staunton's account of Lord Macartney's diplomatic mission , she was thrilled to find a copy of Staunton's rare leather bound volume in George Morrison's private library.

As George III's ambassador to China, Lord Macartney travelled 233 km to Jehol for an audience with the Qianlong Emperor and failed to obtain trade concession for Britain, but he was amazed by the luxury he saw everywhere in the Imperial Palaces and their extensive grounds.

The Imperial Park at Jehol near Chengde its hunting lodges, temples and ornamental gardens had been constructed so that emperors could organise displays of archery and swordplay to impress visiting groups from Mongolia, and Tibet with the wealth of the Manchu dynasty. After Empress Cixi's senile husband, the Emperor Xianfeng died here, Jehol had been shunned allegedly haunted by spirits of those who had died here.

Since there was no proper hotel in the town of Cheng Te Fu, Mary was relying on hospitality from missionaries at the English mission in the centre of the town. To reach Cheng Te Fu she had to cross a high mountain pass in one of those flimsy high wheeled mule carts without springs.

As wayside inns for the mule drivers rarely supplied food, Mr Wang had to cook for them on a charcoal stove Tuan bought with him. At nightfall Tuan announced they would stay at an inn which carried a sign in Chinese characters which Mr Wang translated as *'Room for a thousand merchant guests'*. Looking at the crumbling inn with its mud walls and rotting thatch Mary thought those thousand merchants must all be midgets if they could all sleep in such a tiny building!

Mary had been warned that Chinese wayside inns frequented by the mule drivers were invariably dirty and smelly. But they were the only safe accommodation on offer and she was feeling feverish and feared she was developing influenza. She asked Tuan to tell the innkeeper to have someone clean her room before she entered it.

Tuan went inside and after some time re-appeared, beaming from ear to ear like the Cheshire cat. He assured Mary she had been given the best room in the inn, which had been specially dusted and cleaned for her. Later Mary would learn that Tuan's broad smile owed much to the generous secret commission he had extracted from the landlord which would, in due course, be added to her account.

Mary entered her bedroom with a throbbing head, longing for a good rest. She was dismayed that all the alleged 'cleaner' had done was to raise the dust which swirled around in the musty air. The bedroom was lit by a lattice work window covered in grimy tissue paper and had a *ka'ang* or fireplace in the middle on which she was expected to place her own bedding.

As she changed out of her dusty clothes into her night attire, a Chinese mule driver, hoping to observe the foreign women at her toilette, wetted one finger and poked it through the tissue paper that covered the lattice of the window. Mary saw his eye pressed to the hole he had made and the outline of his face. Angry at being spied upon, she dressed, went outside to find Tuan and insisted he complain to the inn keeper about the peeping Tom. One of the men looking after the mules was then made to guard the window of her room and ensure her privacy.

Mary's allegedly 'superior' room had a stone *k'ang* or fireplace, a platform about three quarters of a metre high, and a small fire lit in it. The resulting warmth was carried by a system of flues to the stone which was covered by stained and greasy coir matting. On the stone platform g was a small table and two uncomfortable wooden chairs. Someone had sprinkled borax powder on top of the *k'ang* against fleas. Just to be sure Mary topped it with a layer of Keating's Anti Flea Powder as this was where she was supposed to sleep on her own bedding roll and pillows.

Tuan had managed to purchase a small chicken about the size of a pigeon, plus a few onions and rock-hard pears. He stewed them in a pan on the charcoal oven, promising a delicious meal. However, the chicken was as tough as an ostrich, tougher than the scrawny chickens Mary had eaten on her African expedition and the pears were old and leathery.

Mary lay on her mattress, bruised from the journey and her head aching with the symptoms of flu. She thought she must have been mad to travel to the imperial summer palaces in a flimsy cart with wobbly wheels that bumped and bounced over the stony ground and could easily overturn.

The next day, covered in bruises, Mary tried to make herself more comfortable by sitting on cushions in the d Peeking cart, but the effect of the bouncing and jolting over bumpy ground was just as bad. The only good thing about her expedition to the summer Hunting Palaces was the fact that so much jolting seemed to have dispelled her threatened attack of influenza but given her an entirely different set of aches and pains.

After a few days of uncomfortable travelling they arrived at the walled city of Tsung Hua Chou (Zunhua), where they looked for a suitable inn for the night. Mary was not impressed by the town and wrote,

...once inside Tsung Hua Chou I saw no beauty in it, for all the romantic walls outside. The evil-smelling streets we rumbled through to the inn were wickedly narrow, and down the centre hung notices in Chinese characters on long strips of paper white and red, and pigs, and children, and creaking wheelbarrows, and men with loads, blocked the way. But we jolted over the step into the courtyard of the inn at last, quite a big courtyard, and quite a busy inn. This was an inn where they apparently ran a restaurant, for as I climbed stiffly out of my cart a servant, carrying a tray of little basins containing the soups and stews the Chinese eat, was so absorbed in gazing at me he ran into the 'cartee man', and a catastrophe occurred which was the occasion of much bad language.

The courtyard was crowded. There were blue-tilted Peking carts, there were mules, there were donkeys, there were men of all sorts; but there was only one wretched little room for me. It was very dirty too, and I was very tired. What was to be done?[2]

The innkeeper's wife kindly offered Mary her own room and said she would sleep at her mother's home. But the wife's room was so dirty and smelly that Mary declined the offer and was obliged to sleep in the 'wretched little room', making it as comfortable as possible with her own cushions.

The following day Mary set out to explore the town but found Tsung Hua Chou just as depressing in daylight as it had seemed the previous evening. The streets were thronged with half-naked children and small-footed women with elaborately dressed hair, tottering along keeping their balance with outstretched arms.

After leaving Tsung Hua Chou Mary's expedition had to cross a steep mountains range before arriving at the river Lan (also known as Lwan or Luan). As they approached the river, wind began to blow and clouds of yellow dust gathered in the sky.

By the time we arrived at the river-banks it was blowing furiously, and a good part of the country, as always seems to be the case in China when the wind blows, was in the air. The river,

> wide and muddy and rather shallow, was flowing swiftly along, and the crossing-place was just where the valley was widest, and there was a large extent of sand on either bank, so there was plenty of material for the wind to play with… There were many other people on that sandy beach, there were other Peking carts, there were laden country carts with their heavily studded wheels cut out of one piece of wood, there were laden donkeys and mules, there were all the blue-clad people in charge of the traffic, and there were tiny restaurants, rough-looking shacks where the refreshment of these people was provided for.[3]

However, there were no refreshments available at the 'rough looking restaurants that was little more than a shack because the wind was blowing hard, causing clouds of dust. Customers were grabbing plates and implements before these blew away or secured them under a stone. Eating here was clearly impossible, and by now very hungry Mary's team moved on.

By the time they crossed the river the storm had subsided. Mary shook the reddish yellow dust from the Gobi Desert from her clothes and out of her hair and eyes.

The road was in a terrible condition and followed the path of a mountain stream. Following Chinese etiquette, Mary's cart always went first because Chinese roads were so dusty the second cart bore the brunt of all the stirred-up dust.

Mary and her team managed to find a meal after passing a decaying stretch of the Great Wall at Hsing Feng K'ou, another little walled city. However even in its s decayed state, the Great Wall looked magnificent and she was told that ramps once led to it so archers on horseback could patrol this particular stretch of wall.

Beyond the Great Wall of Hsing Feng K'ou lay Inner Mongolia where the track went from bad to worse — sometimes following the crest of a hill, sometimes skirting a mountain stream or gulley with no safety barriers to prevent travellers plunging to their death. When the unfortunate mules harnessed to the Peking carts stumbled again and again, Mary decided it was safer to walk. But her progress over e rough stony ground was so lsow she decided to trust the mules again.

At one y steep and stony area disaster struck. The Peking cart with Mary inside turned over and she found herself entangled in the canopy or tilt.

> I was out on to the hillside before I had time to think, and presently was watching those mules make hay of my possessions. They didn't leave a single thing either in or on that cart, camera, typewriter, cushions, dressing-bag, bedding, all shot out on to what the Chinaman is pleased to consider the road, even the heavy box, roped on behind, got loose and fell off, and the mule justified my expectations by, in some mysterious way, breaking the woodwork at the top of the cart and tearing all the blue tilt away. It took us over an hour to get things right again, and my faith in the stability of a Peking cart was gone for ever.[4]

※

After several more days of uncomfable travel they reached Cheng Te Fu [modern Chengde] in Jehol province where Mary had been invited to stay at the Anglican Hsi An Fu Mission in the town's centre.

At the request of George Morrison, President Yuan Shih Kai had written e a letter of introduction to the Military Governor of Jehol province on Mrs Mary Miller's behalf (the name on her passport) The President of the Chinese Republic asked his old friend, the Military Governor, to arrange the visit of an important writer to the now decaying Jehol Imperial Park, which had been closed to the public after the death of Cixi's ageing husband decades previously .

The governor of the Chengde Province, General Hsiung Hsi Ling, was a powerful man whose headquarters were close to the Anglican Hsi An Fu Mission, where Mary was a guest of the missionaries.

She was driven to the general's headquarters over a bumpy road in the swaying Peking cart. After climbing down from the cart, feeling stiff and sore and slightly sick, she was ushered into the presence of General Hsiun. The general's private secretary, a polite young man, who spoke a little English, did his best to act as interpreter for Mary and the governor who spoke not one word of English.

The Military Governor treated Mary with great courtesy, having been told by President Yuan she was a relative of his political advisor. Dr George Morrison. The governor was y happy to make an exception to the rule that the imperial summer palaces of Jehol (the Bishushanzuang were off limits to the public. He confirmed Mary Gaunt and her servants and drivers would be given passes to visit them and asked Mary if thirty admission passes would be enough, clearly imagining she was a wealthy woman travelling with an army of servants to protect her and coolies to carry her palanquin like an aristocratic Chinese lady. Obviously, the governor had no idea that Mrs Miller had only had a handful of helpers.

Mary hid her amusement, remembering George Morrison's warnings on the need to sound as though she was rich and powerful.

So she smiled at the general, said nothing and accepted the thirty passes he offered. She knew that many of the foreign missionaries had servants (some of whom had served the Manchu emperors) and they were longing to visit Jehol, one of the great wonders of China. She would return to the mission station, invite the missionaries and some of their Chinese staff to join her group which would increase the numbers.

The general ordered his private secretary to accompany Mrs Miller and her group to Jehol where only a deaf and elderly caretaker and a few gardeners resided. It was agreed that Mary and her companions would visit the Imperial Park within the next few days.

Back at the Anglican Mission it transpired several mission servants had relatives who had worked for the Manchu emperors at Jehol and were thrilled to be allowed to accompany Mary and their new employers, the missionaries.

Chende and the Hunting Palace of the Manchu   209

Mary had read that Jehol Imperial Park had an evil reputation as a place cursed by the gods. In 1820 the Manchu Emperor Jiaqing had died there, allegedly struck by a lightening bolt and Emperor Xianfeng, the elderly husband of the Dragon Empress Cixi, and father of her only son also died at Jehol. There were rumours that the spirits of the dead haunted the area and brought bad luck to all those who visited the summer palaces but as Mary did not believe in ghosts she pooh-poohed the idea.

She found that the Imperial Park of Jehol surrounded by a high wall with a broad pathway on top, along which guards could walk. Access to the Imperial Park was from the northern side of Chengde. Mary described how

> ...we went along a sordid, dusty street to the principal gate, a shabby and forlorn-looking gate, and the watch-tower over it was crumbling to decay, and we entered the courtyard, a forlorn and desolate courtyard, where the paving-stones were broken, and the grass and weeds were coming up between the cracks. Then there was a long pathway with a broken pavement in the middle... On either side of that pathway were high walls over which were peeping the tiled roofs of buildings, until at last after fully five minutes' walk, after passing through many gates, all in various stages of decay, we came to a place where the path ended with two doors to the right and left... No one save the servants, who keep the place, live in the grounds now, no one has lived there for over fifty years, not since 1860, when the reigning Emperor fled there from the Allies who sacked Peking, and died there. Perhaps it was for that reason that his secondary wife, the great Dowager-Empress whom all the world knew, disliked the place, and went there no more.[5]

General Hsiung's secretary managed to explain in a mixture of broken English and sign language that the complex of pavilions, lakes and temples had been built in this remote mountain area after a hunting expedition, led by the Emperor Kangxi entered the valley of the Jehol River. The emperor had been overawed by its beauty and ordered engineers to dam the river and turn this stretch into a series of small lakes around where hunting pavilions or 'palaces' and temples were to be constructed.

The Manchu emperors hailed originally from Manchuria in the north of China where the summers were more temperate. They found Peking oppressively hot in summer and were happy to spend the hottest months of summer at the vast walled complex surrounded by mountains near the small town of Chengde. Vast sums were spent damn the river, enlarge the lake and over the centuries build pavilions and magnificent temples to various gods in what became known as the High Mountain Pleasure Gardens.

When the Quing emperors left the heat of Peking in summer to travel to the Jehol River they were accompanied by a vast cavalcade of wives and concubines carried in mule litters or palanquins. In addition nine-thousand courtiers, servants, eunuchs and foot soldiers walked or rode on horseback.[6] Mule litters carried silken wall hangings from the palaces of the Forbidden City to adorn the elaborate pavilions of Jehol.[7]

This vast complex consisting of hunting lodges, temples and ornamental gardens, laid out so that wealthy Manchu emperors could organise spectacular displays of archery and swordplay to impress visiting groups from Mongolia, and Tibet with their wealth.

Despite the decay of many of the buildings, Mary was impressed by the beauty of the area and the restrained elegance of many pavilions and pagodas. Acres of gardens, ornamental pools and eight small lakes were dotted with single-storey wooden pavilions, linked by twenty-six causeways or highly decorative bridges. The gardens and ornamental pools were still were tended by a few resident gardeners although some stunningly beautiful palace pavilions and temples had been allowed to go to rack and ruin.

The largest hunting pavilion or 'palace' was built entirely of sweet scented cedar and inside was a carved throne draped in tattered yellow silk. Beside it was the imperial bedroom where the emperor's bed companion for the night had been carried by eunuchs. The selected concubine for that night,(one of whom was

Chende and the Hunting Palace of the Manchu

Cixi, the future Dragon Empress) after being bathed and covered in expensive perfume was carried in by the eunuchs and dumped stark naked at the foot of the emperor's bed. The concubine had to be naked to ensure she was not carrying a knife or any weapon that could harm the sacred person of the emperor, the Son of Heaven although he could do murder the concubine after taking his pleasure if he felt inclined.

Mary saw the Pine Crane Palace where Cixi as a young daughter of a Manchu bannerman or member of the imperial guard had had started her rise to power. She had been brought in to spend the night with the elderly Xianfeng Emperor who was suffering from senile dementia, but thanks to Cixi's wiles the emperor had been able to make love to her and sire a son by her. His other sons had been murdered due to the intrigues that always accompany multiple heirs to great empires. But by selecting the young and allegedly fertile Cixi as a sex toy, the emperor's supporters had hoped that she would bear a male heir to inherit the empire. And so she did but she was far cleverer than anyone had imagined and would soon wielded enormous power as the mother of a future emperor.

As Cixi had always been closely guarded by eunuchs, it was obvious that the senile emperor had managed to impregnate her and was the father of Cixi's son, Prince Toggzhi who was duly proclaimed heir to the Dragon Throne. Cixi, once despised, was now treated with respect as the mother of the heir to the Dragon throne and transformed from concubine and sex toy to 'Noble Consort'. Due to her guile and strength of personality when widowed Cixi, the Dragon Dowager Empress would end her days as the most powerful woman in China. But her only son, the spoiled overindulged Prince Toggzhi became a dissolute youth who e spent his time in brothels and died of syphilis.

Well aware no woman however clever could rule the Chinese empire in her own name Cixi chose the young and often sickly Prince Zaitan as his successor believing he would be malleable. To make certain she was kept informed of his doings she married him off to her shy skinny niece, Princess Long Yu whose funeral rites Mary had recorded. [8]

Aware that Cixi had died in 1908 and her death and that of Long Yu's husband precipitated the fall of the Chinese empire, and pondering what tp wrote about the unloved Princess Long Yu, Mary walked through a courtyard filled with fragrant white peonies to the imperial library which held valuable manuscripts. From there she went to see the great audience hall of various emperors and mounted on another mule was shown the Temple of Happiness and Longevity built on a steep slope looking down over the lake. The Temple of Happimess and Longevity had been built in 1780, before Australia was settled by the First Fleet, to celebrate 45th years of the reign of Emperor Quianlong when the Panchen Lama of Tibet visited Jehol as a guest at the Emperor Qianlong's 70th birthday celebrations.

From the Temple of Happiness and Longevity Mary obtained a superb view over much of the pleasure complex lying along the Jehol River. of the complex.

On an island in the middle of the lake she was shown the pavilion where young Cixi had once lived with the senile emperor and her baby son. The pavilion contained exquisite carved wooden furniture, copied by Chinese craftsmen from original designs by Thomas Chippendale sent out from England. Other pavilions contained red and black lacquered Oriental furnishings inlaid with precious and semi-precious stones but vandals had prised some of the precious stones loose in order to steal them.

George Morrison had told Mary there were beautiful jade ornaments and long wall panels of intricately carved jade and huge wall silk hangings, called *thangkas*, but Mary looked in vain for these valuable items.

One of the missionaries whispered that her the elderly Chinese servant, formerly a maid at Jehol, had told her that the Military Governor of Jehol Province had removed portable items from the pavilions, allegedly, worth a fortune. Mary was very curious about these thefts but realised she could hardly ask the general's private secretary to confirm if indeed the general as Military Governor had stolen the missing valuables!.

She consoled herself with the thought that the artefacts, removed from the pavilions, would be better preserved than those that remained in the complex which had been allowed to decay. Those delicate silk hangings, had they had remained at Jehol would have become brittle and rotted away.

After her visit to the palace complex Mary and the missionaries returned to the Anglican mission in the centre of Cheng Te Fu. She had a few days rest before visiting another temple complex in a nearby valley, which Mary referred to as the 'Valley of the Dead Gods' and had another bumpy journey in a Peking cart.

> ...we went up a valley for perhaps eight miles [and] embosomed among the folds of the hills, hills for the most part steep, rounded, and treeless, are the temples, red, and gold, and white, against the green or brown of the hills.
>
> To the glory of God! Surely. Surely. An ideal place for temples whoever placed them there, artist or Emperor, holy man, or grateful son.
>
> 'Idols. Idols,' say the missionaries at Jehol sadly, those good, kindly folk, whose life seemed to me an apology for living, a dedication of their whole existence to the austere Deity they have set up. But here I was among other gods.[9]

Amongst the temples Mary visited in the Mountain Pleasure Gardens high above the complex was what was known as the 'Temple of the Five Hundred and Eight Golden Buddhas'. There she was shown a huge statue of Guanyin, the Buddhist Goddess of Mercy and beside it rows upon rows of seated Buddhas, covered with gold leaf that shone in the semi-darkness. The temple roof had fallen in,, the hangings were in tatters and the dust of years lay thick on the floor and on the gold leaf covered Buddhas who no one had visited for decades.

Climbing into the bone shaking mule cart Mary ventured even higher into the steep mountains of Inner Mongolia to visit a replica of Lhasa's famous Potala Palace, built by an emperor who had married a Tibetan girl and hoped building this replica would overcome her homesickness. The steps up to the lamaserie were so steep and narrow that Mary had difficulty climbing them but Tuan supported her elbow and a little boy carried her heavy camera. She wrote that she had never seen such steep high walls. This scaled down version of the great Tibetan palace was very imposing and no expense had been spared in its construction. Jehol's copy of the Potala Palace was tiled with gold and its pinkish-red walls formed a striking contrast against the snow capped mountains on the skyline.

The inner temple contained enamelled vases decorated with cloisonné, silken hangings, the golden chair of a Dalai Lama inlaid with lacquer-work, lanterns, incense burners, ' all heaped together in what seemed the wildest confusion. The rich red lacquer had perished, much of the china was broken... and the copper and brass were green with rust.'

The next temple, was a mass of golden brown with green tiles roofs peeped out from among the first and pines... and every bell hanging in the corners of the roofs was chiming musically. I do not know any sweeter sound than those temple bells.'[10] For Mary these temples, 'beautiful beyond dreaming even though their glory has gone,' some of which dated back to the days of Marco Polo were the highlight of her visit to Chengde.

But it was getting late and time to return to the Anglican mission. Even though she was dog tired Mary managed to scramble down the steep steps and climb back into the Peking cart with its lack of springs and be driven past the winding Jehol River and over bumpy ground to the mission compound at Chengde.

✲

In mid June Mary bid farewell to her kind hosts at the Anglican Mission and returned to Peking. To avoid yet another uncomfortable journey in a bruising Peking cart she decided to accompany the missionaries who were going on long leave. They hired boats called *wupan* and were to float down the Lanho also known as the River Luan. Mary l had travel in a mule litter for a distance of eleven kilometres before reaching the Luan River. This was also was a bumpy ride and she felt bruised and sore but consoled herself it was more comfortable than travelling in that torturous and hihgly unstable Peking cart.

> At last we arrived at the river, a broad, swift-flowing, muddy river running along the bottom of the valley and full to the brim… there was not a particle of vegetation to beautify it. There was a crossing here very like the ferrying place I had crossed on my journey up, and there were a row of long boats with one end of them against the bank. It was raining hard when I arrived, and the litter was lifted down from the mules, but the only thing to do was to sit still and await the arrival of Tuan and my baggage in the Peking cart.[11]

Eventually Tuan did arrive and Mary was ready to board the *wupan'*, flat bottomed boat, 10 meters long and 2 meters wide which could be rowed and was fitted with a large cotton sail which at night became a make shift tent for the paying passenger.

From the *wupan* Mary observed rugged mountains, towering over both sides of the river whose steep lopes descended right to the water's edge.

On the second day they reached the heart of the mountains of inner Mngolia and passed through great rocky gorges. Mary described early mornings when .

> … the valley would be wrapped in a soft grey mist, with here and there the highest peaks, rugged and desolate, catching the sunlight; then gradually, gradually, the sun came down the valley and the mists melted before his rays, lingering here and there in the hollows, soft and grey and elusive, till at last the sunlight touched the water and gave this muddy water of the river a golden tint, and all things rejoiced in the new-born day. The little blue kingfishers preened themselves, the blue-grey cranes with

white necks and black points that the Chinese call 'long necks' sailed with outspread wings slowly across the water, and the sunlight on the square sails of the upcoming boats made them gleam snow white. [12]

In the middle of the day the sun beat down on the water and the heat was uncomfortable for all of them . They passed gorge after gorge and the crew had to negotiate dangerous rapids. As they came descended the river so , the hills receded and the country became flatter.

After several enjoyable but cramped days in her *wupan* Mary arrived at the port of Lanchou at the mouth of the river, took the train to Peking and returned to the comfort of the Hotel Wagon-Lits in the Legation Compound.

* * *

By the time Mary was back to Peking it was mid-summer and extremely hot. Many officials attached to foreign legations found refuge from the heat in the Western Hills during the summer, renting accommodation in old and disused temples.

Mary was invited by a friend to stay with her in a house at Tongshan (Tong Xian), on the eastern outskirts of Peking. The house resembled a small fort, because it had been used as a refuge by foreigners during the Boxer Rebellion. It was not a restful place as her hostess had several servants and entertained many friend, so Mary found it hard to concentrate on her writing.

CHAPTER 17

The temple of the Three Mountains

When autumn came Mary returned from her friends' fort-like accommodation at Tongshan to Peking's Hotel Wagon-Lits. By that time she had assembled enough information to write her book *A Woman in China* but needed somewhere quiet and relatively inexpensive where she could spread out her papers and turn her notes into a typed manuscript to send back to her publishers who were waiting for it.

English friends suggested she rent one of the disused temples in Peking's Western Hills, which was a very beautiful area. They found her a delightful place to rent, called the San Shan An, or 'Temple of the Three Mountains'.[1]

Mary rented the disused temple from a priest but had to provide her own furniture, bedding and table linen. There was plenty of room for all her reference books, notes and papers and space to develop her photographs.

The temple, built during the Sung dynasty, was some 30 kilometres from the centre of Peking and an hour's walk from the nearest railway station. It was set among oaks and maple trees and nestled in a hollow on the slopes of a sacred hill.

> …the valley was lovely [in] that autumn weather. Day after day, day after day, was the golden sunshine, the clear, deep blue sky, the still, dry, invigorating air — no wonder everyone with a literary turn yearns to write a book in a valley of the Western Hills. And this valley of the San Shan An was the loveliest valley

of them all. It, too, is a valley of temples, to what gods they were set up I know not, by whom they were set up I know not, only because of the gods and the temples there are trees, trees in plenty, evergreen firs and pines, green-leaved poplars and ash-trees, maples and Spanish chestnuts. At first they were green, these deciduous trees, and then gradually, as autumn touched them tenderly with his fingers, they took on gorgeous tints, gold and brown, and red, and amber, the summer dying gloriously under the cloudless blue sky... I have seen nothing to match this autumn in the Chinese hills and I had not thought to see beauty like this in China![2]

There were several temples in this particular valley but few worshipers. The Temple of the Three Mountains had a large garden in the shadow of Mount Pa-ta-chu, the Holy Mountain. Pilgrims climbed the mountain to make sacrifices to a large ;statue of Buddha, which stood outside one of the temples. On meeting Mary the Pilgrims would bow and smile and seemed pleased that she was living there.

In rural areas hiring servants was cheap and Mary could afford to employ a Chinese 'boy' as a house servant and a male cook. Both were excellent and she was surprised to find that their combined wages plus the rent of the disused temple and all her food cost far less than staying at the Hotel Wagon-Lits. (See plate xxxx)

Mary's book *Alone in West Africa* had been written by hand but in 1912 to make life easier she had brought a portable typewriter with her. She sat at a wooden table under the pergola and typed chapters of *A Woman in China* on the little 'Underwood'.

Like her early married life at Warrnamboul, Mary described her stay at the Temple of the Three Mountains as one of the happiest times in her life. To be able to entertain in style she bought crockery and glasses, had some table linen made out of the inexpensive blue cotton cloth worn by Chinese peasants.

Itinerant vendors arrived carrying their wares in two oval baskets balanced on long poles of split bamboo. Mary remembered seeing Chinese vegetable sellers in Ballarat during her childhood who used similar poles and baskets. The Chinese vendors who had climbed the mountain path to this temple did not sell fresh vegetables. Instead they proffered candied fruits, patties made from fried bean curd and little buns of steamed white dough they called *man-tu*. Other Chinese who made the long climb hoped to earn money by mending broken pots and pans or broken porcelain which they managed to rivet together very skilfully with tiny copper clamps or rivets.

Several of Mary's friends, who worked in Peking, spent weekends with her. One of these friends, whose tour of duty was over towards the end of the year, told Mary he would be happy to take her manuscript to London, so the hazards and delays of the inefficient Chinese postal service would be avoided. The legation official promised to deliver the manuscript in person to her publishers which was a huge weight off Mary's mind, since her letter to the Morrisons had been lost in the post between London and Peking.

A photograph (Plate xx) shows Mary and two friends enjoying an open air meal under the pergola overlooking the surrounding hills. A second pergola overlooked a lily pond where the nightly croaking of frogs at night mingled with the hum of the cicadas. During the day hoopoes and larks joined in a chorus of bird song. Mary enjoyed entertaining friends from the British and other legations and to meals under the pergola and remembered

> ... those sunny days in the mountain temple when we read poetry, and told stories, and dreamed of the better things life held for us in the future! They were good days, days in my life to be remembered, if no more good ever comes to me. Was it the exhilarating air, or the company, or the temple precincts? All thanks give I to those dead gods who gave me, for a brief space, something that was left out of my life.[3]

Kind English friends gave Mary a small fluffy black and white dog, found wandering the streets of Peking, a town where people are not generally kind to stray dogs. She called the dog Buchanan and grew very fond of him. He was a excellent watchdog and Mary was convinced that Buchanan's shrill bark would warn her of any danger. Soon he was allowed to sleep on her bed and became Mary's devoted companion. Her dog would figure in *A Wind from the Wilderness* as McTavish, the much loved little white dog owned by Mary's *alter ego*, Dr Rosalie Gascoigne. a determined woman who finds herself caught up in China's civil war.

At night the isolated Valley of the Three Mountains could be eerie. It was a dangerous time civil war was raging between North and South China and there were rumours that Sun Yatsen's Southern Army might march on Peking, which was defended by President Yuan Shi Kai's troops. Mary had heard many horrific stories of foreigners beheaded or skinned alive during the Boxer Rebellion with fears that similar atrocities could be perpetrated again as foreigners in any future conflict as foreigners were disliked by many of the Chinese. But Mary remembered the family motto 'Gaunts never give up' anmd refused to leave China as she still had a great deal more to explore and hoped to get enough material for a second travel book as well as her novel.

Once Mary's manuscript was typed up and given to the legation official to take to London she had time to concentrate on plans for her return journey across the Gobi desert and along the ancient Silk Road connecting China to Europe which would be the subject of her next travel book.

CHAPTER 18

'Keep your last bullet for yourself'

After three months at the Temple of the Three Mountains, just before Christmas Mary travelled by train to the American mission in Pao Ting Fu (Baoding).

She hoped to spend a considerable amount of time at this mission, run by Doctor Lewis and his wife, the setting for her a novel about a mission doctor who comes to work in China to get away from the small town gossips after being jilted just before her wedding. Rosalie Gascoigne the main character in A Wind from the Wilderness lacks religious faith and like Mary is cynical about organised religion but is a humanitarian . Her reason for coming to the mission is the fact she was jilted by her fiancé just before their wedding and wants to get away from small town gossip. Dr Rosalie Gascoigne has a great deal in common with Mary Gaunt'

Just as George Morrison told Mary to 'Keep your last bullet for yourself' if threatened by the war lord White Wolf so Dr Gascoigne and her companion in distress when the mission is besieged, selfish avaricious Sylvia Chapman, are given the same message when under siege by the brutal henchmen of Mongol war lord, White Wolf.

Mary's observations of the work carried out by doctors at the Baoding Mission hospital is described in detail in her novel.

> Young Chinese girls hiding their eyes from the light, suffering the tortures of in-growing eyelashes, old women gasping with asthma, babies holding to life by a thread' and sores, sores

everywhere, such sores as I never saw in my life.¹

Mary had bought a detailed map of China, which she studied and described her time at the mission station.

> I was living in an American Presbyterian mission station in the western suburb of the walled town of Pao Ting Fu, just beyond European influence... There was plenty to see in Pao Ting Fu, goodness knows. It had suffered severely in the Boxer trouble. In the northern suburb, just about a mile from where we lived, was a tomb, or monument rather, that had been raised to the missionaries massacred then. They have made a garden plot where those burning houses stood, they have planted trees and flowers, and set up memorial tablets in the Chinese style, and the mission has moved to the western suburb, just under the frowning walls of the town, and—is doubly strong... So there in the comfortable mission station I studied the local colour, corrected my last book of China [*A Woman in China*], and instead of continuing to plan a novel [as Mary had intended], looked daily at the atlas of China, till there grew up in me a desire to cross Asia, not by train to the north as I had already done, as thousands of people used to do every year, but by the caravan route, across Shensi and Kansu and Sinkiang to Andijan in Asiatic Russia, the terminus of the Caspian Railway.²

As children, Mary, Ernest and young Guy had planned to follow the Silk Road together.³ But now her brothers were senior naval officers and the world filled with conflict this was impossible. Mary had to fulfil their childhood dream alone. She wrote to George Morrison to ask which was the best of the three ancient Silk Roads to follow.

Morrison wrote back that all three were fascinating, but added the same warning he had given previously when she stayed in his house. She had to cross a very dangerous area when law and order were breaking down. Sadistic bandits in the pay of the war lords who were now taking over and roamed there. To such men rape and murder meant nothing since they regarding human life as cheap.

If Mary insisted on taking such a dangerous journey, Morrison advised her to visit en route the walled city of Hsi An Fu (Xi'an), former capital city of the Tang dynasty which had a magnificent imperial palace, now partially ruineds which she must see.

X'ian had once been one of the most splendid cities in the ancient world but in 1913 the entombed warriors had not yet been excavated so he did not mention them. From X'ian Mary should take the most southerly of the Silk Road through the Taklamakan Desert into the Gobi which was surrounded by snow covered mountains which made this an unforgettable experience — if she survived.

Mary's friends at the Baoding Mission echoed Morrison's warning — the murderous thugs and bandits in the area were as cruel as the Boxers. Pai Lang (White Wolf) employed henchmen, notorious for raping female prisoners before torturing and murdering them.

But not everybody was negative about her proposed desert journey. Mary was introduced to the British botanist and botanical artist, Reginald Farrer and his associate, William Purdom, who were staying at Pao Ting Fu at the time and aiming to collect specimens of flowering plants of north-eastern China to introduce to British nursery gardens. They loved Outer Mongolia and Ithe desert and were sending samples of plants and seeds back to Kew Gardens and planned to write an illustrated book about the plants and flowers found there.

One night Farrer and Purdom invited Mary to have dinner with them. As she told the two botanists about her plans, they declared that, if Mary was prepared for discomfort and hardship, she should undertake her journey and provided her with useful information about travelling through the western regions of China.

Reassured by the advice from Farrer and Purdom, Mary made the necessary preparations for the journey across the Loess Plateau to Hsi An Fu and along the most southerly of the three Silk Routes to Lan Chow Fu (Lanzhou) by mule cart and camel. Fascinated by deserts she hoped to cross part of the Gobi Desert, home of Mongolian horseman who had once terrorized the area from the Yellow River to the Danube.

When Mary outlined her plan to the missionaries at Pao Ting Fu they were pessimistic — one woman missionary said, 'If I wanted to die I'd choose an easier way of doing it!' The only person at the mission fascinated by Mary's proposed trip was Doctor Lewis, who said he would have loved to join her, if only his patients did not need him so badly.

By now Mary had enough of Tuan and his 'squeeze' or secret commissions. She needed a honest tour manager who was a hard worker and a good organiser. He had to be strong enough to lift her into a mule litter and help her down, which was not easy for someone of her age.

The missionaries said they knew just the man for the job, a convert who came from Northern China who had previously worked as a stone mason and was tall and immensely strong. Mary had doubts about hiring Mr Wang again as his English was poor. Unfortunately, at that time good interpreters were hard to come by in China and Mr Wang was the only applicant for the job. Mr Wang, who wore a long blue cotton gown buttoned to his feet, responded even to the simplest remark with 'repeat, pliss' and always ended every phrase with a giggle.

Mary packed her clothes in cloth bags because these were easier to load onto pack mules than a tin trunk. She was determined not to be separated from Buchanan, her faithful little dog.

> Buchanan was a great comfort beside me to me under these circumstances. He had recovered from his accident [having been bitten by a much larger dog] before we left Fen Chou Fu. One thing he declined to do, and that was to walk with the servants unless I walked too, when he became wild with delight.
>
> And if anyone thinks I make an absurd fuss about a little dog, I must remind him that I was entirely alone among an alien people, and the dog's affection meant a tremendous lot to me. He took away all sense of loneliness. Looking back, I know now I

could not have gone on; this book would never have been written, if it had not been for Buchanan.[4]

For her journey Mary had written to various mission stations along her route, telling them of her plans and offering to pay something towards the work of the missions, in return for their hospitality.

She had sent a telegram to the mission at Hsi An Fu (Xi'an), the scene of mass murders of missionaries and Christian converts by the Boxers, several years ago. The missionaries who had replaced those murdered in the Boxer Rebellion, warned her by telegram, 'Do *not* come here. Hsi An Fu threatened by White Wolf'.

Mary took this warning seriously and considered taking a different route to Lan chou fu (Lanzhou), the capital of Kansu. It was a shorter but a far more hazardous route via Fen Chou Fu (Fenyuan), Yung Ning Chow (Lishi) and then across the Yellow River to Sui Te Chou (Suide). From there it would be another 800 kilometres to Lan Chou Fu.

※※※

Once Mary had made her decision she prepared for the long and arduous journey west. In early spring 1914 she went by train to T'ai Yuan Fu (Taiyuan — the word 'Fu' being the Chinese for provincial capital), an ancient walled city at the end of the railway line. She wrote,

> I was met at the station by some of the ladies of the English Baptist Mission who had come to welcome me and to offer me, a total stranger to them, kindly hospitality, and we walked through the gate to the mission inside the walls. It was only a short walk, short and dusty, but it was thronged. All the roadway was crowded with rickshaws and carts waiting in a long line their turn to go underneath the gateway over which frowned a typical many-roofed Chinese watch tower, and as cart or rickshaw came up, the men along with it were stopped by the dusty soldiers in black and grey and interrogated as to their business... The ladies [of the Baptist Mission] lived in a Chinese house close under the

walls. There is a great charm about these houses built round courtyards in the Chinese style; there is always plenty of air and sunshine, though, as most of the rooms open into the courtyard only, I admit in rough weather they must sometimes be awkward.[5]

T'ai Yuan Fu (Taiyuan, capital of Shanxi province) did not welcome foreigners, especially women travelling solo. Mary was warned by the missionaries she was at risk when venturing outside the walls of the Baptist mission station. A European woman travelling by herself, even in a palanquin or mule litter, could easily be attacked. In the streets of T'ai Yuan where she felt herself an alien, she was glared at by those who disapproved of Western women and muttered curses at her.

Aware of the dislike of foreigners and how many missionaries had been murdered here by the Boxers in July 1900, Mary who out of respect for the missionaries and their beliefs who disliked swearing (something Mary did in moments of stress as did her heroine Rosalie Gascoigne) dressed very modestly in a high necked long sleeved blouse and long skirt.

Mary knew that travelling without a husband or a brother, outraged traditional Chinese ideas of the role of women. The Chinese believed women should remain at home and never travel without a male family member to accompany them. T'ai Yuan Fu (now Taiyuan) was a remote and backward place.

> 'This town,' said the missionaries, 'is anti-progressive and anti-foreign.' You feel somehow the difference in the attitude of the people the moment you set foot inside the walls. It seems to me that if trouble really came it would be an easy matter to seize the railway and cut off the foreign missionaries from all help, for it is at least a fortnight away in the mountains.[6]

Mary feared that, if trouble erupted, a similar massacre to the one that took place during the Boxer Rebellion could happen again.

On 27 July 1900, forty men and women working at Taiyuan

mission station and three dozen children, all Chinese converts to Christianity had been murdered by the swords of the Boxers. The missionaries who replaced those who had been murdered showed Mary the doorway where a mission teacher called Miss Coombs was hacked to pieces while trying to protect her pupils from the swords of the Boxers who hacked the younger children to pieces, watched in horror by the older children. Ignoring the girls' sobs and pleas for mercy these Boxer soldiers gang raped them and the rest of the female mission staff before beheading them.[7]

What amazed Mary was that after so many murders, missionaries were still leaving America and Britain to serve at the Catholic and Baptist Missions in T'ai Yuan. Both missions ran schools and orphanages. Hearing the terrible stories of the massacres that had taken place gave Mary new respect for the bravery of the mission doctors and teachers. Baptised as Anglican, the Gaunt family had always attended church on Sunday mornings, but the subject of religion was taken for granted and never discussed at home and certainly none of their family prayed aloud or witnessed to their faith out loud, as they did at the Baptist Missions. Initially Mary found praying out loud very embarrassing but gradually came to accept the missionaries believed they were talking aloud to Jesus since He was so much a part of the their every day lives. She admired the work they were doing helping sick and poverty stricken Chinese. She described how many Chinese were confused by the many different Christian sects who all offered them salvation claiming they were the true faith.

> There are many missions in China, and I often feel that if the Chinaman were not by nature a philosopher he would sometimes be a little confused by salvation offered him by foreigners of all sects and classes, ranging from Roman Catholics to Seventh Day Adventists… The Chinaman, to begin with, sees no necessity for his own conversion, he neither admires nor envies the white man, and is given to thinking his own ways are infinitely preferable. But the Chinaman is a man of sound common-sense, he immensely admires efficiency, he is a great believer in education, and when a mission comes to him fully equipped with doctors,

nurses and hospitals, teachers and schools, he, once he has overcome his dread of anything new, begins to avail himself first of the doctor and the hospital, for the sore need of China is for medical attendance, and then of the schools. Then comes conversion. They tell me that there are many genuine converts.[8]

⁂

Missionaries helped Mary to obtain two mule drivers plus four mules and a donkey, which were to take her across the 1600 kilometres that lay between T'ai Yuan and Lan chow the capital of Gansu province. She paid only eighteen pounds for the cost of two men to take four heavily laden mules and a donkey 1600 kilometres and then travel back along the same route. Mary realized that money went a long way in China.

After her stay at T'ai Yuan Mary travelled a short distance by train to Yu Tze (Yuci), a small town along the railway line to Peking. Her support team had left the previous day for Yu Tze. Mary was intending to travel most of the way in a mule litter, but no litter was available in Yu Tze, so her journey to her next destination, Taiku, turned out to be most uncomfortable. She tried to sit on a chair on the back of a mule, precariously perched on top of the luggage. The chair had no cushioned seat and a rope from it was bound around the belly of the mule. Mary, dressed in her long skirt and high button boots, was hoisted by her porters onto the pack on top of the mule, who disliked this arrangement just as much as Mary and succeeded in throwing her off.

She had no choice but remounting, but Mary regarded that to sit on a mule in a bamboo chair, tied to the top of the pack, was the worst form of transport. By the time they reached the town, Mary was badly bruised by jolting over stony tracks. She wrote,

> I know of no more uncomfortable method. It is not as comfortable as sitting upon a table with one's legs dangling, for the table remains still, the mule is moving, and one's legs dangle on either side of his neck. There are neither reins nor stirrups, and the mule goes at his own sweet will, and in a short time your back begins

to ache, after a few hours that aching is intolerable. To get over this difficulty the missionary had cut the legs off a chair and suggested that, mounted on the pack, I might sit in it comfortably. [But] the mule objected.

It was a sunny morning with a bright blue sky above, and all seemed auspicious except my mule, who expressed in no measured language his dislike to that chair. ...my mule reared on his hind legs and pawed the air with my chair at a perilous angle. He was a true Chinese mule and objected to innovations but stood meekly enough once the chair was removed.

I wanted to cross Asia and was faced with disaster at the outset! Finally I was put upon the pack minus the chair, Buchanan was handed up to me and the procession started.[9]

Having learned to ride as a child, Mary would have travelled on horseback, but mindful of Morrison's words about riding astride being seen as obscene in a woman refrained from dong this. Morrison had warned that riding astride horse or a mule would imperil the success of her journey and degrade her in the eyes of the porters and mule drivers and in China, a woman with her legs astride an animal was regarded as pleasuring herself in an immoral way. If Mary did this she would be the subject of coarse jokes among the mule drivers and lose her authority over them. Riding side-saddle was not an option for Mary not side-saddles were available — traditionally ladies were carried in palanquins or litters and horse riding was reserved for high status men.

Despite her discomfort, she reached the mission at Taiku before nightfall. The following day Mary and her party set off in south-westerly direction to Ping Yow (Pingyoa). They had hardly travelled two kilometres when Mary's back was so sore she could no longer put up with sitting on a chair on the back of a mule. They returned to the mission, where Mary obtained a primitive kind of litter, to be carried between two mules. Between the long poles hung a rope netting, covered by a canvas tilt. The contraption was carried between two mules, one in front and one at the back. Mary's tour master told her this was the safest way to travel through the wilds of rural China, because White Wolf and his thugs would not be able to see she was a women and foreign. Mary wrote,

> ...it cannot be repeated too often that as a conveyance a mule litter leaves much to be desired. Sitting up there on my bedding among my cushions, with James Buchanan beside me, I was much more comfortable than I should have been in a Peking cart, but also I was much more helpless... The missionaries had told me whenever I came to a bad place to be sure and get out, because the Chinese mules are not surefooted enough to be always trusted. They are quite likely at a bad place to slip and go over. This was a cheering reflection when I found myself at the bad place abandoned to the tender mercies of those animals. The mule in the lead certainly was a capable beast, but again and again, as I told Mr Wang, I would have preferred that the muleteers should not put quite so much faith in him...
>
> The only advice I can give to anyone who wishes to follow in my footsteps is to shut his eyes and trust the mule. We went down some slopes so steep they were calculated to take the curl out of my hair.[10]

Ping Yow was a crowded ugly town, surrounded by wheat-growing country. Mary found accommodation on a Baptist mission, and met the missionary's wife who came from a town in Victoria near Chilton, Mary's birthplace and learned that the poorer Chinese suffocated unwanted female babies at birth and then left the little corpses out on the hillsides to be devoured by wild dogs.[11]

After a few days stay at the Ping Yow mission, Mary continued her journey to the four-thousand-year-old hill town of Fen Chou Fu (Fenyang), where she had arranged to stay at the American mission run by Protestant missionaries from Oberlin College, Ohio.

> I came into Fen Chou Fu and went straight to the large compound of the American missionaries, three men and three

> women from Oberlin College, Ohio. They had a hospital, they had a school, they had a kindergarten, the whole compound was a flourishing centre of industry. They teach their faith, for that is what they have come out for, but also they teach the manifold knowledge of the West. Sanitation and hygiene loom large in their curriculum, and heaven knows, without taking into consideration any future life, they must be a blessing to those men and women who under cruel conditions must see this life through. These six missionaries at Fen Chou Fu do their best to improve those conditions with a practical American common-sense and thoroughness that won my admiration.[12]

Mary was told by the missionaries (who had replaced the murdered ones) that the Boxers arrived there in 1900 and declared that all foreigners had to die, because they regarded them as evil. The local people liked the American missionaries who had been very kind to them and did not want the Boxers to behead them within the walls of their city. So Boxer troops took the missionaries seven miles outside the city and butchered them there. To Mary this showed how the citizens of Fen Chou Fu managed to square their conscience and avoided 'blood guilt'.

Despite the massacre that had taken place, Mary felt safe in Fen Chou Fu where t the people were much friendlier than in other towns she had visited on her journey.

> In Fen Chou Fu I could have walked about the town alone unmolested. I never did, because it would have been undignified and often awkward, as I could not speak the language, but the people were invariably friendly.[13]

Mary also attended a wedding at Fen Chou Fu in order to describe the intricacies of a Chinese wedding on a mission station. In company of one of the missionaries she walked on top of the old crumbling town walls and enjoyed the beautiful spring weather but realised that the walls could subside during or after heavy rainfall.

But walls, if often a protection, are sometimes a danger in more ways than in shutting out the fresh air. The summer rains in North China are heavy, and Fen Chou Fu holds water like a bucket. The only outlets are the narrow gateways, and the waters rise and rise. A short time before I came there all the eastern quarter of the town was flooded, the water so deep that a woman was drowned. At last the waters escaped through the eastern gate, only to be banked up by the great ash-heaps, the product of centuries, the waste rubbish of the town, that are just outside the wall of the eastern suburb. It took a long, long while for those flood waters to percolate through the gateway of the suburb and find a resting-place at last in a swamp the other side of that long-suffering town. I must confess that this is one of the drawbacks to a walled town that has never before occurred to me, though to stand there and look at those great gates, those solid walls, made me feel as if I had somehow wandered into the fourth dimension, so out of my world were they.[14]

After staying at the American Mission at Fen Chou Fu for several days, Mary and her porters had to cross a steep mountain range to reach Yung Ning Chow and the eastern part of the Loess Plateau with its rich yellowish-red soil, known as 'loess'.

Most little inns on the way had been built underground and were little more than caves, often with high-sounding names such as 'The Inn of Increasing Righteousness' and 'The Inn of Ten Thousand Conveniences'. The latter was a *yandong* or cave dwelling with a floor of beaten earth. In the one and only room the landlord, his wife and guests had to sleep together and the landlord claimed that *yandongs* were cool in summer and warm in winter. All these uncomfortable inns between Fen Chou Fu and Yung Ning Chou were crowded with mule drives and peasants. The roads outside were littered with mule and donkey packs and inside the courtyard all was hustle and bustle.

To allow oncoming traffic to pass, the narrow road through the Loess Plain had been widened at certain intervals. All villages busy open stalls, were jammed together in the main street. There was no greenery, apart from a few trees, and gardens did not exist. The streets were full of ragged men and children — the men wearing ragged garments in varying shades of blue. Mary saw few young women although elderly women sat on their doorstep in the sun.

As Mary passed down the street, everybody stopped talking and stared at her, because 'foreigners are scarce as snow in summer in that area of China'.

After Mary and her team had passed through the vast Loess Plateau they followed a tributary of the Yellow River up into the mountains. They passed many caravans — strings of ragged camels, strings of pack-mules and still long strings of little donkeys. Mary saw men with bamboo poles across their shoulders with heavy loads slung from either end. Some of them had come from Peking and were bound for the province of Kansu, the other side of Shensi (Shaanxi).

Mary noticed that the heavily laden donkeys and mules were coming from the east, while the pack-saddles of those going west were empty. According to her interpreter, Chinese merchants were reluctant to send goods across the Yellow River into turbulent Shensi fearing they would be stolen. Mary realised that, if she continued her journey into Shensi, she could be stopped by *tufeis*, the local term for robbers and bandits. Nevertheless, she determined to continue her journey and before crossing the Yellow River, find out more about the situation in Shensi.

After the mountains came a high stony plateau, difficult to navigate because every step had to be carefully chosen among the stones. They had to cross many mountain streams with an occasional bridge but generally they had to wade across, which Mary found uncomfortable in long clinging skirts and boots.

At last, after crossing a long bridge across a river, they arrived at Yung Ning Chow (Lishi) which had its narrow, stony streets. Mary went to stay at the Scandinavian mission, run by two missionaries — the other missions were scattered over the mountains to the north.

The following day Mary and her team set off again and arrived at a village called Liu Lin Chen, where she learned more about the movements of the war lord Pai Lang, (White Wolf). Mr Wang, came to Mary and told her that the two mule drivers, who accompanied him, had stated that the gates of Sui Te Chou (Suide) had been closed for the last four days by the townsfolk, terrified of an attack by White Wolf and his cruel henchmen who had murdered hundreds of peasants and taken what few goods they possessed.

Sui Te Chou was the first town Mary proposed to visit after crossing the Yellow River. The only way to get to Lan Chou Fu and beyond was via Sui Te Chou. Mary realised that straying from the main caravan road was impossible so she had to abandon her plan to travel further west into Shensi. But to turn tail at this point, only 40 kilometres from the Yellow River, was anathema e — Gaunts never give up so her father and her eldest brothers claimed so neither would she.

Mary was determined to see this great river before she turned her tracks to avoid being killed by White Wolf's henchmen.

> Almost immediately we left the village [Liu Lin Chen] we began to ascend the mountain pass. Steeper and steeper it grew, and at last the opening in my mule litter was pointing straight up to the sky, and I, seeing there was nothing else for it, demanded to be lifted out and signified my intention of walking.
>
> There was one thing against this and that was an attack of breathlessness. Asthma always attacks me when I am tired or worried, and now, with a very steep mountain to cross and no means of doing it except on my own feet, it had its wicked way… It was hard work, very hard work. When I could go no longer I sat down and waited till I felt equal to starting again.
>
> On one hand the mountain rose up sheer and steep, on the other it dropped away into the gully beneath, only to rise again on the other side. I cannot imagine how man or beast kept a footing on such a slant, and how they ploughed and sowed it passes my understanding. …at the top of the pass was a tunnel bored through it [the mountain], a tunnel perhaps a hundred feet

long, carefully bricked. We, breathless and panting, walked through it and came out on a plateau [Loess Plateau] with a narrow road wandering down a mountain-side as steep as the one we had just climbed.

The hills rose up on either hand and away in the distance; where they opened out were the beautiful treeless hills of forbidden Shensi [Shaanxi], just as alluring, just as peaceful as the hills I had come through. It was worth the long and toilsome journey.

Then we went down, down, but I did not dare get into my litter, the way was too steep, the chances of going over too great, for it seems the Chinese never make a road if by any chance they can get along without. They were driven to bore a tunnel through the mountains, but they never smooth or take away rocks as long as an animal can pass without the certainty of going over the cliff. The dust itself was yellow here.

And at last through a cleft in the hills I saw the Yellow River, one of the world's great rivers [not yellow but muddy brown]. The setting was ideal. The hills rose up steep and rugged, real mountains, on either side, pheasants called, rock-doves mourned, magpies chattered, overhead was a clear blue sky just flecked here and there with fleecy clouds, beyond again were the mountains of Shensi [Shaanxi], the golden sunlight on their rounded tops, purple shadow in their swelling folds, far away in the distance they melted into the blue sky. Close at hand they were green with the green of springtime, save where the plough had just turned up patches of yellowish-brown soil. At their feet rolled a muddy flood, the mighty Hoang-Ho, the Yellow River, China's sorrow.[15]

The phrase 'China's sorrow' referred to the fact the Yellow River transported the soft yellowish fertile silt of the Loess plateau away from the areas where peasants needed it to grow rice to feed their families. Instead of helping the peasants, 'China's Sorrow' carried the precious yellow silt down to the sea or in a dry season the fine silt was blown away as fine dust.

Fort 2,000 years the Yellow River had killed many farmers

when it flooded and changed course many times. This mighty river had brought wealth to those who owned the fertile silt along the riverbanks, but when the river changed course it left small farmers without access to water and unable to grow the rice that kept their families from starving. When times were really bad the only way some families survived was by selling a child into slavery.

Near the Yellow River dirt-poor Chinese families had lived for hundreds of years in the caves in the rocks known as *yaodongs*, overlooking the Loess Plateau. Some caves had window frames fitted into holes in the front of the cave.

As Mary and her team descended into the valley of the Yellow River they arrived at an old temple which had been taken over by soldiers of the People's Republic of China. These shabby-looking soldiers in blue ill fitting unifpr,s swarmed around Mary and demanded to search her baggage for guns. She remembered George Morrison telling her that when he made a long journey across southern China he had givem the impression he was a very famous person and had no trouble with Chinese soldiers.

Mary mentioned that a relative of hers, Dr Morrison of Morrison Street in Peking, was a good friend of President Yuan Shih Kai. Hearing the name of the President of China, the soldiers became friendly and refrained from searching Mary or her baggage.

As they went further down towards the Yellow River her team had to follow a rocky paths, which Mary described as 'reeking of human occupancy'— a ladylike way of saying the paths were used as lavatories by soldiers who were guarding the area.

At last Mary arrived at the bank of the Yellow River. She took one more good look at the river, her farthest point west on the journey. It was so peaceful in the afternoon sunlight and it seemed foolish not to continue. The hills of Shensi beckoned and she wanted to carry on with her journey and see the desert. But reason prevailed. To continue would be madness —the *tufeis or* amred bandits of d White Wolf were swarming all over Shensi. They had had captured several cities, shot or beheaded the most prominent citizens , raped their wives and stolen money from the banks. If they found a European women her end would be very unpleasant.

CHAPTER 19

Last days in China

Mary had to come to terms with the fact that she had failed to reach her goal. She came from a family who despised failure. So as she retraced her footsteps that horrid word 'failure' kept ringing in her ears.

However, Mary did not want to give up altogether and considered an alternative route — to make her way back along the great waterways of Siberia. There were mighty rivers there and they could prove very interesting. On her way back to Fen Chou Fu and T'ai Yuan Fu Mary pondered ways and means by which she might penetrate Siberia.

At T'ai Yuan Fu Mary met the missionary, Dr Edwards, who had written a letter to her before she started her journey to Lan Chou Fu Dr Edwards had been on his way to collect medical supplies from Xi An Fu, but due to the threats of White Wolf and his gang he had turned back. In his letter he had warned Mary against continuing across the Silk Road. He thanked God that she had returned unharmed, realising that to reach Lan Chou Fu would have been impossible.

A few days later Mary met up with the celebrated botanist Reginald Farrer, author of a book on the wild flowers of China. Farrer, as a fellow author had been interested in Mary's progress and told her, 'I often wondered what became of you and how you had got on. We thought perhaps you might have fallen into the hands of White Wolf and then…' He paused, not wanting to utter the terrible words 'raped and murdered'.

Reginald Farrer told Mary that Shensi was seething with bandits and it would have meant death to cross those seemingly peaceful hills.

At T'ai Yuan Fu Mary paid Mr Wang's fare back to Pao Ting Fu and was happy to see the last of him. In her book *A Broken Journey* she wrote, 'There may be worse interpreters in China, but I hope there not many!.'

When Mary returned to the American Mission at Pao Ting Fu [Baoding], the missionaries were delighted to see her alive and said she had been wise to alter her plans and return. She spent several weeks with the missionaries and during that time her plans to travel north-east to the Russian border and beyond crystallised. She decided it would be interesting to take a boat along the River Amur, part of which forms the border between China and Russia and few Westerners had visited the area.

She intended to travel to Tientsin (Tianjin) and from there take the train via Harbin to Vladivostok. Following she would take the train to Khabarovsk to start her river cruise on the Amur, go downstream o Nikolayevsk at the mouth of the river and after visiting the island of Sakhalin return to Khabarovsk and continue further upstream to Blagoveshchensk.

She would return to England by train through Siberia, visit St Petersburgh and travel through Finland and Sweden and catch a boat to England.

Mary was lucky to be invited by Dr Lewis and his wife to join them on their journey aboard a large house boats to the important city of Tientsin (Tianjin). Their predecessors at Pao-Ting Fu had been murdered by the Boxers so fearing repeat attacks by a militant group called The Elder Bretheren, who also hated foreigners they decided to take long leave. As civil war between the reformists and those who supported President Yuan was raging, law and order had broken down.

. The group left the mission station and on the river just outside the south gate of Pao Ting Fu embarked on *wupans*, house boats with cabins made out of canvas.

> Dr and Mrs Lewis and their children had the largest, with their servants, and we made arrangements to eat together on board their boat. Miss Newton and a friend had another, with more of the servants, and I, like a millionaire, had one all to myself. I had parted with the master of transport at Pao Ting Fu, but Hsu Sen, one of the Lewis's servants, waited upon me and made up my bed...
>
> They were pleasant days we spent meandering down the river. We passed by little farms, we passed by villages, by fishing traps, by walled cities. Hsi An Fu, with the water of the river flowing at the foot of its castellated walls, was like a city of romance, and when we came upon little marketplaces by the water's edge the romance deepened, for we knew then how the people lived. Sometimes we paused and bought provisions; sometimes we got out and strolled along the banks in the pleasant summer weather. Never have I gone a more delightful or more unique voyage. And at last we arrived at Tientsin and I parted from my friends, and they went on to Pei Ta Ho and I to Astor House to prepare for my journey east and north.[1]

Tientsin was the second largest city in northern China and like Peking had a special compound where foreigners were allowed to live. To celebrate the fact she was still alive instead of murdered by White Wolf's men, she splurged out and stayed at The Astor Hotel, the best in the city where they kindly allowed t Buchanan to sleep in her room.

Mary enjoyed her stay in Tientsin — she felt safe there and this cosmopolitan trading centre and ic city gave her a delightful feeling of adventure.

After a short stay she boarded the train for Mukden (Shenyang) where she spent the night in a Japanese owned hotel. She was surprised that the Japanese seemed to own and run almost everything in Mukden, even the train on which Mary and her dog departed the following day was Japanese owned.

She had been told that dogs were allowed on the train, so was annoyed when an official from the Japanese rail company grabbed Buchanan and, ignoring her protests, placed the little dog in a filthy box in the luggage compartment. From her own compartment Mary could hear poor Buchanan howling in protest.

The conductor on the next train she caught bound for Harbin said that dogs *were* allowed in the compartment. Mary was amazed when a Chinese soldier wearing the ragged uniform of the republican army threw a cushion on top of Buchanan just before a ticket inspector arrived. Fortunately the inspector did not see the little dog hidden under the cushion.

On the train Mary learned that Harbin, although a Chinese city, had a huge Russian population, many of them Jews who had fled there from pogroms and persecution in Russia. All the street signs in that crowded cosmopolitan town were in Russian and Chinese. Harbin was a lawless place where Chinese or as Russian brigands could rob and kill you without remorse. Mary was glad she had her Smith and Wesson in her bag.

Holding Buchanan and her bag Mary stepped down onto the platform. A man tapped her arm and said something she could not understand: she recognised the Chinese soldier who had hidden Buchanan from the ticket inspector, clearly expecting a tip. Mary's money had run out but not speaking Chinese could not explain this to him and felt embarrassed.

A middle aged man who spoke with a *mittel* European accent, seeing Mary looking lost, enquired politely 'Does ze English lady vant a hotel?'

The European told her his name was Polonteszky, a native of Poland and a courier for the Grand Hotel. Mary explained she had a dog that she could not leave. He told her he had a small house which was far cheaper than the Grand Hotel and he and his wife would be happy to have a dog to stay. Mary replied she would like to accept his offer but had run out of money. She could not withdraw any more until the Hong Kong and Shanghai Bank opened the following morning.

Mr Polonteszsky smiled and replied,

'No matter, *chere madame*, pay me later.'

He added his name was difficult for English speaking people to pronounce so they called him 'Mr Poland'. Would she like to see his house? The Chinese soldier who had hidden Buchanan under the cushion was hovering around, still expecting a tip. Embarrassed Mary asked 'Mr Poland' if she could borrow a rouble. He gave one to the soldier, who smiled, thanked them and went away satisfied.

Mary and Mr Poland climbed into a ramshackle horse drawn *droshky* and were driven through the streets of Harbin to his home.

Mary was lucky in her choice as though Harbin was full of desperate characters, rogues and thieves, Mr Poland and his wife were very honest and kind and did their best to make Mary comfortable and help her.

> ...they gave me a fairly large room with a bed in it, a chair, a table and a broken-down wardrobe that would not open. 'Mr Poland' had the family washing cleared out of the bath, so that I bathed amidst the fluttering damp garments of his numerous progeny, but still there was a bath and a bath heater that could be made to produce hot water; and if it was rather a terrifying machine to be locked up with at close quarters, still it did aid me to arrive at a certain degree of cleanliness.[2]

The day after Mary arrived at Harbin she went to see Mr Sly, the British consul, who thought that she was in need of a loan. Mary was amused and said hastily: 'I'm *not* a distressed British subject and I *don't* want any money.'

Mr Sly happened to know a naval captain named Gaunt. (probably Captain Ernest Gaunt). As a result the British consul asked Mary to dinner and introduced her to the elite of the area. He drove her around to see the sights in his carriage and they ended the evening with a party of friends in the public gardens.

The gardens at Harbin were beautiful — the paths were lined with lamps and there were open-air restaurants. Bands were playing and excellent ice-creams and drinks of all descriptions were for sale. There were crowds of cheerily dressed people —

Mary felt it resembled Monte Carlo in the heart of Central Asia. She discovered that Harbin in summer is very hot while the winter is bitterly cold and the temperature often drops to 30° C below zero. The town had wide streets with houses and gardens and many vacant spaces and Mary was reminded of many outback towns in Australia.

※

Mary prepared herself to go east to Vladivostok first and then north into Siberia. She asked advice of both the British consul and her self-appointed courier 'Mr Poland' who she now trusted absolutely.

> Certainly he took care of me, and the day before I started east he handed me over to his wife and suggested she should take me to the market and buy necessaries for my journey. It was only a little over twenty-four hours so it did not seem to me a matter of much consequence, but I felt it would be interesting to walk through the market. It was.
>
> My Polish Jewess [Mrs Poland] and I laboured under the usual difficulty of language, but she made me understand I had better buy a basket for my provisions, a plate, a knife, a fork—I had left these things behind in China, not thinking I should want them. No self-respecting person, according to her, would dream of travelling in Siberia without at least a couple of kettles. I laid in two of blue enamel ware and I am bound to say I blessed her forethought many and many a time.
>
> Then we proceeded to buy provisions. Mrs Poland engaged a stray Chinaman, to carry our goods. I thought she was provisioning her family against a siege or that perhaps there was only one market a month in Harbin... We bought bread in large quantities, ten cucumbers, two pounds of butter, two pounds of cream in large earthenware jars, two dozen bananas, ten eggs and two pounds of tea. And then I discovered these were provisions for *my* journey to Vladivostok, twenty-seven hours away!
>
> I never quite knew why I bought provisions as the train stopped at stations where there were restaurants even though

there was no restaurant car attached to the train.³

On her trip to Vladivostok Mary had a comfortable second-class carriage to herself. At every station a conductor appeared and asked her if she wanted boiling water to make tea or coffee. Mrs Poland had provided more than enough food to last Mary for her twenty-seven-hours' journey.

The train steamed east through the wooded hills of Manchuria, covered with lush green grass and multi-coloured wildflowers. The sky was deep-blue and the fresh dry air that entered through the open window of the carriage invigorated Mary. As she looked out over the surrounding countryside she got the impression that the Manchus were as industrious as the Chinese — the crops in the fields as carefully tended as those in China

When night came, Mary made herself as comfortable as possible, spread out her rugs and cushions, took off her clothes and put on the silken kimono that had been such a bargain at the Harbin market.

By the following afternoon the train was approaching the Siberian border. Mary saw Chinese and Manchu people at railway stations who looked more like Russians — they still wore pigtails, but had belted Russian blouses and top-boots, and mingled amongst flaxen-haired, blue-eyed Russians wearing similar attire.

By the time the train steamed into Vladivostok it was evening. The name made her think wistfully of her brother Ernest who years earlier had sent her postcards from Vladivostok Harbour, where the Russian fleet was quartered in summer. As part of the British-China fleet he had paid several visits to this large port.

In winter the magnificent northerly harbour froze over and before this happened the Russian fleet would sail south and establish their winter quarters outside Nice in the beautiful harbour of Villefrance where Mary had seen their ships during winters spent in the south of France.

Now she was thrilled to see that the British Fleet was visiting Vladivostock Harbour. Ships flying the white ensign made her remember how decades ago Ernest and Guy had been midshipmen serving with the British fleet.[4] How she wished her brothers were here now. But at least she had Buchanan to keep her company. She wandered around with her little dog making notes for her book *A Broken Journey*, describing this magnificent port, Russia's only outlet to the Pacific Ocean as

> ...a beautifully situated town set in the hills alongside a narrow arm of the grey sea. The hills around were covered with the luxuriant green of midsummer, a land where it is winter almost until June. The principal buildings in Vladivostok are all along the shore lined with all manner of craft. The British fleet had come on a visit, and grey and grim the ships lay there on the grey sea, like a Turner watercolour and for a dash of colour, the flew brightly coloured Union Jacks.
>
> Mr Sly who I had met at Harbin insisted that I should see the Russian port... whose shores were edged with grey mist, and all the old forgotten ships of wood, the ships that perhaps were sailed by my grandfather in the old East India Company.
>
> Large wooden ships were drawn up against the shore or they were going down the bay with their sails set, and the sunlight breaking through the clouds touched the white sails and made them mountains of snow. There was shipbuilding going on too, for there were huge stands of timber in the forests behind the town. There were fishing-boats, hundreds of them close against each other along the shore, and on all the small ships, at the mastheads, were little fluttering white flags. [I learned that] the ships of sealers would soon go up to the seal rookeries to bring away the pelts of the seals.[5]

After staying in Vladivostok for several days, Mary embarked on the thirty-hour train trip to the Russian river port of Kharbarosvk. She travelled first class — the fares were reasonable and, once again had a carriage to herself. At railway stations she saw many Russian soldiers as well as peasants in belted blouses with embroidered collars, most had few teeth but many wore large fur hats. (Plate xxs)

Mary greatly enjoyed the scenery and after travelling through teeming China found the Siberian countryside strangely empty. Most of it was virgin land, practically uninhabited until the Russian Government populated it with a large number of Cossacks. Nevertheless, in the early twenties century the population was still very low.

The wood-fired steam train rumbled through the vast pine forests, so typical of Siberia. In one of the wooded valleys Mary saw clouds of thick blue smoke and when darkness fell distant hills were outlined by flames. In summer bushfires are common in these pine forests and noticed that fire brakes had been made at certain intervals.

CHAPTER 20

Exploring the Amur River and Saghalien

After two days and one night the train arrived at Khabarosvk railway station. Mary intended to make her initial cruise on the Amur River downstream to the mouth of the river, so her first priority was booking a cabin on the steamship *John Cockerill*, which would leave the following evening.
She went to the best hotel in town, run by a German, booked a room and had an excellent meal in the hotel's restaurant. From the windows of her room she could see the Amur, one of the world's greatest rivers. The wide expanse of water was clear as glass and sparkled in the sunshine.

The following evening Mary, with her little black and white dog hidden in a shopping basket, boarded the *John Cockerill*. She was pleasantly surprised to find the ship very comfortable, with a dining saloon and a lounge upholstered in dark green velvet. The steamer was divided into four classes, all packed with passengers — Russians occupied the first, second and third class, along with an occasional German or Japanese businessman and some government officials. Mary's cabin was in second class while the third and fourth classes consisted of a mixture of Russians, Chinese and Mongolians with their long black hair and bushy black beards. Before nightfall the ship steamed towards Nikolayevsk at the mouth of the Amur River, which was a three-day voyage.

Three or four times a day the *John Cockerill* pulled up at some little riverside port, generally only consisting of two or three log-houses with painted doors or windows. There they loaded large quantities of wood, needed to fuel the ship.

> ...it was delightful moving along, the great crowded steamer but a puny thing on the wide river, the waters still and clear, reflecting the blue sky and the soft white clouds and the low banks far, far away. The hills were densely wooded, mostly with dark firs, with an occasional deciduous tree showing up brightly among the dark foliage, and around Blagoveschensk there is a beautiful oak known as the velvet oak, the wood of which is much sought for making furniture.
>
> What struck me was the vastness and the loneliness of the mighty Amur River. I had the same feeling on the Congo River in Africa, another great and lonely river with empty banks. Here in the north the great Amur River went wandering on for ten times as far...
>
> At last we steamed up to the port of Nikolayevsk, set at the entrance of the shallow Sea of Okhotsk, right away in the east of the world. When I set foot upon the wharf among all the barrels with which it was packed I could hardly believe I had come so far east, so far away from my regular beat.
>
> The port of Nikolayevsk at the mouth of the Amur River is on the same latitude as London, but due to pack ice is closed for seven months of the year. Winters in Siberia are lovely, with a bright, clear and cold but the thermometer is often below minus 40° Fahrenheit (minus 40° C) and when that happens life is difficult for man and beast. But in that five months of summer, large steamers run from Nikolayevsk via Khabarovsk to Blagoveschensk and travelling is done in the summer months and in the summer of 1914 those steamers were crowded.
>
> Nikolayevsk is officially supposed to have thirteen thousand inhabitants, but in the winter-time they shrink to ten thousand, while in the summer they rise to over forty thousand, everybody coming for the fishing, the great salmon fisheries.[1]

Mary soon discovered that there was little of interest at Nikolayevsk apart from fish. She looked longingly out over the harbour and wondered whether a visit to the island of Saghalien (Sakhalin) would be more exciting. She booked a passage on the *Erivan*, a steamship that would depart to the island the following day. Mary intended to stay for several days on the island, but on board the *Erivan* she was told that there were no hotels, not even in Saghalien's main town, Aleksandrosvk. She was aware that camping out by herself would be far too dangerous.

> I had gone on board that steamer without any introduction whatever, with only my passport to show that I was a respectable member of society. I knew nobody and saw no reason whatever why anyone should trouble themselves about me. But we carried distinguished passengers on board the *Erivan*. There was the Vice-Governor of Saghalien, his wife and son, with the soldiers in attendance, and a good-looking young fellow with short-cropped hair and dreamy eyes who was the Assistant Chief of Police of the island, and this man, by command of the Governor, took me in charge. Never again shall I hear of the Russian police without thinking of the deep debt of gratitude that I owe to Vladimir Merokushoff of Saghalien.[2]

As a result of that chance meeting Mary was offered accommodation at the police station. The kind Assistant Chief of Police spoke a few words of English and managed to communicate with Mary, telling her a few things about the island and its history.

For centuries Russia and Japan had disputed the ownership of Saghalien. In 1855 Russia had managed to conquer the whole island and used it as a penal settlement. In fact, convict, ex-convicts and their descendants still formed a large part of the population. At the time of Mary's visit, the northern part of Saghalien belonged to Russia while Japan occupied the southern part.

Although there was very little to do on Saghalien, Mary l enjoyed her brief stay on the island. She wrote that

>...the people [on Saghalien] seemed nondescript. The upper class were certainly Russians, and all the men wore military caps and had their hair clipped so close it looked shaven, but it would be utterly impossible to say to what nationality the peasant belonged. There were flaxen-haired Russians certainly, but then there were dark-bearded men, a Mongolian type, and there were many thrifty Chinese with queues, in belted blouses and high boots, generally keeping little eating-shops. There may have been Japanese, probably there were, seeing they hold the lower half of the island, but I did not notice them, and there is, I am afraid, in that place which is so full of possibilities absolutely nothing for that go-ahead nation to do.[3]

On 25 July 1914, at nine o'clock in the evening, Mary left the island of Saghalien. As the ship steamed away she realised that at last, after eighteen months of travelling in the East, she was on her way home. She was counting the days—one day to Nikolayevsk, three days to Khabarosvk, three more days to Blagoveschensk, to be followed by a very long train journey through Siberia and home via Germany, a country she had never visited. At that time Mary was still blissfully unaware of the impending war when travel through Germany would be out of the question.

In Nikolayevsk Mary boarded the *Kanovina*, a post steamer bound for Blagoveschensk. Although the ship was less luxurious than the *John Cockerill*, she greatly enjoyed going up the river again. Because they were steaming south and the fact that the short northern summer was reaching its zenith, it became warmer every day.

It took almost a week to reach the river port of Blagoveschensk, a town with large weatherboard houses and wide streets that intersected at right angles. Mary noted a resemblance to many Australian outback towns. Blagoveschensk boasted an enormous emporium where Mary purchased a few small gifts and a dog-collar with a bell, so she could not easily lose Buchanan.

While shopping Mary met some English speaking people who told her that Russia and Germany were at war — this was the first she had heard of it. Russia as the protector of the Serbs had come to the defence of Serbia, after the country had been invaded by Austrian soldiers seeking revenge for the assassination of the heir to the Austrian empire at Sarajevo. But no one could explain to Mary what this l meant to the rest of Europe. All she was told was that the generals of Tsar Nicholas were mobilising their forces to fight the Kaiser's Army and were busy recruiting young men for the Russian Army.

The problem was that while it was clear to Russians that Mary was a foreigner, no one could tell whether she was English or German. Was she friend or foe?

Her fellow shoppers regarded her with suspicion, fearing she was a German spy. Those Russians who believed Mary to be German, were openly hostile. One of them aimed a kick at Buchanan who yelped and ran to Mary for comfort and people strarted muttering threatening comments . Clearly she had to do something or she could be lynched by a mob as things were turning ugly.

A department store manager who spoke a little English advised Mary to go to the office of the Provincial Governor and seek a Protection Order written in Russian to explain she had a British passport, was an ally of Russia and must be given all possible assistance.

By now Mary's clothes were worn and travel stained but fortunately she had put on her best outfit to go shopping. She felt it was respectable enough to visit the governor at his residence.

Mary hired a horse-drawn *droshky* and drove to the governor's official residence. The office was crowded with anxious people. Mary and her little dog were directed from one room to another by Russian officials who could not understand a word of what she was saying.

Everybody said *'Bonjour'*, and the Governor's *aide de campe* kissed her hand when she told him she came from Australia. But clearly he had no idea of what or where Australia was and she had to explain the difference between 'Austria' and 'Australia.' Mary was travelling on a British passport (there being no Australian passports in 1914).

She tried another tack, showed her passport and explained she was 'Anglisky' which the Russian official understood. She added she was being mistaken for a spy and needed a Protection Order. But as he did not understand what she wanted nothing more happened.

After spending hours in the reception area, by which time Mary was hungry, a tall, good-looking officer in the dark blue and gold uniform of a Russian Hussar entered. The officer clicked his heels, bowed low and kissed her hand and informed Mary in excellent English that he was the Boundary Commissioner for this part of Siberia. They had sent for him because nobody could make out exactly what the English lady wanted.

Mary was so relieved she could have hugged the handsome young man. Instead, remembering her age, she told him she was an author from Australia who was writing a book about China and Siberia and hoped to return to England on the Trans-Siberian Express. But because of the war and fact no one knew which side she was on,. it was vital she had a Protection Order written in Russian saying she was Australian travelling on a British passport.

The Boundary Commissioner drove Mary to his house and introduced her to his wife. It was clear that she was not a spy, so he wrote the requested Protection Order and told Mary she was free to go wherever she pleased.

In answer to Mary's questions the Boundary Commissioner told her as well as he could why Europe and Russia had been plunged into war. He explained that Austrians had invaded Serbia in response to the murder by a Serb or a Bosnian at Sarejevo of the Archduke Franz Ferdinand, heir and nephew to Franz Josef, Emperor of Austria.

Now Russia, as protector of Serbia, had declared war on Germany and Franz Joseph's Austro-Hungarian empire. From all over Russia young men were enlisting into the Tsar's army to fight the combined Austrian and German armies.

Far away in Europe, the Kaiser's army had invaded Belgium, a neutral country, en-route to attack Paris. German soldiers violated

Belgian neutrality and killed Belgian citizens, so Britain had declared war on Germany. The conflict had engulfed France as well. British dominions had declared war on Germany in support of the British Empire.

The Russian officer kissed her hand again, to celebrate the fact they were allies. Her homeland of Australia had entered the war in support of Britain, 'the mother country.'

Mary had a letter of introduction to a Danish gentleman by the name of Paul Barentzen, who was the regional head of the Chinese Customs Service. Mr Barentzen lived on the other side of the Amur River in a Chinese town called Sakalin (not to be confused with the island of Saghalien). Mary asked the kind Russian Boundary Commissioner if he knew Paul Barentzen. As it turned out the commissioner was a good friend to him. When Mary told him that she wanted to visit Mr Barentzen and his wife, the Russian officer wrote out a permit for her to cross the river.

The ferries that crossed the Amur River to the Chinese side were big boats built to carry a large number of passengers. Mary was one of many passengers and they had to wait a long time before they could board the ferry.

But with her permit she had no problem on the Chinese side of the river. She found her way to Mr Paul Barentzen's residence, a comfortable two-storey house and received a warm invitation from the Barentezens to stay with them.

> I was tired in every bone, so a chance like this to stay with kindly people who spoke my own language, was not to be missed, and I accepted with gratitude. Mr Barentzen was a Dane, but spoke excellent English as his wife was English.[4]

In the evening of that same day Mary crossed the Amur River once again, this time in company of Mr and Mrs Barentzen to celebrate Britain's entry into the Great War.

> And that [same] night in the summer of 1914 they [Paul Barentzen and his wife] were celebrating the entry of Britain into

the Great War. He asked me and the Russian Boundary Commissioner and his wife and another Russian gentleman to dinner in the gardens at Blagoveschensk.

The place was ablaze with light, there were flags and lamps and bands everywhere, the whole city was *en fete* to do honour to the new addition to the Grande Entente. When we were tired of walking about the gardens we went inside to the principal restaurant that was packed with people dining, while on a stage various singers discoursed sweet music and waved the flags of the Allies. But the British flag had not got as far as the capital of the Amur Province and was represented by a red flag with black crosses drawn on it, and 'Anglisky 'written boldly across it to make up for any deficiency.

Mr Barentzen had foreseen this difficulty and had provided us all with nice little silk Union Jacks to wear pinned on our breasts. About ten o'clock we sat down to a most excellent dinner, with sturgeon and sour cream and caviar and all the good things that Eastern Siberia produces. A packed room also dined, while the people on the stage sang patriotic songs, and we were all given silk programmes as souvenirs. They sang the Belgian, the French and the Russian national anthems, and at last we asked for the British.

Very courteously the conductor sent back word to say he was very sorry but the British national anthem was also a German hymn and if he dared to play it people would tear him to pieces. I suggested as an alternative *Rule, Britannia,* but theconductor had never heard of it. It was a deadlock. Then the tall Russian who was the other guest pushed his chair from the table, stood up, and saluting, whistled *Rule Britannia!* How the people applauded that Britain had entered the war in Eastern Siberia. We laughed and ate and drank and did not go home till morning.[5]

Mary spent a week with Paul Barentzen and his wife before continuing her voyage along the Amur River and the Shilka River in north-westerly direction. Upstream the river became narrower and shallower, so only very small ships could navigate the upper stretch of the River Amur. In consequence Mary had to embark on a much smaller steamer and the deck that ran round the cabins was only eighty centimetres wide and was overcrowded with children.

Mary became acquainted with the chief mate, who had served on British maritime vessels and spoke English well and was able to discuss the war. But it was not possible to get much reliable information. Radio communication was almost non-existent in Russia in 1914 and there were no newspapers at the little river side ports where they stopped. Russian peasants had never learned to read under the rule of the Tsar and this was an area of woodcutters and small farmers and few literate people lived there.

The Amur River gradually became narrower and meandered through lonely wooded hills and grassy plains. On the Siberian side they occasionally passed little settlements, but on the Chinese side not even a single hut was in sight. While the ship steamed up the Amur River the weather was fine and warm, but soon after they entered the Shilka River it began to rain. They were now further north and among mountains so the air became chillier by the day.

CHAPTER 21

On troop trains through Siberia

Seven days and nights after leaving Blagoveschensk the river steamer finally arrived at Sretensk, where Mary was to catch the train to Irkutsk. To reach the railway station she had to take a crowded ferry across the Shilka River. She engaged a *droshky*, whose horse had to negotiate mud several feet deep to get Mary and her luggage to the ferry.

An avid reader of Tolstoy and other Russian writers Mary had always regarded Siberia as a hell hole where exiles and criminals were sent as a punishment. Now the Siberian port of Sretensk was one of the centres of recruitment for Tsar Nicholas's troops and for the first time Mary saw how the excitement of war affected young men. Along the road to the ferry she saw streams of open carts, packed with tall, fair-haired young man with sun-tanned faces. They shouted, laughed and sang as they drove past her. Mary could not understand what they were singing but could see they were wild with excitement at the thought of going off to war. They had not the slightest idea of the dangers involved and regarded enlisting as a big adventure. Mary wrote,

> ...down the road came endless streams of square khaki-coloured carts, driven by men in flat caps and belted khaki blouses, big fair men, often giants with red, sun-tanned faces and lint-white hair, men who shouted and laughed and sang and threw up their caps... these men were delighted with their lot. I wondered was it a case of the prisoner freed or was it that life under the old regime

in a Russian village was dull to monotony and to these recruits was coming the chance of their lifetime. Some will never come east again, never whether in love or hate will they see the steppes and the flowers and the golden sunshine and the snow of Siberia, they [would] have left their bones on those battle-fields...[1]

Years later Mary would learn from Australian friends that young Australian soldiers departing for Gallipoli or the trenches of northern France behaved in exactly the same way.[2] The young Anzacs left their home towns by train, laughing and singing with no idea that many of them would be dead within a year. All these young Russian recruits could think about were cavalry charges and glory, and like the Anzacs they had no idea of the havoc caused by German machine guns that awaited them.

Initially Mary watched with interest at the cheery soldiers, who kept filling up the ferry. When after two hours there was still no break in the stream of khaki-clad men, Mary became worried. Her only consolation was the fact that the train would not leave until late that afternoon — or so she had been led to believe.

After several more hours Mary became desperate to board the ferry and catch the train for Irkustk. She engaged the tallest and strongest porter she could find to help her to get on board and to carry her luggage. He wore a red blouse, dark trousers and sea boots and on his head was a small hat made of tightly curled black lambs wool. Persuaded by the promise of a very large tip, he managed to get Mary, including her dog and her luggage, aboard the ferry. But her troubles were only just starting.

> ...the ferry came to a full stop in the middle of the stream and a motor boat which did not look as if it could hold half the people came alongside... In a few seconds that boat was packed to the gunwales and I was looking over at it. I had Buchanan under my arm and in my other hand had my despatch-case, and, being far from acrobatic I felt it was hopeless to think of clambering down into the boat. However, that big Russian porter picked me up and dropped me, dog and all into the motor boat on top of the those people [who were] already there... Hanging on to my little dog, I

slipped and...[became] wedged between screaming people.

After me, with my luggage on his shoulder, came my tall porter in the red blouse. Somehow he seemed to find a precarious foothold on the gunwale, and he made me understand he wanted two roubles for our fares. If he had asked for ten roubles he would have got it, but how I managed to reach my money to this day I do not know. The boat rocked and swayed in a most alarming manner, and I thought to myself, Well, we are on top now, but presently the boat will overturn and then what?

I gathered that the passengers were disputing with the boatman the price to be paid for the passage, though this was unwise, for the ferry was threatening to crush us against the rocky bank... Just as I was growing desperate and Buchanan was on the verge of suffocation the problem of the fares was settled and we made for the bank. But we did not go to the usual landing-stage ; that was reserved for the soldiers so we drew up against a steep, high bank faced with granite.

The rest of the passengers began scrambling up. But I was helpless. Whatever happened, I knew I could *never* climb that wall. I could only clutch my little dog and await events. My guardian angel in the red blouse was equal to the situation. The boat had cleared now and there was room to move. Dropping the baggage he was holding,, he picked me up like a baby and tossed me, dog and all, up on to the bank above. [3]

Mary's porter engaged a boy to carry the lighter baggage and shouldered the rest himself. He took her by the arm and raced her up the steep incline to the railway station. As they arrived there, Mary saw thousands of soldiers waiting to board the west-bound train. Once again the military had priority and no one knew when the long line of patient civilians would be able to board the next train to Irkutsk.

Clearly, Mary was in for a long wait. Meanwhile she went to buy her ticket to St Petersburg and tried to pay for it with a ten pound note. The booking clerk looked bewildered and declined to accept it. As Mary offered the note again a man standing beside her whisked it away.

'Madame, are you mad?' he asked in French and explained that all around were thieves, robbers and assassins, and any one of them would cut her throat for a good deal less than a ten pound note. The man, who was wearing a green uniform with red stripes and a military cap, put the offending cash in his pocket, saying he would get the note changed.

The man in the red and green uniform explained to Mary that the train, which was about to depart, was reserved for the troops and civilians who had already boarded it were turned out.

'When does the next train go ?' asked Mary.

The man looked dubious. 'Possibly to-morrow night.'

Mary realised she had to stay overnight and asked where she could find a hotel. He pointed across the river to the centre of Sretensk and said that there were no hotels on this side of the river. But Mary hated to go across the river again after all it had cost her to get to this side.

'Can't I stay *anywhere* on this side of the river?'

The man in uniform made a gesture at the waiting room as if he were offering palatial quarters. 'Here, Madame, here.'

There was no choice, Mary had to stay in the railway station and wait for a train to Irkutsk until the following evening.

When the man disappeared Mary feared she would never see him again.

> I set myself to make the best of the situation. The station was crowded with all sorts and conditions of people, and a forlorn crowd they looked, and curious was the flotsam and jetsam that were their belongings. Of course there was the usual baggage, but there were other things I did not expect to come across in a railway station in Siberia. There was a sewing-machine; the trumpet of a gramophone; the back of a piano with all the wires showing and a dressmaker's stand looking forlorn and out of place among the bundles of the soldiers.
>
> The civilians watched the soldiers getting into the carriages from which they were debarred, waved their hands and cheered them, though the next train would not leave till one-fifteen the next morning. The civilians were content that the soldiers should

be served first. They settled themselves in groups on the open platform, in the refreshment room, in the waiting-rooms, fathers, mothers, children and dogs, and solaced themselves with kettles of tea, black bread and sausages.

...To wait a night and day for a train in a railway station was surely a little sacrifice to what some people were making. How cheerfully and patiently that Russian crowd waited ! There were no complaints, no moans, but here and there a Russian woman buried her head in her shawl and wept for those loved ones who had gone to the war...

I went into the refreshment-room to get some food, and had soup with sour cream in it, and ate chicken and bread and butter and cucumber and drank *kvass* as a change from the eternal tea. I watched the people on the platform and as the shades of night fell began to wonder where I should sleep. I would have chosen the platform, but it looked as if it might rain, so I went into the ladies' waiting room, dragged a seat across the open window, and spread out my rugs and cushions and established myself there. I wanted to have first right to that window, for the night up in the hills here was chilly and I felt sure somebody would come in and want to shut it. My intuitions were correct. Buchanan and I kept that window open against a crowd who wished it to be shut. The room was packed with unwashed human beings and someone stretched across me and did so.

I arose from my slumbers and protested... the sanitary arrangements were abominable, and what the atmosphere would have been like with the window shut. One woman pulled at my rugs and though I could not understand her language her meaning was plain enough I had plenty of rugs, it was they who had nothing. It was a fair complaint, so I shared my rugs with her and the summer night slowly wore on until at last it was morning.

And morning brought its own difficulties. Russian washing arrangements are always difficult as. I had discovered in the house of Mr Poland. I wrestled with the same bad plumbing in the house of the Chief of Police in Saghalien, and I met it... here in the railway station waiting-room.

However, I did the best I could, and afterwards, as my face

was sore from the hot sun of the day before, I took out a jar of face cream and began to rub it on my cheeks. This proceeding aroused intense interest in the women around me who begged for some of it. As long as that pot held out every woman within range had cream daubed on her weather-beaten cheeks.

Having dressed, Buchanan and I had the long day before us, and I did not dare leave the railway station because I was uneasy about my ten pound note and my luggage. I awaited with a good deal of interest the gentleman with peaked cap and the colourful uniform and my ten pound note. He arrived at last, and explained in French that he had the change but he could not give it to me till the train came in because of the thieves and robbers. And God forgive me that I doubted the honesty of a kindly, courteous gentleman.

It was a long, long day with nothing to do save to walk about for Buchanan's benefit. I diversified things by taking meals in the refreshment-room whenever I felt I really must do something. But I was very tired. I felt I had been travelling too long, and… had not been for Buchanan's presence I should have wept. No one seemed at all certain when the next train west might be expected.[4]

It was evening before the train finally arrived. To Mary's relief, the man who had taken her ten pound note turned up again. After declaring that this was the train that would connect with the Trans-Siberian express, he took Mary by the hand and led her to a carriage. He shut the door, drew the blinds and gave Mary her change for the ten-pound note.

'Guard your purse, Madame,' he whispered, 'Guard your purse. There are thieves and robbers everywhere!'

Once Mary's uniformed protector, who could have been a general, was satisfied she had carefully hidden her money, he offered to get her a ticket. Mary asked for a first-class seat but the man returned with a second-class ticket because there was no first-class carriage on the train. The ticket only cost about five pounds and another pound bought a ticket for Buchanan.

Mary's protector in his magnificent red and green uniform also boarded the train for the Siberian town of Irkutsk. She discovered her protector was not a general in some Balkan army but the stationmaster of a small Russian town further down the line.

> I was [travelling] second class and my compartment opened into the other compartments in the carriage all filled to the brim with people. We were four women, two men who smoked, a baby who cried, and my little dog.
>
> I spread out my rugs and cushions, and when I wanted the window open the majority were against me. Not only was the window shut, but every ventilating arrangement was tightly closed also, and presently the atmosphere grew pestilential. I grew desperate. I wandered out of the carriage and got on to the platform at the end, where the cold wind even though it was August and summer time in Siberia sliced through me like a knife. The people objected to that a cold wind coming in, and the next time I wandered out for a breath of fresh air I found the door barred and no prayers of mine would open it. In that carriage the people were packed like sardines, but though I was almost suffocated no one else seemed at all the worse. I couldn't have looked at breakfast next morning, but the rest of the company fed cheerfully although the reek that came from the open door [of the toilet] was disgusting.
>
> I offered tea to a Cossack officer, we became friends and descended from the train and bought cakes to eat at various stations. In Kobdo, ten thousand feet among the mountains in the west of Mongolia, was a famous lama. My Cossack friend was full of praise for this lama and his gift of prophecy. The lama had foretold three emperors foretold the lama would fight a war. Two would be overwhelmed and utterly destroyed while the third would win great glory.
>
> 'The Tsar, madame,' said my friend, 'The Tsar [Nicholas] is the third.'[5]

Years later Mary would remember this prophecy. By the end of the war three emperors *had* lost their imperial thrones. Tsar Nicholas of Russia would be murdered by the Bolsheviks, Emperor Franz

Josef of Austria was dead and Germany's Kaiser Wilhelm had to abdicate at the end of the Great War.

The train reeked of body odour. At a small station in the hills Mary was promoted to a first-class compartment which she had to share it with a Russian lady and then Mary and her dog had the compartment to themselves all the way to Irkutsk.

As there was no restaurant car, Mary descend from the train at various stations and bought from station vendors bread rolls filled with meat or fish and was able to let Buchanan answer the calls of nature.

One such stop Mary became acquainted with the captain of the Swedish ship *Askold*, who occupied the compartment next to her and was impressed by the splendour of his gold braided naval uniform.[6] They communicated in French a language Mary spoke quite well as she had spent numerous holidays in Nice and parts of Provence. The Swedish naval officer was happy to help , Mary, with her naval connections f buy provisions at various stations en route and insisted on paying for them in spite of her protests.

Eventually the train steamed towards Lake Baikal on the outskirts of Irkutsk. Mary remembered arriving at Irkutsk on her outward journey when it had been winter and the lake a mass of glittering ice. Now on her return journey it was summer and the lake blue as the Pacific Ocean.

> ...[the lake] lay glittering now, beautiful still in the August sunshine. There were white sails on it and a steamer or two, and men were feverishly working at alterations on the railway. The Angara was a mighty river, and we steamed along it into the Irkutsk station, which is by no means Irkutsk, for the town is four miles away on the other side of the river.
>
> At Irkutsk we began to be faintly Western once again. And those exiles who had come so far abandoned hope here. All that they loved-all lay behind. I should have found it hard to turn back and go east myself now. What must that facing east have been for them ?
>
> They turned us out of the train and Buchanan and I were ruefully surveying our possessions, heaped upon the platform,

wondering how on earth we were to get them taken to the cloakroom and how we should get them out again supposing they were taken there, when the captain of the *Askold* appeared with a porter.

'Would Madame permit?' he asked 'that her luggage be put with mine in the cloakroom?'

Madame could have hugged him. Already the dusk was falling, the soft, warm dusk, and the people were hastening to the town or to the refreshment-rooms. There would be no train that night, said my kind friend, some time in the morning perhaps, but certainly not that night.

I sighed. Again I was adrift, and it was not a comfortable feeling. If Madame desired to dine — Madame did desire to dine. Then if Madame permits — Of course Madame permitted. She not only permitted she was most grateful.

So we dined together at the same table outside the station restaurant — I like that fashion of dining outside — under the brilliance of the electric light. He arranged everything for me, even to getting some supper for Buchanan. So I forgot the exiles who haunted me, forgot this was Siberia. Here in the restaurant, save for the waiters with Oriental features we might almost have been France.

'Perhaps,' said my companion courteously as we were having coffee, 'Madame would care to take a room at my hotel? I could interpret for her as no one speaks anything but Russian.'

Again I could have hugged him. I intimated my dressing-bag was still in the cloakroom, but he smiled and shrugged his shoulders.

'Not necessary for one night!'

In the morning I saw that Irkutsk, capital of Eastern Siberia, is a frontier town. There were the same wide streets grass-grown at the edges, great houses and small houses side by side, and empty spaces where as yet there were no houses. We went to the Central Hotel.

'I do not go to expensive hotels,' my companion told me, 'This is a moderate one.'

But if it were moderate it certainly was a very nice hotel. Russian hotels do not as a rule provide food, the restaurant is generally separate, but we had already dined. That naval officer made all arrangements for me. He even explained to an astonished chamber-maid with her hair done in two long plaits that Madame must have all the windows opened.

When I tried to get a bath he did his best for me. But again, he explained, Russians as a rule go to a bath-house, and there was only one bathroom in this hotel; it had been engaged for two hours by a gentleman, and he thought, seeing I should have to start early in the morning, it might be rather late for me to have a bath then, but if I liked in the morning it would be at my service.

Had anyone told met on arrival in Irkutsk I would be more interested in a bath than in seeing round the city called the 'pearl of the Russian steppes'— I would not have believed them!

Early in the morning there was a knock at the door. When I said 'Come in,' half expecting tea, there was my naval officer in full uniform smilingly declaring my bath was ready, he had paid the bill, and I could pay him back when we were on board the train.

The chamber-maid, with her hair still done in two plaits —-I fancy she had slept in them —-conducted me to the bathroom, and I pass over the difficulty of doing without brush and comb and tooth-brush. But I washed the dust out of my hair, and when I was as tidy as I could manage I joined the captain of the *Askold* and we drove back through the town to the railway station.[7]

The station was a surging mass of noisy chattering people. Mary and the Swedish naval officer had breakfast together in the pleasant sunlight — fresh bread rolls with butter and honey and the luxury of coffee with cream, cream being something never seen in China.

As Mary had told the captain of the *Askold* that two of her brothers were captains in the British Navy he treated her as kindly as though she was his elder sister. Aware that she was short of money and with war raging it would be hard for banks to exchange foreign currency, he insisted on paying for Mary's breakfast.

While having breakfast, Mary's companion spoke to another

officer who told him that the train to St Petersburg was all reserved for the Russian army. The naval officer passed on the message. 'So sorry Madame, the military authorities will not allow you or any other civilians on board.'

Although Mary was disappointed, she considered that having to stay a day or two at Irkutsk, the Pearl of Russia, could be very pleasant.

But the captain said, 'Wait, wait — I'm not yet finished. They will give me two compartments, one for day and one for night. I cannot sleep in a four bunks at once — you are welcome to sleep in the second compartment.' For the first time Mary realised that he was indeed 'a very great officer', and how lucky she was to have met him as everyone else would be packed as tight as herrings in a barrel.

Before boarding the train Mary had to buy food from the station buffet and take it back to the compartment. To be able to make tea or coffee, the passengers could obtain hot water from samovars in station waiting rooms whenever the train halted.

As the train was overcrowded the conductor asked the naval officer permission to put a Russian Army doctor into Mary's compartment in the empty bunk above hers. As the Swedish captain asked Mary whether she would agree to that arrangement, she could scarcely refuse — having been admitted onto the Russian troop train on sufferance. As a result an exhausted Russian Army doctor, who spoke no English, arrived, climbed into the top bunk and went to sleep and his snores kept Mary awake for hours.

A few nights later the Russian doctor was replaced by an elderly professor from a Siberian university, going ff to Sweden in search of radium for his experiments. While most people believed the war would be over by Christmas the professor, took a more realistic view.

'The Allies will win,' he told Mary. 'But it will be a long war and the world drenched in blood. It last three or four years. Many towns will fall and many thousands will be killed before finally the Allies win.'

The journey seemed interminable. The train, loaded with Russian conscripts, crept slowly across the steppes, past lakes and rivers, herds of cattle. and mobs of horses and companies of Russian soldiers learning to use arms for the first time. Buttercups, daisies and purple vetches were trampled underfoot at areas where armed men were drilling before going off to the trenches. Further west Mary saw fields where the wheat was cut and stacked, waiting to be harvested by women in colourful t headscarves and long skirts, while their men were on the way to the front to fight the Germans.

Mary had to change trains again at Chelyabinsk, where she said farewell to the captain of the *Askold*. The troop train continued as far as Moscow where Mary had to wait for a train for St Petersburg until the evening.

Mary, being a foreigner, was not allowed to watch Russian Army installations or to take photographs from the train. Her films were confiscated and in spite of her protests she never got them back.

> Someone always came in and drew down the blinds in my compartment—I had one to myself since leaving Chelyabinsk—and told me I must not go out on the platform whenever we crossed a bridge. They were evidently taking precautions against spying though they were too polite to say so. There were big towns with stations packed to overflowing. At Perm we met some German prisoners of war, and there were soldiers, soldiers everywhere, and at last one day in the first week in September we steamed into Petrograd [St Petersburg].[8]

As the train arrived at St Petersburg, Mary bundled her luggage and her kettles and baskets together for departure. With Buchanan under her arm and dressed in the only respectable clothes left to her after more than a year in China she , she descended from the train. The steam engine had ejected clouds of gritty smoke over the passengers so Mary was in need of a good bath as they reached St Petersburg.

CHAPTER 22

St Petersburg and after

For years Mary had wanted to see the magnificent city designed by Tsar Peter the Great in 1793 while the Tsar of all the Russias was living in a log cabin. She regarded Peter the Great as a genius for the way he had planned the city on the water, named after him. The city had been built amid marshes that had been drained alongside the Neva River, and provided valuable access for Russians to the Baltic Sea.

With his zeal to modernise Russia, which was still centuries behind the rest of Europe, Peter the Great had visualised a great city built of wood beside the water which would give Russia access to the West. Wile Moscow was a city dominated by the past and cut off from the civilisation of the West St Petersburgh was the new city which would connect Russia with Europe.

The boulevards and wooden palaces of St Petersburg built by the Tsar were eventually rebuilt in stone by Empress Catherine the Great. With boundless wealth at her disposal she commissioned magnificent summer and winter palaces in the European style and due to its canals. St Petersburg became s known as 'the Venice of the North'. Mary loved Tolstoy and had read War and Peace avidly with its descriptions of Moscow and St Petersburg. Petersburg lived up to her dreams and she described it as 'the most beautiful of cities in the world'.

After walking past the Winter Palace with its elegant green and white façade designed by an Italian architect hoping to have time to visit the magnificent interiors later, Mary went to the office of a shipping company who sold tickets for trains and boats from Finland, Sweden and Norway, and across the North Sea to Newcastle-on-Tyne. The tiny office was packed with Poles, Lithuanians and Russians and naturalised Americans all wanting tickets to go home, yelling and shouting in different languages.

As Mary bought her ticket, the man in charge asked whether she was intending to take her dog with her.

When she replied, 'Of course', the ticket officer said sternly 'You will *never* get that dog through Sweden. The Swedes are extremely strict about dogs.'.

> Poor Buchanan. Despair seized me... Here was I in St Petersburg and instead of exploring streets and canals and cathedrals and palaces my whole thoughts were occupied with the fate of my little dog. ... All the while I was in Petrograd—and I stayed there three days looking for a way out—my thoughts were given to James Buchanan. I discussed the matter with the authorities in the hotel who could speak English, and finally Buchanan and I made a peregrination to the Swedish Consulate. And though the Swedish Consulate was a deal more civil and more interested in me and my doings than the English, in the matter of a dog, even a nice little dog like Buchanan, they were firm—through Sweden he could not go.[1]

Mary had hoped to visit the St Peter and Paul Cathedral, containing the sepulchre of Peter the Great and to the Church of the Holy Blood, which had been built on the place where the reformist Tsar Alexander II had been murdered as he was about to carry out essential reforms. However, Mary's her preoccupation with the fate of Buchanan meant she saw less of St Petersburg than she had intended.

> My dear little companion and friend had made the loneliest of places pleasant for me. Now I could not get him out of the country!
>
> I went back to the office where I had bought my ticket. Everyone was interested in the tribulations of the cheerful little

black and white dog who sat on the counter and wagged his tail. The consensus of opinion was that he should be drugged and smuggled across Sweden in a basket!. Buchanan might be given sleeping tablets and covered up in a basket so I bought one, went back to the Astoria Hotel and asked the porter to get a vet to visit me. The vet gave me Sulphonal tablets and assured me Buchanan would be all right...[2]

After a four day's stay at the Astoria Hotel and a quick look at the wonders of the Hermitage Mary took a train to Raumo in Finland. Its second and third class carriages were packed with men, women and children, desperate to get out of Russia. Men in fur hats with broken teeth breathed black tobacco and garlic over her.

The railway officials refused to allow Buchanan to stay in Mary's compartment and banished him to the luggage-van. Because Mary felt he would be lonely, she went and sat in the van to keep him company.

Moving through the train Mary met up with another charming Russian naval officer, a tall, broad-shouldered, fair haired man who spoke English well. At the Finnish border the Russian officer took Mary (whose money was running low) to the station's refreshment room. Apart from having an excellent breakfast, she bought eggs, sausages, bread and scones and a supply of fruit, to take with her aboard the train. Despite Mary's protest the naval officer insisted on paying for her breakfast and her purchases.

'Madame! In Russia when a gentleman takes a lady for refreshments he pays!' he told her.

> [The Russian captain asked] had I heard about the sea fight in the Mediterranean? Not heard about the little *Gloucester* attacking the *Goebenn*! A battle between a dwarf and a giant! Madame! It was a sea fight that will go down through the ages! All Russia is talking of nothing else!
>
> 'Do you know anyone in the English Navy?'
>
> I said I had two brothers in the British navy although they were Australian born like myself.
>
> 'Then tell them,' he said 'We Russian sailors are proud to be

Allies of a nation that breeds such men as manned the *Gloucester!*

The Finnish border was soon reached. The Russian naval officer left us, and travelling through Finland discipline relaxed and I brought Buchanan into the carriage and made friends with the people who surrounded me. And once again did I bless the foresight of the my Polish Jewish friend in Harbin who had impressed upon me the necessity for *two* kettles. They were a godsend in that carriage. We commandeered glasses, got hot water at wayside stations and I made tea for everyone within reach.[3]

> The Finnish scenery was very different from that of Russia. The train passed huge lakes, crossed a wonderful salmon river and skirted Finland's inland sea. Here and there a castle stood out amongst the farmhouses and little towns.
>
> The passengers in the train spoke many different languages: English, French, German, Polish, Russian, Latvian and Yiddish, but not one amongst them spoke Finnish or even understood a single word of it. Unfortunately, the Finns spoke no language but their own and seemed to have a grudge against all foreigners. They turned all the passengers out of the train in the middle of the night in a railway station in the heart of Finland and left them to discover that every hotel in that little Finnish town was full.
>
> Once more Mary was faced with spending the night on a bench in a railway station waiting room and shared her predicament with others who spoke English.

There was the Oxford man and the musician with a twang, there was the wife of an American lawyer with her little boy and the wife of an American doctor with three little girls and four Austrian girls making their way back to some place in Hungary. Of course, technically, the Austrians were now our enemies, while as yet the Americans were neutral. The Russian-American musician had studied in Leipzig and boasted of the strength and power of the Kaiser's Germany. And so we ignored him.

The refreshment rooms were shut, the whole place was in darkness, but it was a mild night, with a gorgeous September moon sailing out into the clear sky, and y I should not have minded spreading my rugs and sleeping outside...,but the tales of the insecurity of Siberia still lingered in my consciousness. When the Oxford graduate said that one of the porters would put us up in his house I went with all the others and took along my bundles of rugs and cushions.

How many strange place I have slept in!

That porter had a quaint little wooden house set in a garden which might have been lifted from a story by Hans Christian Andersen. We had the freedom of a very clean kitchen. We made tea there and ate what we had brought in our baskets. The Austrian girls had a room to themselves, I lent my rugs to the young men who made shift with them in the entrance porch, and the best sitting-room was turned over to the women and children and myself Two very small beds were put up very close together and into them got the two women and three children, and I was accommodated with a remarkably Lilliputian sofa.[4]

The next morning the group continued their journey across Finland which took another two days.
Towards the end of the journey Mary made friends with a Finn who had Scottish relatives and spoke excellent English on his way to England to buy sheepskins for the Russian army. He took great interest in Buchanan and offered to 'borrow' him till they reached Sweden as he was known to the authorities and Finnish dogs would be allowed to enter Sweden, while a dog that had come from Russia would be barred.
Mary thanked the man for his kindness and handed over Buchanan in his basket without a qualm.

Fate seemed to have turned against Mary and her travelling companions as once again there was no accommodation. Finally a Finn who spoke English appeared, saying he was the agent for the Swedish steamship company but had not expected passengers in wartime so he had gone to bed. He was annoyed at having been woken in the night to deal with a bunch of troublesome travellers intent on disturbing the peace of this Finnish village. They showed him their tickets for the Finnish steamer *Uleaborg*, whereupon the official smiled in a supercilious fashion and said the Finnish were enemies of Germany and the lot of them were likely to be captured by a German ship.

> We didn't believe much in the Germans, for we had many of us come through a country which certainly believed itself invulnerable. Then an American woman travelling with her daughters, who spoke English with a most extraordinary accent, proclaimed that if there was a Swedish steamer she was going by it as she was afraid of 'dose Yarmans'. She and her daughters would give up their tickets and go by the Swedish steamer. Protest was useless. She was not going by the *Uleaborg*. Besides, where were we to sleep that night? The Finnish steamer was three or four miles away down at the wharf.
>
> The Swedish agent claimed there were no hotels; there were no boarding-houses; no, it was not possible to get anything to eat at that hour of the night. Something to drink? Well, there was plenty of water in the station cloakroom and he would arrange for a train for us to sleep in. The train would leave at ten o'clock next morning and take us down to the steamer.
>
> We retired to the train. Only one of the carriages had electric light. By general consent we gave up to the lady whose fear of the Germans was profound and she in return asked us to share what provisions we had left. We pooled our stores and dined off tinned sardines, black bread, sausages and apples. The only person left out of the universal friendliness was the Yiddish lady. Out of her plenty she did not offer to share.

After they had eaten their shared meal, Mary retired to a darkened carriage, wrapped herself in her eiderdown and went to sleep.

The next morning the train steamed up to the wharf, and there lay white ships that were bound for Sweden on the far side of the Baltic Sea. There were Customs inspections and all luggage was examined before it was allowed to leave Finland.

Near one of the goods sheds tables had been set out where coffee, bread rolls, butter and hard boiled eggs could be bought. There was a nip in the air and the hot coffee was very welcome.

Mary and the other passengers met that Finn with Scottish relatives again. Nobody paid attention to his suggestion that the *Goathied*, the Swedish steamer, was very much smaller than the *Uleaborg* and that there was a wind getting up they would all be seasick. Mary replied that at she preferred being seasick to being captured by the Germans.

It was midday before they were allowed on board the little white ship. By now Mary was weary and longing for her journey to end. She heard a broad Scottish accent and watched as fifty Scottish sailors climbed the gangplank and arrived on board. They were part of the crews of four British ships that had been caught in the fortunes of war and laid up at St Petersburg. Now they were returning to Britain via Sweden, leaving their ships behind in dry dock in St Petersburg until the war ended, Russia being Britain's ally.

Just as they sailed out of the bay the captain announced that he was not going to Stockholm but to the Swedish harbour of Gefle which lay further to the north of Sweden. He had received orders to change course. to the north. He did not know why, but he it was wartime and he had to follow orders.

CHAPTER 23

Captured by the Germans

The air was clear and clean as if every speck of dust had been washed away by the rain of the preceding night. The wind was strengthening, breaking the sea into white-crested waves. It was not long before the little ship was tossing about like a cork.

As the half Scottish Finn — who had 'borrowed' Buchanan for the duration of the voyage — had predicted, most of the passengers including Mary, became seasick. She watched them going below deck to hide their misery but stayed on deck, feeling better in the fresh air as she watched the sun set and spotted a sinister blac vessel steaming round the *Goathied*/+

. The black torpedo boat, came so close Mary could see the gaiters of a German officer m who stood on the bridge and must be the captain. The decks were crowded with men and the muzzle of a large deck-mounted gun was pointing in the direction of the Swedish ship.

The *Goathied* slowed down and passengers came scrambling on deck crying 'Germans!'

> ...from the torpedo boat came a voice through a megaphone. 'What are you doing with all those young men on board?' it asked in English with a German accent, English being the language of the sea.
>
> The sinister black torpedo boat was lying up against us. Seasickness was forgotten, and the violinist who had studied at Leipzig came close and said, 'They are going to take the young

Englishmen,' sounding partly sorry and partly pleased, because he had been so full of the might of the Germans.

I thought of the Oxford man in the prime of his manhood.

'Have you told him?'

'I didn't dare,' said he.

'Well, I think you'd better, or I'll go myself. They are going to search the ship and he won't like being caught unawares by the enemy.'

So he went down below, and presently they came up together. The Oxford man had been very sea-sick and thought all the row was caused by the ship having struck a mine. However he felt so ill with seasickness that he was accepting his fate calmly. He was the only one with a British passport travelling first class, and when we heard the Germans wanted all the men of fighting age it was likely they would take him as well as the young sailors.

Leaning over the rail of the *Goathied*, we could look down upon the black decks of the torpedo boat, blacker than ever now in the dusk of evening, A rope ladder was flung over the side and it up climbed a couple of German naval officers armed with pistols. They spoke very correct precise English, and went below, demanded the passenger list and studied it carefully.

'We must take those young Englishmen,' said the leader, and he went through every cabin to see that no more were concealed.

The captain made as much remonstrance as an unarmed man can make with three cruisers looking on and a torpedo boat close alongside.

'We are at war,' said the German officer curtly.

In the dusk he ranged the sailors along the decks, all fifty-five of them, and picked out those who were between nineteen and forty. Indeed one luckless lad of seventeen was taken, but he was a strapping fellow and they said if he was not twenty-one he looked it.

It was tragic. There must have been treachery at work or how should a German torpedo boat have known that British sailors were on board?

But a few moments before they had been counting on getting home and now they were bound for a German prison! In the gathering darkness they stood on the decks, and the short, choppy sea beat the iron torpedo boat against the ship's side, and the captain in the light from a lantern wailed in despair.

'My ship cannot stand it! She cannot stand it much longer! '
Crash ! Crash ! Crash on the hull !
'She was never built for it ! And she is old!'

But the German paid no attention. The possible destruction of a passenger ship was as nothing weighed in the balance with the acquirement of 36 English men of fighting age, a trophy for them.

The sailors were very quiet as they handed letters and small bundles to their comrades or to the onlookers and dropped down that rope ladder. No one but a sailor could have gone down, for both ships heaved up and down, and sometimes there was a wide belt of heaving dark water between them, bridged only by that frail ladder. One by one they went, landing on the hostile deck, and were greeted wit jeers at their misfortune by the German crew. Once a bundle was dropped into the sea and there went up a sigh that was more like a wail, for the passengers looking on thought the man was gone, and there was no hope for him sandwiched between two ships.

Darker and darker it grew. On the *Goathied* there were the lighted decks, but below on the torpedo boat the men were dim figures, German and English undiscernible in the gloom. On the horizon loomed the sombre bulk of the cruisers, each with a bright light aloft, and all around was the heaving sea, the white tops of the choppy waves showing sinister against the darker hollows.[1]

The Oxford man was anxiously waiting to be arrested but was lucky as the Germans did not realise his nationality, because he had entered himself as Scottish rather than British on the passenger list. Mary d described herself as Australian and possibly the Germans mistook this for Austrian and ignored her. Those Scottish sailors who embarked at St Petersburg had been listed on the register as British since they were serving in the British Navy. The Germans. with instructions to arrest all British citizens took at gunpoint the sailors wearing British naval uniform onto their torpedo boat as prisoners of war.

The opinion on board the Swedish boat was the Germans would use the prisoners to stoke their warships and they might die if the torpedo boat was hit by a British warship. Those Scottish lads were very brave and did not show fear.

As the torpedo boat drew away, the Swedish captain of the *Goathied* said he was relieved that the German torpedo boat had not blown a hole in the side of his ship and thankful that none of *his* crew had been taken. A gloomy man he predicted the Germans had gone 'to take the *Uleaborg*,' he said, 'They will blow her up and before tomorrow morning Raumo will be in flames!'

In those days Sweden had great faith in the power of the Kaiser, convinced German efficiency would win the war. However the Swedish captain had the decency to warn all British ships he could contact in the area they could be in danger from the German torpedo boat.

※

Mary would adapt the drama with the German torpedo boat and use it in el *The Wind from the Wilderness* as a dramatic ending to the novel. Dr Rosalie Gascoigne and Martin Conant have managed to escape from an attack by White Wolf and other hair raising adventures in China and are returning to England on a Swedish ship which is threatened by a German submarine which has surfaced beside them. Martin. has finally revealed his love for Rosalie and she for him. But faced with the fact the German U-boat may blow them sky high with a torpedo, Martin sacrifices his own safety to save the Swedish ship and its passengers. Mary Gaunt's most appealing novel for contemporary readers, has a dramatic and totally unexpected conclusion with no standard happy ending.

※

In real life Mary's ship, the ss *Goathied*, entered the neutral

Swedishg harbour of Gefle where all passengers were instructed to bring their belongings onto the lower deck for a Customs' examination. Mary had been unsuccessful in her attempt to drug her little dog who was still wide awake and hid him in his basket, under her pile of luggage, where the Swedish Customs failed to find him. Mary piled her luggage including Buchanan onto a handcart and managing to get Buchanan into Sweden and was overjoyed.

Leaving their luggage at the railway station, the passengers went across the road to a restaurant for breakfast and Mary described how .

> Gefle reminded me of a town in a Hans Andersen story even more than Finland had done. It had neat streets, neat houses, and fair-haired women, and Gefle was seething with excitement because the *Goathied* had been stopped [by the Germans]. It was early days then, and Sweden had not become accustomed to the filibustering ways of the Germans, so every poster advertising a newspaper had the tale written large upon it, and the whole town was talking about it.
>
> I was nearing the end of my long journey and it did not seem to me to matter much what I did. We were all untidy and travel-stained, the violinist had a huge rent in his shoe, and, having no money to buy more, he went into a shoe-shop and had it mended. I, with Buchanan somewhat recovered, sat beside him while it was done.
>
> And in the afternoon we went by train through the neat and tidy country to Stockholm. I felt as if I were resting, because I was anxious no longer about Buchanan, who slumbered peacefully on my knee. Should anyone think I am making a fuss about a little dog, let them remember he had been my faithful companion and friend at the ends of the earth and had stood many a time between me and utter loneliness and depression.
>
> Stockholm for most of us was the parting of the ways.
>
> The American consul took charge of the people who had come across Finland with us and the Oxford man and I went to the Continental Hotel, which, I believe, is the best hotel in that city. We had an evening meal together in a tea room that

reminded me very much of the sort of places we used to call coffee palaces in Melbourne when I was a girl. We drank tea served in cups with milk and cream. I felt I was nearing home. I was tired and I didn't want any more adventure and had had a surfeit of travel.²

Later in the day Mary boarded the night train to +Oslo. As she crossed the border into Norway, a customs officer entered her carriage. Seeing Buchanan he asked sternly, 'Have you got a certificate of health for that dog?'

Mary had to admit she did not. The customs officer telegraphed the police in Oslo to meet her and take the little dog to a veterinary surgeon for a health check. On arrival in Oslo she took a room at the Victoria Hotel, while Buchanan dog was taken to the vet. Next morning a Norwegian policeman returned with Buchanan, handed Mary the dog's health certificate and demanded five shillings.

Greatly relieved, Mary continued her train journey through Buskerud, an area of snow-capped mountains. Arriving at Bergen, a city of wooden houses set at the head of a fiord she and the other passengers boarded the *Haakan VII*. On board ship Mary learned to her amazement that British and Anzac troops had landed in France and were fighting against the Germans.

The Norwegian ship took them to Newcastle-on-Tyne and from there Mary caught a train to London. At that time in Britain there was no quarantine for dogs so she was able to bring Buchanan into England without any problems and she and Buchanan returned to *Mary Haven*, her home at Eltham in Kent, where at last the little dog could freely in her garden.³

CHAPTER 24

The Gaunts in wartime

After years of travelling under harsh conditions , Mary enjoyed the t rural atmosphere of Eltham. Petrol was rationed but she was able to catch a train to central London in order to visit her literary agent, old friends and favourite bookshops and attend meetings of the Royal Geographical Society.

In the first year of the war the plight of homeless Belgian refugee families became urgent. The Kaiser's troops had invaded neutral Belgium en route to attack Paris provoked Britain to declare war on Germany.

German troops, claiming the Belgians had blocked their route and slowed down their conquest of Paris and shot at them from rooftops (which was untrue) s, torched ancient Belgian towns like Liege and the ancient cathedral city of Louvain and its university library, leaving thousands homeless and with no possessions.

The Germans had shot Belgian civilians and taken thousands of Belgian men in cattle trucks to Germany to work in German factories. and their wives and children fled on ferries or fishing boats to Dover and Folkestone or crossed the Dutch border and were fed by the Dutch government and houses in tents.

Bewildered Belgian refugees were directed by British police to Dartford, a town where male factory workers had had to enlist in the war and the factories needed labour and had nothing but the clothes on their backs. Mary and other kind hearted residents formed a committee to raise money and rent homes for the refugees, provided them with food and warm clothing, and gave

English lessons to French or Flemish speaking children. Those Belgian boys spared by the German and young women were given work in the armaments and lorry making factories of Dartford like J and E Hall and some were billeted at Eltham.

In 1915 a hospital for wounded and crippled Anzacs was established at Dartford, No 3 Australian Military Hospital using Australian nurses. Mary volunteered to become a regular visitor at the convalescent home for amputees and went there too write letters for disabled Anzacs back to their families in Australia. The nurses many of whom had been nursing under terrible conditions in France were overworked so civilian volunteers like Mary Gaunt helped out by taking the wounded outside in wheelchairs , reading to them and talking of Australia to them. Young wounded officers well enough to leave the hospital were entertained by Mary and other volunteers in their homes, aware how good it was for 'our boys' to feel they were in a private home rather than an institution.

On her hospital visiting days Mary noted the comfort obtained from reading to the wounded in the convalescent home. She organised a library for Anzacs with books she supplied and Lucy Gaunt sent parcels of Australian books from Melbourne.

In 1916 the first 'Super Zeppelins' (large airships), capable of dropping bombs, appeared over the night skies of southern England. These Zeppelins attacked a range of targets, including Tilbury Docks on the Thames. Cenral London and the town of Dartford near Eltham with its factories and the Joyce Green Military Airport., a target of interest to the Germans/ Bombing civilians was something entirely new.

On the night of 8 August 1916 the Germans Luftwaffe :launched thirteen Zeppelins on southern London, aiming for Deptford Dry Dock and the factories of Dartford busy making armaments and Army lories. Some of the Zeppelins went off target and their bombs fell on private homes in the Eltham areas.[1] Nine people were killed and forty more badly injured. Mary's house had its roof blown off and windows shattered — neither her insurance company nor the British Government covered civilian bomb damage, a very new concept in warfare Mary had to pay a substantial sum to render her house liveable.

As winter approached Mary suffered from severe attacks of bronchitis. The fact that the repairs to her house were still not completed as so many tradesmen were fighting in France caused her even more discomfort.Mary thought longingly of the warmth of southern France or Italy and vowed that when the war was over she would sell her house and rent somewhere cheap in the warmth of the Mediterranean.

As the war dragged on supplies of imported sugar, fruit and nuts became scarce as German submarines were blockading the ships which tried to bring supplies to Britain. In response the British navy retaliated by blockading German ports. The war which had been expected to last only a year seemed endless and the death toll was horrendous.

The news of the sinking of several hospital ships and the stalemate in the trenches intensified the belief that these disasters were due to inefficient political leadership. There was talk of appointing a 'Food Minister' to supervise rationing of essential foods and the official establishment of 'meatless days' to make what meat there was go further.

The spring of 1917 was one of the coldest ever recorded in Britain, coal was scarce and Mary continued with her hospital visiting and work on another novel. The price of eggs and butter soared and became scarce — a proper system of food rationing was still to be worked out by the British Government/.

Paper rationing now meant few books were published so Mary's income from royalties plummeted. Before the outbreak of war Mary had been one of the most popular female 'quality authors in the English speaking world with a good income and a nest egg of savings for her old age since at that time there were no such things as age pensions.

Despite Mary's meagre royalties, she could not refuse the plight of the homeless refugees and continued to donate her time and what remained of her savings to help the unfortunate Belgian war victims. After German attacks on towns in western Flanders such as Ypres and Poperinghe, widows and orphans flooded into the area who had no clothes other than those they stood up in and needed financial help.

By the summer of 1917 trench warfare across the north of France was at a stalemate and peace seemed a distant dream. That winter was even colder than the spring, coal still in short supply and once again Mary suffered from bronchitis. By now she had finished *A Broken Journey*, but due to paper rationig e this and her Chinese novel *The Wind from the Wilderness* would not be published until the war had ended. Mary had begun work on *The Wind from the Wilderness* as a guest at an American Baptist Mission and the novel incorporates many of her own feelings about missions in China. The principal character mission doctor Rosalie Gascoigne is dedicated to ending the practice of foot binding. White Wolf, who had made a huge impression on Mary features in the novel. Another character is a disreputable Englishman, a man who had gone down in the world and became an arms dealer. When he seeks hospitality at the mission the missionaries learn he is travelling through the region to sells guns and ammunition to White Wolf.

The novel was gripping with a vivid description of an attack on the mission by xenophobic Chinese and the escape of , Dr Rosalie Gascoigne and Englishman Martin Conant and the flirtatious Stella Chapman. Dramatic tension is provided by the fact Rosalie Gascoigne refuses to acknowledge how attracted she is to Martin Conant. Stella Chapman's husband is shot by bandits throws herself at Martin Conant and the three of them escape from White Woolf together. Mary Gaunt's gripping novel aroused enthusiasm from Werner Laurie but was published until 1919.[2]

Lance Gaunt, her youngest brother had abandoned his successful legal practice in the Far East to join the British Navy as a reserve officer and was eventually given command of a cruiser. Mary's nephew Pat Archer, son of her sister Lucy and living in Victoria volunteered to join the Anzacs and was sent to France. Whenever Pat managed to obtain leave he stayed at *Mary Haven*, which he regarded as a home from home.

Guy Gaunt, as a very successful Head of British Naval Intelligence was subsequently knighted for his war effort. Ernest Gaunt also enjoyed a stellar career and in 1917 was given command of a squadron of the British Fleet ating the Battle of Jutland close to the Danish coast. Jutland was a largest naval battle of World War One with many ships sunk and a huge death toll.

Every time Mary opened *The Times* she felt a chill when looking at the Casualty List, fearing that Ernest or her nephew Pat could be on it.

Ernest Gaunt proved himself a brilliant tactician, his ship sunk several German battle ships but Ernest did not lose a single sailor under his command and was knighted by George V at Buckingham Palace.

Mary continued her hospital visiting at Dartford, in summer the rows of wounded men sat outside in the pale English sunlight and she read to them and wrote letters 'home' for men with no arms or no legs. Like everyone else she wondered when would this dreadful war end?

***

Finally at 11 am on 11 November 1918 the Germans requested an armistice and the fighting ended. Very soon prophecy that had been made to Mary on her Siberian journey that three emperors would lose their thrones proved to be true. The Kaiser, the Tsar of Russia and the Emperor of Austria all lost their thrones in what the newspapers called 'The Great War to End All Wars.' The wounded Anzacs at Dartford Australian military hospital went home to Australia on transport ships.

One result of the peace was soaring inflation to pay for the war. Mary's second book on China was published and republished.

Sir Ernest Gaunt, honoured with a KCG (Knight Companion of the Order of the Bath) was given command of *HMS Majestic* and made Commander-in-Chief of the Western Approaches Fleet and in addition honoured by a KBE.

Guy Gaunt was posted to Washington heading British Naval Intelligence there and helped run an international spy ring based in Budapest .On his return to Britain with his charm and good looks Guy was chosen to serve as ADC to King George V at Buckingham Palace and knighted for his services. After retiring from the Navy he became a Conservative Member of Parliament for Buckrose in Yorkshire.

Mary and Ernest kept in touch with Jennie Morrison who had returned with George Morrison from China since he was ill. The Morrisons were guests of Lance and Violet Gaunt at their country house at Forest Row in Sussex so George Morrison could consult with Harley Street specialists. He was eventually diagnosed with chronic pancreatitis and gall bladder problems which were not operable. He and Jennie moved to a rented house on at Sidmouth on the coast and after prolonged illness George died there on 27 May 1920. Sir Ernest Gaunt, now retired from the navy, his wife daughter Sheila, (who had married a grandson of the fourth Lord Ventry) and Mary attended George Morrison's funeral.

Also in 1920 Messrs Werner Laurie brought out a collection of Mary Gaunt's short stories, *The Surrender and other happenings*, including 1 stories set during World War One, some set in Tasmania, two in Victoria and another in a Chinese town under siege by the bandits working for the war lord, , White Wolf, who had made a deep impression on Mary during her ttempt to reach the Gobi desert.

Once again the reviews were excellent. The London *Daily Chronicle* for April 1920 and the *Brisbane Courier* for 15 May 1920 described Mary Gaunt as 'a gifted author' with a similar talent for depicting character that she displayed in *A Wind from the Wilderness,*

During the British winter of 1920, Mary's asthma became worse and she suffered a severe attacks of bronchitis. Keen to free up money and live in a milder climate but aware she must remain reasonably close to her London publishers she decided to sell *Mary*

Haven and move to the south of France. She rented accommodation at St Agnesse en Provence, having invested most of the money from the sale of her house in southern England and received a small but regular income from her investments. In England once the war was over inflation had soared.

Relieved by milder winter days and nights, Mary found that living in southern France was considerably cheaper. She still published novels of adventure set in wild places in Africa.

CHAPTER 25

The final years

By 1922 Mary, now in her sixties was determined to continue writing, ill her main source of income and pleasure.

Perhaps it was the fact that Italy was now chapter than France which caused her to move from the French village of St Agnesse en Provence and rent the Villa Camilla at the holiday resort of Bordighera on Italy's Ligurian coast. Bordighera had an excellent international library which was one of its attractions for Mary and a mild climate. The excellent yacht harbour meant that Ernest and his wife who loved sailing, would come to stay with her. .

Mary had been fond of Guy's wife -Margaret but knew from Ernest that her dashing brother, a former Head of Naval Intelligence, a still handsome man, greying at the temples was attacted by beautiful women and was discretely unfaithful to his wife. . Mary and Ernest feared Guy was playing with fire as a Member of Parliament and when he was cited as co-respondent in a scandalous society divorce and Guy had to resign as a Member of Parliament. Mary was unhappy about the press reports of Guy's infidelity and his divorce from Margaret but Guy was such amusing company and Mary so proud of him she could never be angry with her younger brother for long. To avoid scandal Guy left England and lived in Tangier.

Guy liked Bordighera which was twenty kilometres to the east of the Italian-French border at Ventamiglia. Around the long narrow harbour of Bordighera were wide boulevards known as *lungarnos* lined with palm trees. Bordighera was proud of the fact it supplied palm fronds to the Vatican for the Palm Sunday services.

By 1922 when Mary rented the *Villa Camilla,* No 6 via Sant'Ampelgio, with its view over the harbour, Bordighera was an affluent holiday resort. It had a large British community and an interesting group of Russians and Russian Jews.

Mary's next door neighbours were a couple of charming Russian-Jewish artists who had met while working in Paris. They gained a precarious living by selling paintings and doing some work in a local antique shops. Mary enjoyed sharing meals with the two of them, hearing their memories of Russia and Monparnasse where they had known the Russian-Jewish artist Moise Shagall, who had taken French citizenship under the name of Chagall.s.

Queen Margharita of Savoy owned a summer villa at Bordighera as did many Italian aristocrats who frequented the Internatioanl Library and its book circle. Bordighera's international library-cum- museum had been founded by the Reverend Bickford, an Anglican clergyman. It had shelves of English books and subscribed to *The Times* and other English newspapers and magazines. Through the library Mary now in her late seventies and starting to feel her age made friends with other elderly English ladies, the widows of diplomats and Army officers. .

Living at the *Villa Camilla,* .Mary felt so well cared for by the faithful Anselma that she planned to spend the rest of her life there. Mary restored the villa's garden. Anselma, a widow from Reggio Emilia near Bologna, resided in the villa and was an excellent cook and housekeeper. Anselma enjoyed telling Mary's neighbours that she worked for a famous author.

After a lean period after the war Mary had two more successes in April 1925 when *The New York Literary Review* and *The Saturday Review of Literature* acclaimed her powers of narration when reviewing her latest book, *Where the Twain Meet*, which concerned the slave trade between Africa and the West Indies. In 1926 she had an unexpected success when urged on by brother Guy one Christmas they wrote a crime novel, *The Mummy Moves* sparked by Mary's visits to the Egyptian galleries of he British Museum. The detective novel written to amuse friends and family aroused the interest of Mary's agent who claimed it would sell well on both sides of the Atlantic, which turned out to be correct. Mary, urged on by Guy had written the crime novel with her usual competence but somewhat ,tongue in cheek. She was surprised to find it had turned into a best seller in America and Britain where it was published in London by T. Werner Laurie and in New York by Edward Clode with enormous success.[1]

At the *Villa Camilla* Mary finally found the time to complete a historical novel set in Sydney, started when she was living at Warrnamboul and only stopped working on when it became clear that her husband was suffering from mental and physical illness. She had not looked at it since butdecided to finish it.

Mary was a versatile author and her novel *As the Whirlwind Passes* — begun years earlier in Warrnamboul and put away during her husband's fatal illness now attracted her attention again. It was set in Sydney in the time of Governor Hunter. It charted the struggles of the fledgling colony to survive, the machinations of the Rum Corps and the struggles of , convicts who had served their time to build a better life for themselves and their children on the far side of the world. Published in London in 1923 and dedicated to her niece, Sheila Gaunt, the novel proved popular with Australian readers and had two colonial editions shipped to Australia by the London publishers.[2]

Mary's novel *The Forbidden Town*, also published in 1926 received excellent reviews. Set in West Africa the heroine was a hardworking feisty young woman who struggles to run a large rubber plantation in a colony composed of British bachelors or married men separated from their wives. A critic of *The Times Literary Supplement* praised Mary Gaunt's handling of plot and narrative and called it 'an exciting story of West Africa by the writer of several other tales of African adventure' *The Forbidden Town* had huge success in America where it was published in three separate American editions.

By now Somerset Maugham had become by far Britain's most financially successful novelist and writer of short stories. Maugham's turbulent marriage to Syrie, a cover for his homosexuality had become unbearable to him. Maugham's relationship with handsome young American, Gerald Haxton would lead to his divorce. Gerald Haxton's trial for illegal homosexual activities caused Maugham a large outlay in lawyers' fees to get Haxton off. Maugham warned that his homosexual activities could cause him to be jailed also left England. He bought the Villa Mauresque at St Jean Cap Ferrat where Maugham, now at the height of his creative powers also became an expatriate author domiciled in Europe.

In 1929 the bubble of the soaring economy finally burst. Mary's investments in England from the sale of her house were badly affected by the stock market crash. Fortunately a book r, designed for schools and libraries as well as the general public, *George Washington and the Men who Made the American Revolution*, brought her a steady stream of royalties. Shortly after the New York and London stock markets crashed Mary's novel *The Lawless Frontier* appeared in print and it went to two paperback editions in 1930 and 1932.[3]

In 1929 Mary spent a summer holiday in Cornwall with her brother Guy. They stayed at a former smuggler's inn at the picturesque harbour of Polperro which in Mary's novel, *Joan of the Pilchard* (the name of the inn), was about a young kitchen maid at the inn whose boyfriend is press ganged aboard a ship commanded by Captain Bligh. Mary wrote about the subsequent voyage of Bligh and his crew on the *Bounty* with accurate details of the ship's rigging and the hazards of a sailor's daily life. Most of that information was supplied by Guy Gaunt, whose hobby was maritime history. The hardback, published in London in April 1930 was dedicated 'To my brother Admiral Sir Guy Gaunt' and with its accurate accounts of life at sea in the era of Captain Bligh was sold to book clubs and a paperback edition appeared the following year.

In the winter of 1930, after a severe bout of bronchitis, Mary Gaunt sailed to Jamaica for a holiday in the warmth of the West Indies. But her Jamaican travel books are not nearly as fascinating as those earlier works set in Africa and China.

Mary had been invited to visit Jamaica by an English speaking Frenchman who owned a newspaper there as she was fascinated by the dark history of the island. Monsieur Delissier had become interested in Mary and her books when he had met her at a function at Bordighera's international library. Delissier provided entrées to the homes of wealthy Jamaican plantation owners, most of whom were of upper class English background. They told Mary about the eighteenth and nineteenth century plantations and the lives of their ancestors who had grown rich on slave labour. They showed Mary the miserable rows of wooden huts were their slaves had been housed, while their masters lived in large and elegant plantation homes, waited on by the slaves they had bought and the more attractive black women were usually taken as mistresses by the master of the house and his sons.

Mary would never forget these stories about the sufferings of black slaves who had been shipped from African slave forts to American plantations. Clearly the plantation owners did not understand that she had seen the slave forts in Africa where this terrible trade began and she wrote about it with the same passion and conviction she had written about the evils of foot binding in China which made her unpopular in the West Indies.

Monsieur Delissier owned a copy of the diary of a titled English lady of the eighteenth century who had paid an enjoyable visit to Jamaica and loaned it to Mary and based on it she produced *Harmony, A Tale of the Slave Days*. The novel portrays the degrading effects of slavery, not only on black women but also on the wives of plantation owners. Many of these wealthy planters had black mistresses as well as children of these unions. Their long-suffering wives were expected to put up with the situation and stay silent in return for a comfortable life. *Harmony, A Tale of the Slave Days* roused a furore in Jamaica and in England. Scores of England's titled families had made their fortunes out of the slave trade from which they had extended or built stately homes and become inordinately wealthy. Mary depicted British colonists using their female slaves as sex objects at a time when such things were covered up in 'polite society.' By writing these *three* books Mary made enemies among those Jamaican plantation owners who had entertained her and local reviews of her books on the West Indies were blistering with anger against her. But Mary was ageing and although she had many readers of her own age younger feminist writers like Rebecca West and Virginia Woolf were taking over. However Mary still had a solid core of readers with twenty novels and travel books published in Britain and America and copies shipped to Australia by her London publishers so in the International Library she was regarded as Bordighera's star expatriate author.

After a long visit to the West Indies Mary sailed back to London, where she paid a brief visit to her literary agent and several London publishers. It would be her last visit to London. Back at the *Villa Camilla*, Mary concentrated on finishing *Reflection in Jamaica which contained descriptions of visits to* , elegant white colonial houses, and their former slave quarters, a reminder of Jamaica's brutal past and the involvement of prominent English families in the slave trade, something they wished to forget .

Fears of yet another world war were beginning to preoccupy Guy and Ernest, both of whom had had close contacts with British Naval Intelligence. They realised that Hitler was building up his armed forces in contravention of the Treaty of Versailles. Sir Guy Gaunt wrote letters to *The Times w*arning of the dangers of National Socialism and Fascism.[4] Mary was now of a person of interest to Mussolini's secret police, the OVRA (Organisation for Vigilance against Anti-Fascism).

Guy Gaunt visited his sister at the *Villa Camilla*, and his presence as a former head of British Naval Intelligence no doubt meant the OVRA suspected she was a British spy. Without thinking of the consequences Mary took photographs of the navl harbour of Bodighera for a projected travel book on the Ligurian coast.⁵

During one of his visits to *Villa Camilla,* Guy introduced his second wife to his sister — a difficult situation as Mary had been very fond of Guy's first wife Margaret. and had dedicated one of her novels to her.

Sir Guy Gaunt's marriage had foundered amid scandal when he was cited as the lover of a wife of a fellow Member of Parliament in a society divorce. After he had been cited his wife Margaret had left him and, according to the conventions of the era, Guy was obliged to resign from Parliament.

, Guy Gaunt spent several years on his own in Tangier, writing his memoirs, before marrying a wealthy widow named Sibyl Grant White. His visit to introduce his second wife to Mary at Bordighera was purely a social visit but the OVRA (Mussolini's answer to the Gestapo) believed that Sir Guy Gaunt still had connections to M15 and Mary was part of his former network of spies.

After terrorist bombings in Italy in the early 1930s Mussolini enlarged his secret police and ordered them to report on the activities of all foreign residents in Italy. If Mary had not fled to France she would almost certainly have been arrested.

Guy had warned his sister to return to England once Mussolini declared war on England, but well cared for by Anselma she was reluctant to leave Bordighera. Mary's final novel *World's Away* dedicated to Ernest Gaunt had appeared in London in 1934 but did not do as well as her previous novels. Mary's era was the period of authors like Conrad, Wells nad , Galsworthy she was not attuned to spirit of the Jazz Age and she spent her time working on her memoirs using her diaries and personal papers.

Following the collapse of France in 1940 many English expatriates wanted to leave and return to England

Meanwhile at Bordighera Mary and her expatriates friends were convinced that Mussolini despised Hitler so would never enter into any alliance with the Nazis. ⁶ France was divided into two zones — the north under the Nazis while Southern or Vichy France with its capital at Vichy which was allegedly neutral.

Although the French secret police worked hand in glove with the Gestapo counterparts, arresting Jews in house to house searches and sending them to harsh concentration camps like Le Gur near Bordeaux.[7]

Sheltered by Mary Gaunt in the secluded hilltop village of Vence which was a brave thing to do her Russian Jewish friends escaped on forged documents to America with the help of Varian Fry, an American Oscar Schindler. During the eighteen months he spent working in Marseilles Fry helped to escape some 1,500 Jews and anti-Fascists, some fled over the mountains to Portugal or Spain and others took ships to the French colony of Martinique and from there went to America.

From his Marseilles HQ Varian Fry worked closely with the American consul, Hiram Bingham who defied instructions from the American State Department and endorsed identity documents he knew were forged by Varian Fry's organisation.[8] Mary may have continued to act as a 'safe house' for more Jews awaiting forged papers from Fry's Emergency Committee to leave France but there is no written evidence of this since Varian Fry ordered his helpers to destroy all written records in case the French secret police searched their houses. s

Cecil Gaunt, retired from his position of colonel of a cavalry regiment had predeceased Ernest. Clive now retired from his position of Government Advocate for Rangoon had bought a house in England. Lance and Violet were living in Sussex home and Lucy was still in Melbourne.

***

Only a brief record of Mary's last years can be gleaned from letters written to her brother Guy and to Ernest's daughter, Sheila but being wartime many letters did not get through.

Ernest, seriously ill was admitted to a London hospital. His daughter, Sheila) kept in touch with Mary about her father's progress. Sheila was by now married to Captain Evelyn de Moleyns, a grandson of Lord Ventry. He died in London late in September 1940 aged 75. Mary now in her late seventies and increasingly frail was devastated by his death. She, Ernest and Guy had been so close in her early childhood that it was hard to come to terms with the fact he was dead. Ernest's funeral was held at Chelsea Old Church in London attended by family, naval friends and colleagues. Admiral Sir Ernest Gaunt's obituary in *The Times* summed up his stellar naval career, culminating with his success at the Battle of Jutland, near Denmark in World War One.[9] The obituary also stated that his estate went to his only son with a smaller bequest to Sheila Gaunt and his younger daughter.

Although Mary was now frail although her mind was still alert. She was short of money, having given what money to her Russian friends to escape, was confined to a wheelchair and dependent on well wishers to wheel her around the steep and narrow streets of Vence.

She made fruitless efforts to contact mayors of northern Italian towns where Anselma might have been living but never found her. Her diaries, papers and manuscripts saved by Anselma vanished. I made enquiries in Vence about diaries or notebooks written by an Australian author during World War 2 but had no success.

In 1941 Mary Gaunt suffered a heart attack and was taken by ambulance down the steep road from Vence to an English-funded hospital in Cannes. She died there on 19 January 1942 with very little money in the bank having given most of what she made during her career as a leading novelist to others.

Mary Gaunt, although raised an Anglican was agnostic and had indicated she wished to be cremated. The hilltop village of Vence lacked a proper burial ground so Catholics used the cemetery in the larger adjacent village of St Paul de Vence. French friends requested Mary Gaunt's ashes be scattered in the St Paul de Vence cemetery. Marc Chagallafter spending the war in America would also request to be buried in the cemetery of St Paul de Vence.

Mary Gaunt's obituary published in *The Times* of 5 February, 1942 called her as 'cosmopolitan Australian writer'. It acknowledged that hard work and talent had given her considerable success in Britain, America and Australia. *The Times* praised Mary Gaunt for her courage in travelling alone through some of the world's wildest areas.

But they ignored the fact Mary was a humanitarian who wrote about the horrendous cruelty of the slave trade in Africa and Jamaica, about maltreated native women she observed in her travels in Africa and China.

She was generous to causes in which she believed. During World War One when paper rationing meant few books being published Mary generously donated money saved for her old age at a time when there were no pensions to help Belgian refugees whose homes had been burned by German soldiers. By 1919 she was so short of funds she was forced to sell her Kentish home and move first to Provence and then to Italy where life was far cheaper and the mild climate helped her avoid attacks of asthma and bronchitis.

Mary Gaunt began her literary career in the 1880s, an era when few women dared to write under their own names. The much younger Australians 'Henry' Handel Richardson and Sarah 'Miles' Franklin were not as brave as Mary and sheltered from criticism behind male pen names.

Edith Wharton was undoubtedly a better novelist than Gaunt but her travel books are not as lively as those of Fanny Trollope, Mary Kingsley or Mary Gaunt. Unlike these three pioneer travel writers Wharton, cushioned by a large personal fortune travelled in the utmost luxury surrounded by servants. It was s the adventures and disasters that overtook brave pioneer female globe trotters like Mary Gaunt, Fanny Trollope, *The Domestic Manners of the Americans*, Kate Marsden *By Sledge and Horseback to Outcast Siberian Lepers* Mary Kingsley's two amusing accounts of travels in West Africa that made their books memorable to the reader. These clever enterprising women were not content to write mere guidebooks to other lands. . They were not afraid to criticise things that shocked them or the treatment of their fellow women by abusive fathers and husbands. They endured deprivations that no modern traveller would put up and this helps to make their travel books so memorable...

Mary Gaunt did not see herself as a writer of the usual style of romances in the late Victorian and Edwardian and on into the 1920 when mores were changing. She always insisted on women's right to be taken seriously and earn their own money. Like her fellow exile Edith Wharton she used some novels to illustrate society's discrimination against women..

In *The Uncounted Cost* Mary Gaunt described the vastly different sexual standards demanded of unmarried men who could 'sew their wild oats' with impunity while unmarried girls had to guard their virginity or would be seen as 'spoiled goods' Her novel was banned by prudish British circulating libraries due to its frankness. Edith Wharton in *The Age of Innocence* also shocked her readers with accounts of discrimination against divorced women banned from 'polite' society and regarded as outcasts while her *House of Mirth* depicted the cruelty of New York society to a clever young woman whose family had lost their money who comes to a terrible end. Few of Mary Gaunt's novels have the conventional happy ending.

In 1913, Mary Gaunt became the first female writer to spend a year in Peking and write a book about her experiences which opened up the previously closed world of China to Western readers. Mary's books about China were written almost twenty years before in 1932 in her novel *The Good Earth* American author Pearl S. Buck shocked her readers with descriptions of primitive life in rural China.

Mary Gaunt also amazed readers when describing life in Chinese villages, where few people had enough to eat, baby girls were routinely strangled at birth in poor families or endured agony by having the bones of their feet broken so they could be married off at a tender age to elderly men and never leave the matrimonial home.

A Wind from the Wilderness which Mary Gaunt began in China in 1913 has stood the test of time well as has her contemporary author, Somerset Maugham's novel *The Painting Veil,* also set in rural disease ridden China. . The film of The Painted Veil kindled the interest of younger readers in Maugham with a superb performance from Naomi Watts as the female protagonist,. Mary Gaunt's *A Wind from the Wilderness* set against magnificent Chinese scenery could make an equally stunning film with an actress of the calibre of Watts or Cate Blanchett playing Gaunt's heroine and *alter ego,* the courageous and somewhat cynical Dr Rosalie Gascoigne. .

In view of Gaunt's many adventures in foreign lands and her lifelong support of women it seems surprising that a biography of this remarkable woman has not been published earlier. .

Mary's travel books demonstrates her empathy with the harsh lives of African and Chinese women and the coolness and courage she displayed in dangerous situations. Another of her strengths was her sympathy to what Tolstoy described as 'the universal human vulnerability to pain and loss.' For that as well as for her courage in travelling in disease ridden areas under appalling conditions and writing vivid prose about her experiences, Ballarat born Mary Gaunt deserves to be remembered by Australians who love books and writing.

ENDNOTES

INTRODUCTION

1. The author's father, Commander J.G.Adamson, fought at the Battle of Jutland off Denmark in World War One with Mary Gaunt's brother, later Admiral Sir Ernest Gaunt, and also knew Admiral , Sir Guy Gaunt over many years from reunion dinners at London's Naval and Military Club. Commander Adamson and his family lived at Chislehurst, near Eltham in Kent where Mary Gaunt had once owned a house in the grounds of the former palace of her ancestor, Prince John of Gaunt. Sir Guy Gaunt told author's father about their fearless sister and her travels. Susanna de Vries attempted without success to find Mary Gaunt's missing diaries and notebooks which vanished from her Bordighera home amid the chaos of World War 2. A visit to the hill villages of Vence and St Paul de Vence produced photographs for this book but no diaries or notebooks by Mary Gaunt. It seems significant that biographies of Varian Fry (including one published by the Jewish Holocaust Museum) record Fry issuing instructions to all his helpers and owners of 'safe houses' to burn all written records for fear of house-searches by the French secret police who were working with the Gestapo. Fry knew that any written evidence against him would mean he would be deported thus ending his escape network, ensuring the capture of the Jewish artists and shot down British airmen Frey and his team of volunteers including Mary Gaunt were helping to escape from internment camps.

PRELUDE — Outwitting Mussolini

1. Mary Gaunt had no pension and had donated all her savings to war victims in World War One so ended the war considerably poorer than at the beginning of the war when she had earned good money from her books. She had never liked the chilly British climate which made her asthma worse so sold her Kentish home, invested the money and spent a year in Provence perfecting her French and writing another novel before taking a long lease on the *Villa Camilla*. .

2. The famous inn and restaurant Le *Colombe d' Or* still had examples of works by Leger, Picasso and Matisse on its walls when visited by Susanna and Jake de Vries when researching Mary's time in Provence...

3. At that stage Matisse was working in Nice and not until the following year would he come to the village of Vence, to convalesce from an operation and be persuaded by his nurse, a former Dominican nun, to dedicate the famous

Matisse Chapel of the Rosary in Vence which at the time when Mary rented a house there was a very quiet but attractive village.

4. The sad fate of elderly foreign residents in Florence who did *not* escape and were jailed in a disused convent in San Gimignano by Mussolini where they were cold and hungry was related by young Italian boy named Franco Zeffirelli in a film called *Tea with Mussolini*. f Mary's elderly friends who remained in Bordighera were jailed on a remote island off the coast where some died from cold and malnutrition as food was very scarce in wartime Italy and prisoners half starved.

5. In 2006 there was a large mural by Leger in the courtyard restaurant and various post World War 2 works were added later. We could not find a work on the walls by a Russian artist called Igor but were told that some work s had been sold off by Monsieur Roux and others added.

6. The Leger mural now resides in the courtyard restaurant of *le Colombe d'Or* and valuable works by Matisse, Derain and Picasso are inside the building.

7. In 1935 as a young journalist on an assignment in Berlin Varian Fry had been shocked by Nazi brutality towards Jews. In August 1940 he was chosen by the American Escape Committee to travel to Marseilles with US$3,000 in cash and a list of 'significant' Jews he was to try and help escape, taped to his inside leg. Varian Fry was helped by his Escape Committee consisting of female volunteers and they aided the Jewish author Arthur Koestler, Jewish film director Max Ophuls, , Wanda Landowska, the Polish-Jewish harpsichordist and Alma Mahler-Werfel, Austrian born widow of Gustav Mahler, who was a composer and married to Jewish writer Franz Werfel. Varian Fry personally escorted Alma Mahler and her husband and the author Heinrich Mann and his wife over the Pyrenees to freedom. He worked closely with Hiram Bingham the American Vice-consul in Marseilles at a time when the US State Department actively discouraged emigration of Jews to America. In December 1940 Fry was arrested by the French police but released. When the American govt. refused to renew his passport and bravely Fry continued working without one. For safety. Fry kept no paperwork and after 'his' Jews had departed destroyed what was left but it is estimated he helped over 1,000 Jewish and anti Fascist artists and intellectuals to escape. It seems Mary Gaunt's rented house in in Vence like Chagall's house in the village Gordes became s a temporary 'safe house for Jews and shot down British airmen while Varian Fry and his helpers paid for forged papers and arranged sea passages for them. .

8. In the 1930s my parents used to holiday in St Paul de Vence and often ate at the le *Colombe d'Or*, Monsieur Roux told them about Chagall'ss escape to

America and a Russian artist whose broken fingers helped convince Chagall he must leave France.

9   On a visit to Vence I was told about an elderly English speaking lady who sheltered wounded British airman until they could be escorted over the Franco-Spanish border and reach England which seems likely to have been Mary Gaunt.

10 Mary Gaunt's unfinished memoirs, titled *A Victorian Girlhood*. Appear in her s entry in the Australian *Who's Who for 1942* and various literary guides. The remote village of Vence, since Matisse decorated a chapel there has now become a busy tourist spot. .

11 Sir Guy Gaunt, *The Yield of the Years, a Memoir*, Hutchinson, London, 1940.

12 Sir Guy Gaunt, an excellent *raconteur* enjoyed telling stories about his sister and her bravery to his naval colleagues. Guy's memoirs were published in 1940 so this escapade does not appear in *The Yield of the Years*. Varian Fry warned his volunteer workers not to keep any diaries or written evidence of their activities. If discovered could jeopardize his rescue network and perhaps this explains why no diaries or notebooks written by Mary have been found at Vence.

13 Anselma was devoted to Mary Gaunt so must have hidden Mary's diaries and personal possessions once the *Villa Camilla* had been requisitioned by the Italian Army. . Various authors have tried to find the diaries keen to write her biography but at the time of writing none have done so..

14 A letter from Mary Gaunt to her sister Mrs Lucy Archer, dated 1940, claimed the villa 'is in chaos due to Anselma have taken refuge at Reggio Emilia [near Bologna]. I came back to find all my furniture wrapped up... Anselma believed that young soldiers could not be trusted not to ruin everything. She has served me faithfully for eighteen years. I cannot walk at all now.' Extract from Lucy Archer Papers, Melbourne University.

CHAPTER 1 — 'Gaunts *never* give up'

1   William Henry Gaunt left England for Melbourne in 1851.Hiss entry in *The Australian Dictionary of Biography* gives his English address as Melton Hall, Melton. See note 11 below re Melton Hall in *The History of Staffordshire*, Volume 7.

2   Mary's paternal grandfather was christened John Gaunt after his famous royal

ancestor, Prince John of Gaunt.

3   Prince John's long term mistress Katherine de Roet Swynford o three years before his death became his third wife, Katherine Swynford was the well educated young widow of Sir Hugh Swynford, a landowner to whom she had been married at the age of sixteen. Widowed till young Katherine de Roet Swynford was employed by Blanche, Duchess of Lancaster, the first wife of Prince of John of Gaunt as governess to their children. Theirs had been a dynastic marriage as was customary for royalty. Prince John and Katharine fell in love and finding herself pregnant she left the court, and bore Prince John three sons and a daughter out of wedlock. As princes only married girls with royal blood she remained a mistress and on the death of the Duchess of Lancaster, Prince John married a Spanish princess who also died young. The English court were horrified when in his old age the twice-widowed Prince John of Gaunt, now second in line to the throne married Katherine Swynford in order to legitimise their three sons and one daughter who had been given the name of Beaufort rather than Gaunt so they could never claim the throne of England.

As a result, the red lions of England on the coat of arms of Katherine's children and subsequent Gaunts bore a bar sinister across them denoting illegitimate descent.

Prince John's sons by Katharine had been banned by Parliament the right to call themselves Gaunt for fear they might try to usurp the crown from the future King Henry IV) but later an illegitimate grandson of Prince John and Katharine would challenge the ruling and call himself Gaunt and the Shropshire Gaunts descended from him.

4   Staffordshire Records Office, Stafford, 1867 in a document cited on page 94 of Ian F. McMcLaren's annotated bibliography of Mary Gaunt, published Melbourne University Press, University of Melbourne Library, Melbourne 1986.

5   Details from Judge William Gaunt's obituary in *The Argus*, (Melbourne) 6 October, 1904, published when Mary Gaunt was living in London. Additional details about the Gaunt family supplied by Admiral Sir Ernest Gaunt to the author's father, Commander James Guthrie-Adamson, RN at London's Naval and Military Club and later Sir Guy Gaunt provided details of the trip to the *Villa Camilla*.

6   Mary Gaunt, *Reflection in Jamaica*, Ernest Benn, London, 1932, page 141.

7   Mary's mother grew up in modest circumstances at Tawonga, in Victoria's 'high country. Information on William Henry Gaunt (1830-1905) appears on

page 80 of *Mary Gaunt, a Cosmopolitan Australian,* compiled by librarian Ian F.McClaren and in The *Australian Dictionary of Biography,* Volume 4, Melbourne University Press, 1972, pp 238-239.

8   Vere Arnold Gaunt born 1870 died 1871; Alice Maud Victoria Gaunt born and died in 1877; William Henry Gaunt(Junior) born and died in 1881. Clive survived and became a champion rower at Melbourne Grammar and did well academically but asthma always plagued him.

9   Verbal information from Sir Ernest Gaunt to James Guthrie-Adamson.

10 Mary Steele, *Beside the Lake. A Ballarat Childhood,* Page 25. In 1879 the entire estate was sold to the Anglican Church as a residence for the bishop and renamed Bishopscourt.

11 Mary Gaunt, *Alone in West Africa,* London and New York, 1912.

12 Kumasi is now a self governing area in Ghana.

13 Henry Moreton Stanley wrote this and a further book *Two Commands* describing the Ashanti who he admired for their courage in battle and regarded as being as brave as the far better known Zulu warriors.

14 Mary Gaunt, From the Foreward to her book *Reflections in Jamaica,* page vii. London, 1932.

15 Interview with Mary Gaunt (Mrs. Miller) by E.M.F. *Sydney Mail,* 26 February 1898, reprinted in the *Warrnambool Echo,* 26 February, 1898.

16 At the start of World War 1 Clive Gaunt, as asthma sufferer tried to enlist but was rejected on health grounds.

17 For an account of *Strathalbyn House* when it was known as *Bishopscourt,* see, Mary Steele, *Beside the Lake, A Ballarat Childhood.* Hyland House, Melbourne, 2000 pages 22-33. Research into Bishopscourt courtesy of Edith Fry, Historian, Ballarat Library.

18 A few very wealthy families still provided daughters with dowries though this custom was now dying out.

19 The chief proponent of the theory about women's brains being smaller than those of men was Dr Henry Maudsley, a neurologist and pioneer psychiatrist at the height of his fame in the 1870-1880s who had the London psychiatric clinic,, the Maudsley Hospital named after him is today seen as a man with h repugnant and repressive views on the capabilities of women so must have been detested by Mary Gaunt and other British and Australian women who supported women's write to vote and attend university.

20 Judge Gaunt's portrait in the Ballarat Club shows him with a large black beard as does a portrait held by one of his descendents.

21 This demand was not outlandish for its era. Queensland politician Thomas Murray Prior after his career ran into difficulties and his wife died, told his daughter Rosa he refused to support her, and she must accept the first suitor to offer her a wedding ring. Rosa did as her father demanded, married Campbell Praed, an Englishman and their marriage was a disaster.

CHAPTER 2 — Fighting prejudice at university

1 Ian McLaren. Annotated Bibliography, Mary Gaunt. University of Melbourne Library, 1986 entry on chronology on page 81.

2 According to *The History of Staffordshire*, Vol 7 on line, Judge Arthur Gaunt worked in Bombay but spent his long leave at the home of his sister *Melton Hall* in Staffordshire.

3 All that first intake of thirteen female students at Melbourne University were failed or like Mary Gaunt, dropped out in disgust.

4 For other examples of discrimination against women in Australian universities see Susanna de Vries, *Strength of Purpose*, HarperCollins, Sydney, 1998. pp 56-63 and pp 89- 100. These pages relates the university careers and discrimination against f Drs Dagmar Berne and Constance Stone who had to study medicine at universities in London and America in order to qualify as doctors in Australia.

5 Mary's sister, Lucy Gaunt and Bella Guerin, journalist and social reformer, were the first women to be awarded arts degrees from Melbourne. University As the discrimination and attempts to fail women continued by some university lecturers continued unchecked, it took these two clever young women *five years* to complete what was supposed to be a 3-year university course.

6 See Ian McClaren's bibligraphy of Mary Gaunt's work page xiv and Margaret Bradstock, entry on Mary Gaunt from *Dictionary of Literary Biography* online, My own interest in Gaunt began in the year 2004 when I applied to the Literature Board of Australia (without success) for funds to find the missing papers and diaries and memoirs of Mary Gaunt , a topic we continued to pursue in Provence in the summer of 2008 but found nothing.

7 Cassells of London published *Picturesque Australasia* with Mary *Gaunt* as the main writer on the colony of Victoria.

8   See Margaret Bradstock's entry on Mary Gaunt in *The Dictionary of Literary Biography* on line and Ian F McLaren's *Annotated Bibliography of Mary Gaunt*.

9   The author's adoptive father, Commander James Guthrie Adamson, RN trained at Dartmouth Naval College with the future George VI. He served at the Battle of Jutland under Ernest Gaunt and they were good friends when they were both member of the Naval and Military Club at 49 Piccadilly, London.

10 The Gaunts travelled on English passports since there were no Australian passports at that time. As William Gaunt had been raised in England his children spoke with English accents as did many educated Australians of that period. ,

11 Mary Gaunt. *A Broken Journey*. T. Werner Laurie, London, 1919. Page l.

12 Judge Arthur Gaunt is mentioned in the *History of Staffordshire*, Volume 7, published in Staffordshire. Volume 7 about the Leek area cites Judge Gaunt spending his leaves at *Melton Hall* owned by his sister. Family lore says William Gaunt's father was a banker but indicates no address for him.

13 The archives of London publishers, Edward Arnold contain letters from Mrs Mary Miller (her married name) written an address at 52, Hampton Road, Pitsmoor, Sheffield where she often stayed as a guest.

14 Contrary to family legend, *The history of Staffordshire for Leek and district* (internet edition) has William's relatives buying *Melton Hall* the year before William departed for Australia from total strangers making it unlikely William stayed there as a child.

15 Sydney author, Louise Mack who sailed to London in 1901 the same year as Mary had had her first contribution to the Sydney *Bulletin* accepted as she sent it in under a male sounding name of M.L. Mack.

16 Louise Mack sailed to London in 1901, the same year as Mary Gaunt. Louise abandoned 'serious novel writing' due to cold and hunger and 'sold out' to the Daily Mail writing sloppy romantic serial stories for women readers unlike Mary Gaunt whose novels were esteemed by literary editors of newspapers like The Times.

17 Australian critics praised *The Other Man* which was published in monthly instalments starting in 1894 and continuing through the first months of 1895.

18 Mary Gaunt intimated discord between her mother and herself in Chapter One of *Alone in West Africa*.

19 Mary's fictitious Jenny Carter was denied a good education through poverty

and accepted an offer of marriage from a police sergeant, new to the district. Jenny's husband taunted her that her father was earning money from sly grog and he would have him arrested. Eventually Jenny had enough of this abusive marriage and ran off with a handsome gold miner named Black Dave who turned out to be violent and alcoholic.

CHAPTER 3 — Finding Doctor Right

1. *Dave's Sweetheart* was published by Melville, Mullen and Slade, of Melbourne. In spite of a 'romantic' title the novel reflected Mary's concern over the lack of educational and work opportunities for women. See Margaret Bradstock's entry on Mary Gaunt and her entry in *The Dictionary of Australian Literary Biography* in Volume 8 and on line. There was al reprints of *Dave's Sweetheart* in the twentieth century and a digitized edition. j

2. Dr Miller married Annie Isabella Murphy in 1883, later she fell ill (Mary did not elaborate on her symptoms). Dr Miller's first wife was daughter of surgeon Sir Francis Murphy of South Yarra.

3. In *Alone in Africa*, London and New York, 1912, Mary opened this non-fiction book by describing her handsome husband and her happy marriage and explained that she only went to London because she was so lonely after her husband's death but is careful not to mention Kew Lunatic Asylum or discuss his case.

4. Australian born Stella Miles Franklin had to write *My Brilliant Career* under a male pseudonym and Joice Loch aroused the wrath of her in-laws about the same time when she published under her single name.

5. Mary's short stories included *Christmas Eve at Warwingie, The Yanyilla Steeplechase* and a seafaring story *The Loss of the Vanity'* which later appeared in a collection of Mary Gaunt's short stories titled *The Moving Finger*.

6. *Kirkham's Find* became an Australian classic, was reprinted several times between 1897 and 1902 and has several reprints in paperback notably one by Penguin, Ringwood in 1988 had a forward by the eminent female author Kylie Tennant. Copies of this are in is in many school and public libraries and *Deadman's* and *The Moving Finger* have also been reprinted by Dodo Press and are sold on amazon.com.

7. Interview with Mary Gaunt from the *Warrnamboul Echo*, 26 February, 1898.

8. Mary's articles from the *Argus,* Jan 28, 1893 promoted the work of the Austen Hospital; 25 March, 1893, *Melbourne's Deaf and Dumb Institution,* April 29,

1893, *Land of Darkness, Institute for the Blind;* August 12, 1893, *The Women's Hospital;* September 23, 1893, *In the slums with the district nurses;*October 28, *The Kindergarten;* November ll, *The Little Sisters of the Poor;* January 27, *The Nuns of the Good Shepherd.* For details of Melbourne Women's Hospital see Susanna de Vries, *Strength of Purpose,* giving details about Drs Constance and Clara Stone both denied the right to qualify by Melbourne University.

9   The novelist, Somerset Maugham, when studying medicine at St Thomas's Hospital in London felt sorry for the poor and for prostitutes but this compassion according to Maugham's biographer, Jeffey Meyers, did not stop Maugham him patronizing them. Dr Samuel Jenkin Evans, father of my late husband, Professor Larry Evans,(MB. BSc Edinburgho studied medicine at Edinburgh University and his tales of wild nights in the pubs of the Grassmarket, included drunken medical students paying group visits Edinburgh brothels or picking up prostitutes which they regarded as an initiation rites into manhood and doubtless Mary's husband had been part of the same macho culture. .

10   Death Certificate No 13385 for the district of Kew, October, 1900.

11   Ethel's father, Dr Walter Richardson, the progress of whose mental and physical decline was recorded by his horrified daughter Ethel in her famous novel *Ultima Thule,* written in 1929, After being praised by Somerset Maugham and other British writers, Richardson's s story of her father thinly disguised as 'Dr Richard Mahoney' an Edinburgh trained physician who migrated to Victoria, enjoyed the respect of his peers and during a time when there were no clinical tests for syphilis is alleged to have suffered from 'Cupid's disease, acquired decades earlier as a medical student in Edinburgh . The shameful diagnosis of syphilis would not be applied to a distinguished doctor even if suspected. Until 1906 the link between grand paralysis of the insane and syphilis, though suspected was not properly documented by research Dr Richardson and Dr Miller were classified as 'lunatics' in Kew Lunatic Asylum where Dr Richardson according to the records of Kew was briefly transferred from the Yarra Bend Asylum and had to endure the horrors of the cells where public patients were kept.

12   The author of this biography was married for sixteen years to the late Dr Larry Lawrence Evans, MRC Psych, Professor of Psychiatry at the University of Queensland.and at the University of Edinburgh they gave a joint lecture ion *'Treatment of Tertiary Syphils and Madness in the works of Hogarth up to the days of Gauguin and Manet'.*

13   Letters from Jennie Churchill to her sister indicate that she feared she might have been infected though for years Lord Randolph had turned elsewhere for

sexual relief and Jennie Churchill had taken other lovers. Violet Hunt's fears over her syphilis are from Jeffrey Myers, *Somerset Maugham, A Life* page 73, Vintage Books, London, 2002..

14   These details provided in Jenny Seba's biography of Lady Jennie Churchill when nursing Lord Randolph Churchill and by Henry Handel Richardson, describing her mother Mary Richardson. Dr Walter Richardson had also been a patient at Kew Lunatic Asylum, transferred there from Yarra Bend Asylum with which it was associated. Kew Lunatic Asylum was the largest in Victoria.

15   The rental of a house in Princess Street is mentioned by Bronwen Hickman in her collection of the short stories of Mary Gaunt, *Life at Deadman's, Stories of Colonial Victoria,'* published by Hat Box Press, Melbourne in 2001. The details about eating off tin plates in the public lunatic asylum at Yarra Bend are from Henry Handel Richardson in *Ultima Thule*. Dr Rush's restraining chair and other methods in force in the late 1900s are detailed in 'Conditions in Nineteenth Century Mental Hospitals and Lunatic Asylums in *The British Army Medical Journal*, October 1967 by Dr Larry Evans, late husband of Susanna de Vries).

16   Dr Lindsay Miller was declared a lunatic, unable to manage his own affairs and died intestate and insane at Kew Lunatic Asylum (Death No 4554, Certificate with the verdict e No 1335 given as 'Unknown' to spare embarrassment to patients' family, a usual practice at that time. Professor John Tyrer, Professor of Medicine University of Queensland and Professor Derek Whitlock, Professor of Psychiatry confirmed that this was the diagnosis often presented to spare pain to the relatives especially when the reputation of an eminent medical colleague such as Dr Lindsay Miller was involved asi t.

17   Mary Gaunt, *Alone in West Africa*. Page 5.

18   Mary Gaunt, *Alone in West Africa*, page 45.

CHAPTER 4 — Mary postponed her visit to China

1   Mary Gaunt. *Alone in West Africa*, pages 6.

2   Mary had several ghost stories published in the *English Illustrated Magazine* (one republished in *The Moving Finger*). Between 1903-1905 to support herself in London Mary wrote and had published two serialised novels in the *Empire Review*, the first, *Susan Pennicuik, a story of country life in Victoria* ran for eleven episodes. In 1905 a chapter by Mary Gaunt on the voyages of Captain Cook in appeared in Cassells, *Pictorial New Zealand*.

3   This Gaunt progenitor used the Gaunt coat of arms with the lions of England on it but had the bar sinister imposed across it which in heraldic terms signalled illegitimacy.

4   This and others facts about Mary related to the author's father by Admiral Sir Ernest Gaunt and Admiral Sir Guy Gaunt, at the Naval and Military Club in London.

5   R.R. de Crespigny, *China this Century (20th Century)*. Nelson, London, 1975. pp 33-36.

6   Marina Warner. *The Dragon Empress*. Weidenfeld and Nicholson, London, 1972, page 7 cites a quote from Dowager Empress Cixi claimging she is more interesting and more powerful than Queen Victoria as *'I have over 400 million people, all dependent on my judgement.'*

7   Australian soldiers from New South Wales and Victoria also sailed to the port and arrived around the time Ernest arrived there. A combined force of British, German, Austrian, and Russian troops helped to quell the Boxer Rebellion and execute captured Boxers.

8   Lance Gaunt and Violet Morrison would marry in 1906 and in a strange twist of fate Violet's sister Hilda would in 1915 marry Lance's *older* brother, Clive Gaunt.

9   Mary Steele, *Beside the Lake*. Thanks to Edith Fry, Ballarat Central Library for information.

10 Mary Gaunt. *Travels in West Africa* relates her reasons for visiting West Africa.

11 Ian McLaren F *Mary Gaunt A Cosmopolitan Australian* ,An Annotated Bibliography p 82 University of Melbourne Library 1986 McLaren states Lance Gaunt married Violet Morrison sister of George Morrison in 1906 and their younger sister Evelyn Hilda married Clive Gaunt at Colombo in October 1915.The Gaunt-Morrison marriages are also documented in Peter Thomson and Robert Macklin, *The Man who died Twice, Morrison of Peking*, Allen and Unwin, Sydney, 2004. pages 281 and 342. :

12 Over a decade later Mrs Eliza Gaunt arrived in England and used her capital to buy herself a house near Folkestone. She died there in 1922.

13 These stories included Mary Gaunt's *The Pot of Gold, An Australian story* published by George Newnes in 1904.

14 Mary Gaunt's house at Eltham would not be completed until after her return from Africa.

ENDNOTES 311

CHAPTER 5 — Africa — the Dark Continent

1. Date of departure confirmed in Ian F. McClaren's bibliography of Mary Gaunt, page xvii.

2. Daisy Bates had chosen holland linen when she made trips in the deserts of West and Southern Australia around the same period and encountered the same kind of prejudice for a woman camping alone near naked natives.

3. Mary Gaunt *Alone in West Africa,* page 10-30, describes her visit to the colony known as the Gambia.

4. Mary Gaunt, *Alone in West Africa,* page 26

5. Mary Gaunt , *Alone in West Africa,* page 61

6. Mary Gaunt, *Alone in West Africa,* page 72

7. Mary Gaunt, *Alone in West Africa* ,extracts pp 75-77

8. Mary Gaunt, *Alone in West Africa,* page 91

9. Mary Gaunt, *Alone in West Africa, pp 111-112*

CHAPTER 7 — 'Madame, you have the heart of a lion'

1. Mary in fact wrote an article on the slave forts and would incorporate much of this information on the slave forts into two of her books on Jamaica published in the early 1930s as Jammaica and the rest of he West Indies received a large supply of slaves from West Africa for British owned sugar plantations but many plantation owners resented Mary Gaunt exposing a past they wished to cover up.

2. Mary Gaunt *Alone in West Africa,* London and New York, 1912

3. Mary Gaunt, *Reflection in Jamaica,* Ernest Benn, London, 1932, pages 94-96 incorporate some of the observations of Dr Duff on the slave trade between West Africa and the West Indies.

4. For a more details see Robin Law, *The Slave Coast of West Africa and its Impact on African Society.* Clarendon Press, Oxford, 1991.

5. Mary Gaunt. *Reflection in Jamaica,* page 95.

6. Mary wrote an article on West African slave forts in an article dated 35 April 1911 published in London' s *'The Morning Post'.* Her novel *Every Man's Desire*

was published in London in 1913, concerned a colonial administrator, married to a white woman who entered into a bigamous marriage with an African woman. Two characters in this book were based no stories told her by Dr Duff.

CHAPTER 8 — 'Murder Hill' and Togoland

1. Mary Gaunt, *Alone in West Africa, page 205*
2. Mary Gaunt, *Alone in West Africa*, page 214. Since Mary Gaunt visited the area the Volta Dam was built, creating the vast Lake Volta and changed the geography considerably.
3. Mary Gaunt. *Alone in West Africa*. Page 238.
4. Mary Gaunt, *Alone in Africa*, page 234
5. Mary Gaunt, *Alone in West Africa*, page 243
6. Mary Gaunt, *Alone in West Africa*, page 276
7. The flukes and eggs of snails and a species of flatworm found in ponds and rivers were believed to cause a parasitic disease eventually to be known as schistosomiasis or 'snail fever. But in 1909 when Mary Gaunt was in Africa this was only a theory on which work was still being done but Mary was well aware of the dangers of drinking river water which had not been boiled.

CHAPTER 9 — Black magic among the Ashanti

1. The Long Dane musket was the principal firearm exported from Europe to West Africa. The Danish flintlock musket was one and a half hands longer than the English flintlock, made by a Danish firm called Schultz and Larsen. According to legend these muskets had severe manufacturing defects which ensured that, however skilful a marksman fired it, the musket rifles rarely hit their target. Mary thought the Ashanti were poor e marksmen but it seems likely the fault lay with the musket rather than the Ashanti owners but just seeing the muskets terrified rival tribes.
2. Mary Gaunt, *Alone in West Africa*, pages 351-2
3. Mary Gaunt, *Alone in West Africa*, pages 324-5
4. Kumasi, in southern central Ghana, is 300 miles north of the equator and 100 miles north of the Gulf of Guinea Today it is the second largest city in Ghana and the largest ethnic group there are Ashanti. Part of Kumasi was destroyed

by British troops in the fourth Anglo-Ashanti war of 1874.

5   Mary Gaunt. *Alone in West Africa*. Page 353.

6   Mary Gaunt. *Alone in West Africa*. Page 356.

7   Mary Gaunt. *Alone in West Africa*. Page 361.

8   Unfortunately the quality of her film stock was poor and possibly the humidity did not help. Some would be reproduced in Alone in Africa but are not very good. By the time she reached China her photos and the film stock were far better.

9   Years later Mary read in *The Times* that Matron Oram had distinguished herself nursing in France during World War One.

CHAPTER 10 — The male dinosaurs of London's R.G.H.

1   Ernest Frederick Gaunt, born in March 1865 served in Peking from 1898-9 as Naval Attache at Peking. In Somaliland he was promoted to commander. In World War One he was promoted to rear- admiral and on retirement lived in London and t Monte Carlo with his wife. He died in 1940 survived by a son and two daughters. (See *Vol 8, The Australian Dictionary of Biography* for details on Guy and Cecil Gaunt and an entry on Ernest Gaunt by Sally O'Neill.)

2   Places in Africa visited by Mary are mentioned in the Magazine of the Scottish Geographical y, and in a review of her book in *The Chicago Booklist* and *Bookfellow, the Australian Review*, Sydney, 1912.

3   Gertrude Bell's biggest success was creating the Bagdad Museum with her own money, so it seems sad she took her own life in a fit of depression at the age of fifty-six.

4   An autopsy years later revealed high levels of arsenic in the body of the Emperor Zaitan.

5   Clive and Hilda Morrison would not marry until October 1915 in Colombo, and they returned to Burma.

6   Thompson, Peter and Macklin, Robert. *The Man who Died Twice, the Life and Adventures of Morrison of Peking*. Allen and Unwin, Sydney, 2004 cites the marriages between the Gaunt brothers and Hilda and Violet Morrison referred to by Mary Gaunt in *A Woman in China.*, on page 4. George Morrison was the author of *An Australian in China*.

7   Peter Thompson and Robert Macklin, *The Man who died twice*, pages 288- M89.

8   On page 4 of *A Woman in China*, Mary states 'when he [George Morrison] came to London he came to see me and we talked about China. I asked if it would be worth my while to go there and he was quite of the opinion it would and he and his newly-wedded wife gave me a cordial invitation to stay with them and the thing was settled. I would go to Peking'.

9   At that time Peking's Summer Palace was still being restored.

10   Hermione Lee. *Edith Wharton* details Whartons' extravagant lifestyle, her homes in France and her travels in Europe.

CHAPTER 11 — Through Tsarist Russia to Peking

1   Mary Gaunt. *A Woman in China*, pages 6-9.

2   Before the Bejing Olympics Morrison Street was pulled down and replaced by a pedestrian shopping mall now known as Wangfujing and there is no plaque to mark the house of 'Chinese' Morrison. For details of Morrison Street see Claire Roberts, 'George Morrison's Studio and Library'. *China Heritage Quarterly*, Australian National University, Canberra, No 13, March 2008.

3   Decades later it would be revealed the corpse of Emperor Zaitan contained abnormally high levels of arsenic. It is generally agreed he was poisoned by persons unknown on the orders of the dying Empress Cixi so that Zaitan's proposed reforms would not be implemented.

4   Morrison's letters to John Otway Bland about his friend and fellow journalist reveal Morrison d disliked Mary's friend and fellow explorer Gertrude Bell and claimed she talked too much on the only occasion he met her.

5   In 1917 Morrison sold his library to a large Japanese collector as no Chinese collector would put up sufficient money to purchase it.

6   Melissa Katsoulis, *Telling Tales, A History of Literary Hoaxes*, Hardie Grant, Prahran, 2010 which contains a chapter on the hoax books of Sir Edmund Backhouse and his dodgy Chinese manuscripts with Morrison the only person to spot Backhouse's deception which would only come to light years after Backhouse's death in Peking. See pages 72-73.

7   Mary Gaunt's description of the Legation Compound in 1913 and its American guards are on pages 58-61 of *A Woman in China*.

8   The term 'vegetable sex' refers to the practice of eunuchs using cucumbers or gourds for vaginal penetration which also occurs in accounts of concubines and eunuchs of various Ottoman Emperors at Istanbul's Topkapi Palace.

CHAPTER 12 — Inside the Forbidden City

1. For the full story of Empress Long Yu see Marina Warner. The Dragon Empress, Pages 153- 157 amd 245 – 256.
2. Extracts from Mary Gaunt, *A Woman in China*, pages 80 and 81
3. Extracts from Mary Gaunt, *A Woman in China*, page 83.
4. From *A Woman in China*. Page 85.
5. Extracts from Mary Gaunt, *A Woman in China*, pages 88 and 89

CHAPTER 13 — A political assassination

1. By now the police had restored law and order in Peking. See also *China: Tradition and Transformation* by John K. Fairbank and Edwin O. Reischauer. George Allen and Unwin, Boston, 1979, page 418.
2. Peter Thompson and Robert Macklin. *The Man who died twice. Morrison of Peking*. Page 285.
3. Mary Gaunt, *A Woman in China*, page 73.
4. Morrison Papers, Mitchell Library, Sydney and National Library of Australia, Canberra.
5. Morrison now regretted he had ever left *The Times* and said as much to his good friend W.H. Donald, of *The Bulletin*.
6. George Morrison to J.O.P. Bland, 24 April, 1903, Bland Papers cited in . irl, P.
7. Mary Gaunt, *A Woman in China*. Pag 24.
8. In 1913 Peking rebuilt after the damage and looting during the Boxer rebellion and after was still divided into four walled cities, the Forbidden City, the Tartar or Manchu city with its shops and offices, the ethnic Chinese quarter to the south and the Legation Compound or Zone which was allied to the Tartar City.
9. Extracts from Mary Gaunt, *A Woman in China*, pages 28, 47, 50 and 51.-
10. Extracts from Mary Gaunt, *A Woman in China*, pages 92 – 96.

CHAPTER 14 — The Great Wall of China

1   Presently some of the most visited stretches of the Great Wall have been well restored by the Chinese government, which promotes mass tourism to the area.

2   Born Prince Di-Zu, after taking the title of Emperor Yong Lo or Yongle, he was careful to kill off everybody who threatened his succession.

3   Another version of the event is that Jianwen had fled, disguised as a monk, after setting fire to the palace.

4   The figure of 26,000 hand decorated porcelain bowls and saucers is quoted in the catalogue of the Percival David Collection of Chinese ceramics.

5   From Mary Gaunt, *A Woman in China*, page 128.

6   Yongle's memorial was in great contrast with the relatively modest one of King Henry IV, at Canterbury Cathedral. Mary suspected John of Gaunt's eldest son, Henry IV, had been buried at Canterbury rather than in Westminster Abbey because, liker Yongle, he was a prince who had taken his crown by force.

7   They had been imported from Yunnan but no one told Mary this.

8   Mary Gaunt. *A Woman in China*. Pages 124-25 recounts Mary's visit to the tomb of Emperor Yongle. At the time of writing, the area under Yongle's burial chamber has not been excavated and is no longer open to the public.

9   In 1979 Jake de Vries visited the Ming Tombs. In separate pavilions to the tombs magnificent golden artifacts like golden crowns, golden bowls and vases from various tombs were on view to the public.

CHAPTER 15 — 'Behind every small foot is a jar of tears'

1   As Mary observes the recent legislation on foot binding by the republican government was often ignored in backward areas. In 1930 the English missionary Gladys Aylward arrived in China and worked as a 'foot inspector' employed by the Chinese government to enforce laws against foot binding/. Aylward's remarkable story and her rescue of 94 children from Japanese invaders was told by Alan Burgess, *The Small Woman*, Pan Books, 1957. When the Communist Party gained power in 1949 they re-enforced the prohibition on foot binding.

2   Mary Gaunt, *A Woman in China*, pages 167 -174 deal extensively with foot binding as do several references to mis/sion doctors dealing with the side effects in women in Mary's sequel, *A Broken Journey*.

3 Study into foot binding by Dr Xu Ling, MD,MPH< Peking Union Medical College, Beijing, Dr Steven Cummings, MD, UCSF Professor of Medicine and Katie Stone, Department of Epidemiology of University College, San Francisco at www.sfmuseum.org who examined 193 elderly women in Beijing and the incidences of hip or spinal fractures, walking and climbing steps. These women tended to stay in the home and come from residential communities which were not visited by tourists.

4 Mary Gaunt, *Broken Journey*. London, 1919, page 80. Mary used aspects of some mission doctors to create characters in her short stories set in China and in *A Wind from the Wilderness*, a excellent novel set in China in which Mary's best loved female protagonist appears Dr Rosalie Graham shares many of Mary's character traits is well read, fiercely independent and gives long homilies on the evils of foot binding.

5 Extract from Mary Gaunt, *A Broken Journey*, page 81

6 Mary Gaunt created the character of Dr Rosalie Gascoigne, as part of her own crusade against out foot binding. This cruel practice continued in many areas but would finally banned by the Communists in 1949. However this still left many Chinese women hobbling around on tiny bound feet. The last factory that manufactured tiny silk shoes for women announced in 1998 they had ended production of 'lotus'shoes' for these women with bound feet.

CHAPTER 16 — Chende and the palace of the Manchu

1 This would be rectified late in 1913 when she was allowed to become a Fellow of the Royal Geographical Society.

2 Extract from Mary Gaunt, *A Woman in China*, pages 188 and 189

3 Extract from Mary Gaunt, *A Woman in China*, page 213

4 Extract from Mary Gaunt, *A Woman in China*, page 231

5 Extract from Mary Gaunt, *A Woman in China*, pages 288 and 289

6 A mule litter is a type of sedan chair on long poles which is harnessed with one mule in the front and another in the rear.

7 George Staunton, *An Authentic Account of an Embassy from the King of Great Britain to the Emperor of China*,3 vols. George Nichol, London, 1798. See also Sir Joseph Banks, Papers of, Section 12. concerning publication of the account of Lord Macartney's Embassy to China, 1797.

8 The best description of Long Yu's marriage and the role of Dowager Empress

Cixi in English is not the dubious book by Edmund Backhouse and J.O.P. Bland *Under the Empress Dowager* published in London as Mary left Peking for Siberia but a scholarly biography by Marina Warner, *The Dragon Empress* published in 1972 in London.

9 Extract from Mary Gaunt, *A Woman in China*, page 306

10 Extract from , Mary Gaunt, *A Woman in China*, pages 319-320.

11 Extract from Mary Gaunt, *A Woman in China*, pages 328

12 Extract from Mary Gaunt, *A Woman in China*, page 331

CHAPTER 17 — The temple of the Three Mountains

1 The Italian diplomat and author Daniel Vare rented the Temple of the Three Mountains or San Shan Yur the summer after Mary Gaunt had departed. He arrived in Peking in 1908 and saw the overthrow of the Manchu dynasty, China swept by civil war and the effects of the Russian Revolution on China. He describes the temple in The Gate of Happy Sparrows. Methuen, London, 1937, pages 210-222

2 Extract from Mary Gaunt, *A Woman in China*, page 375

3 Extract from Mary Gaunt, *A Woman in China*, page 379

CHAPTER 18 — 'Keep your last bullet for yourself'

1 Mary Gaunt, *A Wind from the Wilderness*, London, 1919 Page 11.

2 Extract from Mary Gaunt, *A Broken Journey*, page 2

3 The term Silk Route (or Silk Road) was first used in the 19th century by a German geographer named Frederick von Richthofen.

4 Extract from Mary Gaunt, *A Broken Journey*, page 96

5 Extract from Mary Gaunt, *A Broken Journey*, page 24.

6 Extract from Mary Gaunt, *A Broken Journey*, page 26

7 Mary Gaunt, *A Broken Journey*, page 26.

8 Mary Gaunt, *A Broken Journey*, pages 49 and 50

9 Extract from Mary Gaunt, *A Broken Journey*, page 31

10 Extract from Mary Gaunt, *A Broken Journey*, pages 95 and 96

11	This would be confirmed by the Chinese born American author, Pearl S. Buck in her book The Good Earth, published in America two decades after Mary wrote *A Woman in China* and *Broken Journey*.
12	Extract from Mary Gaunt, *A Broken Journey*, page 51
13	Extract from Mary Gaunt, *A Broken Journey*, page 57
14	Extract from Mary Gaunt, *A Broken Journey*, page 56
15	Extract from Mary Gaunt, *A Broken Journey*, pages 120-123

CHAPTER 19 — Last days in China

1	Extract from Mary Gaunt, *A Broken Journey*, page 142
2	Extract from Mary Gaunt, *A Broken Journey*, page 153
3	Extract from Mary Gaunt, *A Broken Journey*, pages 155 and 156
4	The white or St George's Ensign is a white flag with a red St George's Cross with the Union Flag in the upper canton. The ensign is flown on British Navy ships and shore establishments.
5	Extract from Mary Gaunt, *A Broken Journey*, pages 159 and 160

CHAPTER 20 — Exploring the Amur River and Saghalien

1	Extract from Mary Gaunt, *A Broken Journey*, pages 168-183
2	Extract from Mary Gaunt, *A Broken Journey*, page 189
3	Extract from Mary Gaunt, *A Broken Journey*, page 194
4	Extract from Mary Gaunt, *A Broken Journey*, page 211
5	Extracts from Mary Gaunt, *A Broken Journey*, page 211-213

CHAPTER 21 — On troop trains through Siberia

1	Extract from Mary Gaunt, *A Broken Journey*, pages 227 and 228
2	Australian troops who would end up at Gallipoli thought they were bound for England and were surprised to find they were off to Egypt for training and then to Gallipoli.
3	Extract from Mary Gaunt, *A Broken Journey*, pages 231 and 232

4   Extracts from Mary Gaunt, *A Broken Journey*, pages 234-238

5   Extracts from Mary Gaunt, *A Broken Journey*, pages 240-148

6   The *Askold* was a Russian cruiser, which served in the Russian Pacific Fleet during World War I

7   Extracts from Mary Gaunt, *A Broken Journey*, pages 248-251

8   Extract from Mary Gaunt, *A Broken Journey*, pages 259 and 260

CHAPTER 22 — St Petersburg and after

1   Extract from Mary Gaunt, *A Broken Journey*, pages 264 and 265

2   Extract from Mary Gaunt, *A Broken Journey*, page 265

3   Extract from Mary Gaunt, *A Broken Journey*, page 268

4   Extract from Mary Gaunt, *A Broken Journey*, page 270

CHAPTER 23 — Captured by the Germans

1   Extracts from Mary Gaunt, *A Broken Journey*, pages283-285

2   Extracts from Mary Gaunt, *A Broken Journey*, page 289-291

3   *Mary Haven,* New Eltham the address that appears under the foreword of *A Broken Journey,* her gripping novel set in China.

CHAPTER 24 — The Gaunts in wartime

1   See wikipedia.org.wiki/Zeppelin page 9 of 21.

2   *Wind from the Wilderness* is a gripping story which has dated far less than most novels of the period. Written from four different viewpoints it is Gaunt at her best with a great deal of tension, good descriptions and believable characters. The narrators of this exciting plot of a mission station menaced by White Wolf and its workers fleeing for their lives are Dr Rosalie Gascoigne, the mission doctor loathe to acknowledge she is in love with the Englishman also working at the mission an Oxford educated Englishman Martin Conant, who seems to be as skeptical about fundamentalist religion as Rosalie and clearly ahs a past and Silas and Stella Chapman, the wealthy merchant she has married for his money who initially fancies Martin Conant and is jealous of Rosalie.

ENDNOTES   321

1   From 1925-1928 *The Mummy Moves* was reissued in hardback by Edward Clode of New York and once again received enthusiastic reviews in *The New York Tribune*, 8 Feb, 1925, and the Saturday Review of Literature in the same years.

2   Between 1925 and 1928 *The Mummy Moves* was reissued three more times in America, first in hardback by Edward Clode and then in two paperback editions by Grosset of New York.

3   Noted by Ian McClaren in his Annotated Bibliography of the works of Mary Gaunt, University of Melbourne Library, Melbourne, 1986.

4   *The Times*, (London) 'Obituary column, Admiral Sir Guy Gaunt, , 20 May, 1953.

5   Details of this period of Mary Gaunt's life aren described in detail by Margaret Bradstock of the University of New South Wales in *The Dictionary of Literary Biography* 2005/ The projected book on the Ligurian Coast like Mary's memoirs was never published.

6   Brief details of the escape of Mary and the Russians from Bordighera and the escape of the Russians to America aided by Varian Fry's Escape Committee are in letters written towards the end of 1940 by Mary to Sirr Guy Guant and to her r niece, Sheila Gaunt (de Moleyns) held private collections in England see note 86. Searches s at Bordighera have revealed no further details and l Mary's personal papers and manuscripts from the Villa Camilla were never recovered. Sir Guy Gaunt's memoirs, *The Yield of the Years, Adventures Ashore and Afloat* was published by Hutchinson, London before trip by motor cruiser with Mary to Bordighera.

7   See www.wikipeadia/varian fry, biography for the names of 30 of the 1,500 thousands of Jews and anti-Fascists saved by Varian Fry and his Escape Committee.e. Varian Fry, *Surrender on Demand*, Random House, 1945 and the 1997 edition published in conjunction with the US Holocaust Museum give an account of the work of Varian Fry and his s Emergency Rescue Committee but many of their stories have still to emerge. Mary's account of the Russians and their departure is brief and contained in letters to her brothers Guy and Ernest. An exhibition of the papers and photographs of Sir Ernest and Sir guy Gaunt was organized by the Library Committee of the London' Naval and Military Club (members only) in 1969. To the best of the author's knowledge the various photographs and letters including those from Mary Gaunt were returned to their owners after the exhibition.

8   Among the many Jews saved by Varian Frye's committee were Alma Mahler Gropius,former wife of Gustav Mahler, Max Ernst (aided by money from

Peggy Guggenhiem). The only reference to the Russians was their first names in a letter to Sheila Gaunt and by the time they arrived in New York Mary was very ill and would soon die.

9   Obituary of Sir Ernest Gaunt, *The Times* September 22 1940.

www.ingramcontent.com/pod-product-compliance
Lightning Source LLC
Chambersburg PA
CBHW030230170426
43201CB00006B/166